High Performance Computing

High Performance Computing

Challenges for Future Systems

David J. Kuck

Kuck & Associates, Inc. and
University of Illinois, Emeritus

New York   Oxford
OXFORD UNIVERSITY PRESS
1996

Oxford University Press

Oxford   New York
Athens   Auckland   Bangkok   Bombay
Calcutta   Cape Town   Dar es Salaam
Delhi   Florence   Hong Kong   Istanbul
Karachi   Kuala Lumpur   Madras   Madrid
Melbourne   Mexico City   Nairobi   Paris
Singapore   Taipei   Tokyo   Toronto

and associated companies in
Berlin   Ibadan

Copyright © 1996 by Oxford University Press, Inc.

Published by Oxford University Press Inc.,
198 Madison Avenue, New York, New York 10016

Oxford is a registered trademark of Oxford University Press.

Library of Congress Cataloging-in-Publication Data
Kuck, David J.
High performance computing : challenges for future systems /
David J. Kuck.
p.   cm.
Includes bibliographical references and index.
ISBN 0-19-509550-2 (cloth). — ISBN 0-19-509551-0 (pbk.)
1. Parallel processing (Electronic computers)   I. Title.
QA76.58.K82   1996   004f.35—dc20   95-47796

2 4 6 8 9 7 5 3 1

Printed in the United States of America
on acid-free paper

To Sharon,
Julianne, Jonathan, and Ryan

CONTENTS

PREFACE

When the Cedar system was completed and we had finished an initial series of performance experiments, I was quite satisfied with the results and decided that CSRD should produce a book that explained Cedar and its performance. To discuss Cedar's performance in the context of the rest of the high performance computing (HPC) world, I began to use the Perfect benchmark suite for comparative analysis. Knowing that there was little Perfect data for massively parallel processors (MPPs), I searched the literature for other benchmarks that would allow MPP analysis, but found nothing useful for comparison beyond the level of simple algorithms. This reinforced my belief that MPPs were being oversold as general-purpose computers, and that only very special purpose successes existed. Nevertheless, by 1991, Cedar's 32 processors seemed outdated to many people who had been overcome by an MPP fever.

I had many discussions with colleagues everywhere about the state of the HPC world. For example, in a discussion of the subject at a Supercomputer Systems Inc. (SSI) board meeting, after explaining my position to an agreeable audience, I recall the group (which included the presidents of SSI and IBM's Enterprise Sytems Division, Steve Chen and Carl Conti, respectively), saying to me "You have to do something to explain this to the world." I also had discussions with top people in many other companies and found general confusion and frustration about the understanding of performance in parallel computing. I did not have all the answers for solving the problems of practical parallelism, but I did have some good questions and a few answers. So I began to accept invitations to lecture about Cedar, and worked into my talks the performance of MPPs and other architectures as well.

After giving distinguished lectures at a number of universities, and keynote lectures at conferences on supercomputing, computer architecture, performance evaluation, and parallel processing, I had spoken with many people. In publicly challenging the sometimes outrageous claims made by various HPC groups, I found a great deal of support: people would say that they privately agreed with me but that they had felt alone in their opinions, in view of existing trends. My message was that technology and performance, about which there was much disagreement

– and little understanding in the case of performance – were only part of the story. The business, politics and even psychology of HPC were also major contributors to what was happening in the HPC world. In 1992, George Cybenko and I published a brief article about the subject in IEEE Spectrum [CyKu92], and it too evoked much agreement as well as controversy.

At one point I had a call from Danny Hillis, the founder of Thinking Machines, who wanted to discuss our differences of opinion. In an hour-long discussion that ranged widely, it turned out that we really had no serious basic disagreements, as far as I could see. At another point, in Washington D.C., I debated a panel that included the HPC technical leaders of most of the major government agencies [?]. Although there were many points of contention about details, there seemed to be agreement about basics. Thus one could not easily point to a list of conceptual problems to be solved to reach consensus on HPC goals or general directions.

The difficulties arise in the execution of specific plans and delivery of HPC technology. Parallel systems are very complex and there are many ways to design and sell the resulting products. Making and executing plans under the pressure of economic and technical competition can lead to strong disagreements, missteps from the basic consensus of the community, and in the end disservices to the community. At the inception of one major MPP project, its leader told me essentially the following: "I don't care what it is or how well it performs, as long as it has more processors than TMC and we can get it out in 18 months." The idea of selling peak speeds via large numbers of processors became a consuming desire.

High performance computing has been moving into a more and more confused state over the past decade. Proof that this is so can be found in the popular press and in the technical literature. Contradictory opinions or approaches in science and technology are quite normal. But for a technology that has seemed precise and pacesetting for half a century, and that the entire world now relies upon in their daily lives, everyone should be concerned upon learning that the next steps are not nearly as clear as they were in past decades.

Opinions abound about what is causing the confusion and about what to do to move the field ahead. In testimony before the House Committee on Space, Science and Technology in 1989 as they explored HPC, I pointed out some of the performance related problems of HPC. The chairman, Cong. Doug Walgren, replied that they had never heard anything like this before. What they did hear just before me was Sen. Al Gore advocating more money for computer networks while saying little about HPC specifically, and just after me was Cray Research CEO John Rollwagen advocating more protection for computer exports. It was D. Allan Bromley, science adviser to the Bush administration, who caused the high performance *computing* initiative to be renamed and reorganized as the high performance computing *and communications* initiative (HPCCI). This is one of several examples of Federal government involvement in HPC policy which has muddied the water and focused on important but peripheral points.

A major problem in the HPC field is that some very hard, unsolved problems have been looked upon as merely small gaps in moving to the next era in parallel computing. For example, "scalability" is a buzzword that has come to be associated with every aspect of parallel computing. It connotes ever-increasing performance through expanding parallelism. However, it does not have any generally agreed upon definition, and worse yet, in most situations where it is talked about, intuitively defined and promised, it doesn't really exist beyond the specific topic discussed. To compare my scalability to yours, meaningfully, is impossible today.

This book has turned out to be something quite different from the Cedar performance analysis book that I had planned to write. Instead, I have tried to assess why the field has moved in the directions that it has. Government, industry and academia have all been responsible, in part, for the many amazing successes, but they have all contributed to the present confusion, as well. To move the field ahead, I believe that a return to basics is necessary on certain fronts. The first half of the book discusses HPC in simple terms that should be readable by anyone interested in the topic. The second half is technical and presents some simple remedies using Cedar, Cray computers and others as examples in comparative performance studies.

The book is not a plea for more HPC R & D money. $50M to $200M projects have been common in the past. I have been seriously involved with half a dozen such projects and peripherally involved with a number of others; this has convinced me that it is not for a lack of money or ideas that parallelism still has so many open questions. Instead, what is lacking is the rational, systematic, and comprehensive use of what is already know. Twenty percent of a project's time is used to decide what to build, eighty percent is used to build it, and no time is spent in trying to understand deeply, how well the design decisions were made in terms of the resulting performance delivered to users, and hence, how best to proceed on the next system design. There *is* usually designer sensitivity to knowing what users want and need, but the problems are so complex that users cannot "know" what is needed nor how to communicate needs effectively to designers, who in turn do not know how to translate the conflicting requests that they do hear into better systems for everyone.

Progress in computer system design over the past 50 years can be viewed as an evolutionary process driven by expanding applications and software, shrinking hardware, performance defects, and the natural selection of systems by users. During the past decade, some of the design constraints imposed by technology have shifted dramatically, causing the process to fail with alarming frequency. As with natural evolution in which selection, not mutation, controls the direction, rate, and intensity of evolution, computer system designers need to concentrate less on producing more variety in systems, and more on the users' natural selection process. This presents important new *challenges for future generations* of computer systems and their designers.

This book is a critique of the state of the HPC art in the 1990s, a view of the growing future importance of parallelism, even in desktop computing, and an outline of the most important steps that can be taken now to move effectively toward practical parallelism. The book's primary motivation is the enormity of the failure rate among HPC companies in the past 5 years, and the concern that as parallelism becomes crucial in desktop systems, the very effective "technology trickle down" from supercomputers to desktops in the past decade will become a "technology disaster avalanche" in the future.

Despite the fact that I propose decision making based more on gathering and analyzing performance information and less on intuitive and imitative decision making, this book itself is mostly opinion. However, I have successfully used these ideas to some extent in various projects, and the need to base science and technology firmly on quantitative facts and experimental evidence is so obvious, that I believe it is hard to argue with the basic recommendations. The problem is that "the experiments" involve 5 to 10 year efforts that include hundreds of system designers and users, and there are no standard metrics to quantify the field.

Much of this book is based upon my experiences with Cedar and other projects of the Center for Supercomputing Research and Development (CSRD) at the University of Illinois. CSRD was founded in 1984 to build the Cedar system. This was made possible by the intellectual, financial, and facilities contributions of many people and organizations. The ideas that led to Cedar arose in the 1970s within our research group in the Department of Computer Science. These ideas included the development of the Parafrase program restructurer, the Omega network, various parallel algorithms, and ideas about hierarchical parallel system control. Many people contributed to this including Dan Gajski, Duncan Lawrie, and Ahmed Sameh. In the early 1980s there was a nationwide discussion about how to develop parallel systems, and our group was motivated to submit identical proposals to the National Science Foundation and the Department of Energy, both of which had been supporting us in the 1970s. We learned in 1984 that both proposals would be funded, and both agencies provided strong CSRD support from 1984 to 1992. Substantial support also came to CSRD from the Air Force Office of Scientific Research and the Department of Defense Advanced Research Projects Agency.

Upon hearing of the strong Federal support planned in mid-1984, we received vigorous support within the State of Illinois from Gov. Jim Thompson, and within the university from President Stan Ikenberry. This continued over the years through a number of chancellors ans vice chancellors, including Tom Everhart, Mort Wier, Ned Goldwasser and Bob Berdahl. Money and excellent staff were provided in good times and bad, and eventually a new building, CSRL, was built for us.

From the beginning, CSRD received important technical and financial support from a number of industrial firms. Our industrial affiliates' membership reached over a dozen companies providing half a million dollars per year, and included more than 20 companies over the years. Most important were Alliant Computer

Systems and the IBM Corporation. Ron Gruner and Craig Mundie of Alliant offered offered broad support over many years, including special hardware and software modifications to the Alliant FX-8 to support Cedar's needs. Fran Allen and others at IBM provided much help, including a $1M cash grant and a large computer system upon the founding of CSRD.

I would not have been able to organize and lead CSRD without the outstanding cooperation of the founding Associate Directors Ed Davidson, Duncan Lawrie, and Ahmed Sameh. Their technical leadership was crucial and their administrative skills allowed us to build up a 125 person organization in about 2 years. They graduated to CS and ECE department headships at the Universities of Michigan, Illinois, and Minnesota, respectively, and were ably followed by Mike Farmwald, David Padua and George Cybenko.

Through the design, construction, and operation of Cedar, CSRD innovated in several parallel processing directions. The Cedar design demonstrated a memory hierarchy that incorporates 8-processor clusters with shared coherent caches and shared cluster memory, and among the four clusters offers a shared global memory plus software transmission between cluster and global memory. Two high-speed pipelined shuffle-exchange networks provide interconnection between global memory and clusters, and a prefetching mechanism allows block moves to overlap with computation. Control of the system is also organized in a hierarchical fashion; parallel control of the system globally is via software (compiler plus OS) and within clusters processors proceed independently, but when each loop iteration ends a hardware bus assigns the processor a new iteration to execute. The Cedar Fortran compiler, the Xylem operating system, many innovative numerical algorithms (including the BLAS3 which were widely copied), and new approaches to parallel applications programs were all first developed for Cedar. CSRD led the Perfect 1 benchmarking effort in an attempt to develop a suite of broadly representative programs to use in the design and testing of the system. Beyond the above, CSRD developed sparse matrix algorithms, tools for parallel programming and visualization, parallelizing C and Lisp compilers, parallel system simulators, and innovative parallel computer design techniques.

It is from this background that my views emerged, and I am as opinionated as the next technical person. What I have tried to do in writing this book is to answer one question: Since it is now obvious that no one knows how to deliver practical parallel systems, what simple steps can be taken to direct the community along a path that will eventually lead to practical parallel systems? In developing an answer to this question, I supressed many of my opinions and tried to restrict the discussion to rational, universally useful issues. In the end, those who design practical parallel systems will do it using intuition, of course. My goal is to help direct the community toward a path that will eventually lead to the necessary facts about parallel systems and their performance, so that future designers will be able to succeed where so many others have failed in the past.

I have been influenced by many people, computer systems, compilers, and source programs, over the years, and this book reflects what I have learned from them all. Several people, through recent discussions or comments on book drafts, have directly influenced certain parts of the book. I am particularly indebted to George Cybenko, Ed DeCastro, Stratis Gallopoulos, Karl Hess, William Jalby, Lyle Kipp, Bob Kuhn, David Padua, Constantine Polychronopoulos, Ahmed Sameh, Joe Throop, and Alex Veidenbaum for specific book ideas. Four parallel HPC systems and their design teams have directly shaped my views over the past 30 years – Illiac IV, the Burroughs BSP, the Alliant FX-8, and Cedar – and two restructuring compilers have clarified many of my ideas over a 25 year period: Parafrase and KAP. To the many students and colleagues with whom I have worked on these projects I am deeply grateful.

INTRODUCTION

Everyone is affected by computers today, and every computer today is affected by the supercomputers of a few years ago. There is currently much confusion about what approach to use in building the next generation of supercomputers, and this seems to cloud the future of lesser machines. When contrasted with countless observations about the growth of power and capabilities in new commodity-level computers, concern about the future may seem especially puzzling.

It is not hard to understand that technology trickles down from supercomputers to commodity computers, and it is obvious that there are ultimate limitations to all technologies, so one might expect that, like the Concorde and the Superconducting Super Collider (SSC), computer technology may hit certain walls. On the other hand, the capabilities of computers have grown so steadily over the past 50 years that most people have come to expect that this progress will continue forever. People know that computer progress depends partly on software and that it therefore is less limited by the laws of physics than most other engineering fields. Furthermore, computer prices have dropped so dramatically in relation to increasing performance that it is hard to imagine a computer analogy to the air travel market rejecting the Concorde or Congress terminating the SSC.

Nevertheless, the computer field is in turmoil. Top management is regularly forced out at leading computer companies, and small, innovative, high performance computer companies regularly become bankrupt. These failures may be merely matters of business cycles and technology leadership change, or they may reflect deeper issues of technology limitations and high performance computing design-complexity barriers. Furthermore, academia and government have not demonstrated strong HPC leadership in recent years.

Succinctly put, high performance computing (HPC) is about performance. Unless performance is very well understood, no one can solve the difficult basic HPC design problems. Without deep performance insight, in the complex HPC domain, people often pursue superficial or narrow issues that may be difficult and expensive to solve, but do not really move the field ahead.

This book proposes a number of ways of understanding performance more precisely and more globally than we do today. The fundamental assumption is that

1

by determining and opening the use of the pertinent basic facts, everyone — HPC system designers, top managers, and end users, as well as politicians, investors, and marketers — will benefit by increasing their decision-making ability. **Open performance understanding will be as important in the future as open system standards were in the past.**

While basing decisions upon facts may seem to be an obvious approach, it is too seldom followed in HPC because it is more difficult and less glamorous to gather and analyze performance facts about existing computers than it is to rush into designing new computers using only intuition and opinions. The HPC field is difficult because, like a good mystery story, it is full of misleading clues and unimportant superficialities. However, unlike most detectives, we do not seek a single criminal, but rather a good balance between many competing "criminals." Furthermore, the "crime" is dynamic and continues to evolve over time.

Examples of the HPC Problem

The scope and magnitude of the HPC problem may be demonstrated by recalling the histories of five companies: Alliant Computer Systems, Cray Computer Corporation (CCC), Kendall Square Research (KSR), Supercomputer Systems Inc. (SSI), and Thinking Machines Corporation (TMC). Their very names suggest the diversity of their management and perhaps of their goals. The first was founded as Dataflow Systems (a technical buzzword intended to confuse outsiders) and metamorphosed into Alliant, which connoted harmony among multiple processors as well as between users and problem solutions; it was never shortened to a three-letter name. CCC was named after its founder, a pioneer in the field whose name stood for fast hardware technology. KSR was named after the location of its initial offices in Cambridge, Massachusetts, and proceeded to operate in great secrecy (the name revealed absolutely nothing). SSI leveraged a glamorous current buzzword and connoted a synthesis of supercomputing ideas. Initially, TMC appeared to believe that it would deliver computer systems for the artificial intelligence community (although it never did) and chose a name connoting visions of some distant future.

Each company operated long enough (the canonical seven years) to produce a working system; each was well funded, with perhaps an average of $200 million invested over time in research and development; three (Alliant, CCC, and KSR) had public stock offerings, which attracted many individual investors; and Alliant even made reasonable profits for several years. The list of investors who committed a billion dollars to these and other companies demonstrates the scope of the problem this book addresses; they included some of the most savvy and well-funded East and West Coast venture capital firms, the largest computer (IBM) and most successful HPC (Cray Research Inc.) companies in the United States, the most well-funded and aggressive high-tech government agency (Department of Defense Advanced Research Projects Agency), as well as one of the most experienced HPC agencies (National Security Agency), leading corporations that have long records of using HPC systems in their R & D efforts (e.g., Boeing, Ford, and DuPont), wealthy individual investors with long experience in high-tech investments, plus many mom and pop NASDAQ investors. While $1 billion may be a small amount in terms of the total R & D investment of the United States, or relative to the several hundred billion dollar annual world-wide computer business, these companies and their employees constituted a major representation of the HPC leaders.

Each of these companies was founded by highly motivated individuals. Some were leaders in the field, others were new to it, and all brought innovative ideas to the field. Three of the five companies produced more than prototype computers for end users: KSR sold fewer than 50, TMC perhaps several hundred, and Alliant nearly 1,000 systems. But by the end of 1995, all of them had failed as computer manufacturers. All had run into much more severe technical and financial problems than they had anticipated or could deal with.

These failures among the best of our technical people and the most knowledgeable of our investors in a setting of insatiable demand for more computing power is a cause for genuine alarm. Why has this happened? What does the future hold for HPC? What does it imply for future technology trickle-down to other computer systems, including personal computers?

Questions About Performance Progress

Fifty years after the invention of computers, and a decade after the popularization of personal computers, everyone now takes continued explosive performance progress as a given. Quantitatively the changes in computing have been much greater than in most other engineering fields, and qualitatively they have also been different, as entirely new kinds of uses continue to appear. Perhaps biotechnology and materials science are currently closest to high performance computing in offering ever-changing *types* of innovations, as electronics and chemistry have done for the past century. However, there are major differences between the foundations of these industries and HPC.

Vigorous debates surround many technical aspects of HPC, as debates exist in all active branches of science and engineering. However, because most opinions about HPC are offered without sufficient backup facts, cutting through the technical fog to decide whose proposed solutions are best or even to understand who is working on the right specific problems, becomes difficult as the number of approaches grows. This book arose from the following specific questions:

- What can be done to enable better decisions to be made so that HPC can progress more rapidly?

- How can we focus on those HPC approaches that are best for developing practical parallelism?

The answers must be useful to nontechnical people, but they are obviously highly technical in nature.

To clarify the nature of these questions, we must realize that HPC has a number of differences from most other engineering fields. To explore the future of aviation, for example, one may have to examine the approaches of half a dozen manufacturers worldwide, and we naturally assume certain physical limitations, including the speed of sound, the force of gravity, the principles of combustion and fluid dynamics, the physical properties of materials, and the dynamics of rigid structures. Human factors, economics, and political issues must also be examined. Modern HPC designs have many similarities. The physical constraints on system hardware include the speed of light, the principles of electronics and circuits, and the electrical and mechanical properties of materials. These same constraints have existed over the years, but engineers and scientists have continually probed nature's secrets to develop faster clock speeds and smaller devices, and hence boost system performance. Although these issues constrain the physical design of computers, once the machine is built — unlike most other engineering designs — a computer can be used in an unlimited number of ways.

The runway length, weather conditions for flight, and even the number of passengers are essentially uncontrolled for an HPC system. Users regard computers as general-purpose machines, and the universality of computer use is what has made them revolutionary instruments. Computer systems are designed for unspecified uses, and in terms of the software loads presented to them, they sometimes fail to perform satisfactorily. In the past, however, if computers have had performance shortcomings, the world has only had to wait a few years for a hardware solution. Furthermore, computer uses have expanded as performance grew, but to invent and perfect new uses takes time, so the stepwise performance growth has seldom been noticed. As performance has progressed, users have seen the appearance of software that solves increasingly difficult problems in more user-friendly ways.

It is the software that enables computers to perform effectively in various applications and, as is well known, it is not constrained by physical design principles. It is an invention of the human mind, constrained by certain logical and mathematical principles, and of course subject to the performance constraints of particular computer systems. **The crisis in computing today is about the architectures of parallel systems, which are hardware based, and about the requisite software to exploit those architectures.** The constraints on architectural design are more like those on software than those on hardware. Thus, the era of parallel computing moves HPC design to a new degree of complexity. To hardware based on physical principles and software based on human synthesis, we add architecture based on human synthesis. To the well-known software crises of the past decades [Broo75], we are now adding architectural crises.

On Finding Solutions

Returning to the questions about how to make high-level decisions in this field, it seems obvious that to improve computer systems as a whole, we must:

1. *Define* system-level performance metrics,

2. *Measure* systems according to the definitions,

3. *Compare* computations and system-design concepts in terms of the measurements, and

4. *Make decisions* based on these macroperformance comparisons.

Although this strategy sounds straightforward and simple, it is not, and therefore it has not been followed in the past. This book was written to improve the processes of understanding HPC performance and decision making.

Just as I do not attempt to explain much of the basic technology of parallel computing, neither do I attempt to provide detailed opinions about many specific open issues in high performance computing. The former is a difficult task, but the latter would violate my basic belief that opinions are much weaker than facts as a basis for decision making. The principles advocated in this book *are* applied in the later chapters to indicate how they should be used in making quantitatively reasoned decisions. In the end, intuition and judgment are always needed to make decisions, but today most decisions are based more on opinions than data about the macroperformance of systems, because there is little useful macroperformance data available. This lack of data retards progress in the field, and the book attempts to right this wrong by dealing with issues in a technical sense (e.g., by presenting definitions and equations to use), in an organizational and management sense (e.g., by discussing what academia, government, and industry can do individually and collectively), and in a social sense (e.g., by discussing how technical people can better coordinate their efforts).

Taken in the broadest sense, the book is not about supercomputing, but about everyday commodity-level computing. The PC revolution was based upon the legacy of more than three decades of supercomputing system research and development, together with new human interface software. Now that the hardware technology of PCs has caught up with the hardware technology of supercomputers, new software innovations on PCs await more performance, and computer system architecture is crucial in providing new performance levels. Because supercomputer architecture and system software are in a state of turmoil today, there can be no confident predictions of growth for tomorrow, which in turn implies that the PCs of 2000 and beyond may need to be rethought in terms of growth of user services and functionality. Unless practical parallelism is developed, it appears that performance limitations will limit future computer functionality. Future PCs would become more like today's hand-held calculators; they would provide specific, limited, no-growth functionality and would compete in the marketplace only in price.

If, on the other hand, practical parallelism can be achieved, decades of future performance growth and resulting computer functionality growth are assured. This will hold for supercomputing as well as desktop systems, and technology interchange will continue across the hierarchy of computer system types. In fact, if all types of systems are built from the same hardware technology, and use the same architecture and software technology, then technology and functionality ideas will flow in all directions. In this scenario, future progress may look even brighter than it has in the past. There is just one conceptual hurdle — one technology wall — to get over, and this book is dedicated to providing a push toward achieving practical parallel computing in the near future.

Reading the Book

This book provides a technology-oriented examination of the HPC field. It is written in part for any informed person, and in part for the expert. I believe that combining two levels of discussion about HPC in one book is important, even though some readers may not easily be able to read the whole book. Nontechnical readers are provided with a broad introduction to the problems of high performance computing and can skim the more technical parts of the book. Technical experts — who tend to be polarized and extremely focussed — will be reminded of a number of nontechnical background ideas and principles that guide our field. Both will be exposed to core ideas that are important to the future of the HPC field.

The process of designing high performance into computer systems today is in a prescientific state. In lieu of comprehensive, focussed performance data, designers intuitively and hopefully combine old and new concepts to build new systems. This book may be regarded as an attempt to integrate ideas and move high performance computer design to a level where new designs can be done systematically and confidently, just as natural philosophy treatises helped to systematize our understanding of earth, fire, water, and wind in earlier centuries. Specific aspects of HPC system design are very well understood, of course, but systematically delivering high performance remains beyond our current reach.

The book was not written as an introduction to the field; that is, it does not attempt to provide comprehensive technical background material or explain how high performance computers work. Furthermore, it is not as scholarly or exhaustive as it could be in treating the subject. Some of the successes of the field are presented, but there is a major focus on the remaining problems. The book errs on the short side with references, presenting some for background ideas and others as sources for further reading. Because the field is in a crisis and needs to have certain issues sorted out, the latter half of the book outlines certain steps that I believe are necessary as a basis for this sorting out.

Nontechnical readers should be able to read Chapters 1, 2, and 3, and most of 4, 5, and 10, without difficulty. They can skim other parts of the book to grasp the overall ideas. A number of forward and backward pointers (and the index) help promote reading parts of the book out of order. In fact, some of the issues may be best understood by reading scattered parts of the book together. Because the background and context of HPC are so broad, a short book cannot be complete; however, the book contains more than 100 figures, tables, and "word pictures" in the form of sidebars that supplement the text and are intended to help readers understand the issues. The sidebars include background information ranging from human-interest to technical examples.

Expert readers should skim Chapters 1 through 4 to be reminded of why we are doing what we are doing in HPC, and how we have arrived at the present state. Experts can read Chapters 5 through 10 to understand what the book proposes for moving the field ahead. Chapter 1 outlines many of the ideas of the book, and Section 1.9 summarizes the four main problem areas addressed in the book.

Overall the book does not go into great detail about any subject. The idea was to sketch the historical background and context of HPC, isolate the key problems, and offer ideas about how to solve them. The subject is constrained by a complex mixture of physical and mathematical principles, engineering necessities, end users' needs, and the pragmatics of business, politics, and the economy. No one can aspire to provide solutions that address all of these aspects in detail. Nevertheless, the book touches on all of these factors and offers ideas to help most of the various types of people who have contacts with the subject.

CHAPTER 1

THE TECHNOLOGY, POLICY, AND BUSINESS OF COMPUTERS

Unlike many other inventions, computers embody a very broad and rich range of potentials for new and evolving uses. These new uses arise only through major commitments of creative human effort that produce fundamental changes in computer software. To support the software functionality advances and more complex problem solutions that users demand, there is a constant need for hardware that delivers more speed. In the past, speed advances have required that we unlock nature's secrets to build faster circuits, but as that approach yields diminishing returns, we are faced with a new problem. Human creativity must now produce parallel computer architectures *and* software that will allow future speed advances to match historical progress, without relying on faster circuits.

1.1 Growth Potential of Computer Development and Use

Television is about as old as computing, and automobiles are about twice as old. In their 100-year history, cars have become faster, more efficient, and more comfortable to use, but to a first approximation they have become as fast, efficient, and comfortable as people need or are willing to pay for. In 50 years TV sets have gotten easier on the eyes, programming has widened considerably, and prices have dropped to the commodity level, but there is little new to expect from TV sets themselves in the future beyond the level of high-definition TV (HDTV) (easier, still, on the eyes) or more cable and satellite channels.

Computers can serve us at a different level from that of automobiles conveniently moving us about or TV sets entertaining and informing us; they can interact with us intellectually. Artificial intelligence researchers have promised since almost the beginning of computing, to produce software that would allow computers to think and reason in such a way as to augment and amplify our own intelligence, and perhaps eventually even to compete intellectually with humans. With some notable exceptions (e.g., chess and focussed expert systems), this has not happened

9

Invention	Technology Breakthrough
Automobile	Internal Combustion Engine
Television Set	Cathode Ray Tube Control
Electrification	AC Generators
Computer Hardware	Integrated Circuit

Table 1.1.   Single Technology Inventions

and probably will not happen in the foreseeable future; in addition to better insight, progress on such difficult problems probably depends on progressing to much higher performance computer systems. But even ignoring AI's claims, computers have already broadly amplified and enhanced our understanding, insight, and productivity by simulating real-world phenomena (e.g., molecules, airplanes, or the weather) and by providing new tools for traditional work (e.g., word-processing, spreadsheets, or databases). Computers now pervade the workplace, schools, and homes, and their uses in each of these settings varies greatly. The same can be said about the pervasiveness of automobiles and TV sets, but each auto and TV set is doing approximately the same thing as every other one. The key distinction is that people are continually inventing new and radically different uses for computers.

This multifaceted functionality of computer use, as well as the wide range of forms and sizes that computers can take, are major contributors to the disagreement and confusion that frequently surround parts of the field. The use, performance, and even organization of high performance computer systems are subjects that currently engender great debate among computer designers and users.

1.1.1   Technology Enables Inventions

New product or system inventions have usually been based on either technology breakthroughs or system synthesis breakthroughs. Table 1.1 shows four examples of single-technology inventions and the corresponding technology breakthrough that enabled each of them to be produced and popularized. In each case several technologies were combined to produce the invention, but without that one *necessary* breakthrough the resulting products would not have succeeded. For example, vacuum tubes and discrete transistors enabled us to build the early, room-sized computers, but the integrated circuit enabled us to miniaturize and reduce costs so that computers became commodities.

Table 1.2 shows four examples of inventions that required a systems approach. No single technology item can be pointed to as the key that enabled these complex system inventions. Rather, several difficult technologies (of the type in Table 1.1) came together for their success. Notice that each of the first three diverse systems (as well as most other modern complex systems) depends on computers

Invention	System Technologies
Modern Airplane	Jet Engine, Airframe Structures, Computer, Telecommunication
Apollo Moon Landing	Rocket Engine, Telecommunication, Lunar Lander, Space Suits, Computer
Modern Particle Accelerator	Powerful Magnets, Computer, Bubble Chamber, Other Instrumentation
Computer System	Computer Hardware, System Software, Applications Software

Table 1.2.   Complex System Level Inventions

plus technologies specific to the application of the system. Computers are used as components at many points in such systems, and also as overall system integration and control devices. The success of computer systems depends on computer hardware plus two different kinds of software, which, in turn, depend on years of algorithmic thought, language development, and other basics. Future parallel systems will depend on sequential computers plus some new architectural features and many new software components.

1.1.2   Systems' Use: Uniqueness to Ubiquity

Some systems have a unique purpose, some have a few uses, and some are universally usable. The Apollo system (as a whole) could only be used to land humans on the moon. Particle accelerators can find the next few subatomic particles that high energy physicists seek. But there is still no end in sight to the manifold uses of computer systems. Thus, computers may be the only system-level invention whose wide utility rivals the ubiquity of non-systems such as the wheel or refined oil.

Over time, computers have become necessary components of all complex systems, and they are now being used to enrich single technology inventions such as automobiles and TV sets. This ubiquity can be claimed for few other complex systems. Each application area, of course, has inherent ideas that must be incorporated into application software which then provides a segment of the supporting technology for the new computer use, just as other technologies were necessary for each invention of Table 1.2. This dependence of systems technology on computers, and the universal potential use that uniquely characterizes computer systems in today's world of technology, has complicated our understanding of how best to make progress in the computer field, because the field is simultaneously being pulled in many different directions.

Sidebar 1: Relative Benefits/Cost of HPC

It is difficult to measure the benefits of any technology R & D advance, but this book highlights the fact that computing has broader applicability than most other technologies. To quantify the cost of R & D, let us consider U.S. government expenditures on several of the technologies in Tables 1.1 and 1.2. The computing R & D expenditures of industry are, of course, very high compared to government expenditures, whereas industrial expenditures on the other technologies we discuss may be relatively much higher or lower than government expenditures. The current High Performance Computing and Communications Initiative (HPCCI) has been ramping up toward $1 billion per year for supercomputing and networking the nation over an (initially defined) five-year period from 1992 to 1996.

The Superconducting Super Collider (SSC) had an estimated construction cost of more than $10 billion over a decade, with the potential of finding the Higgs's boson or new puzzles. NASA's scaled-down Space Station Freedom has been estimated to cost $100 billion over 30 years, and the current shuttle program has consumed $6 billion per year or an average of $1 billion per launch. In this sense, HPCCI can be regarded as a relatively minor Federal government expense, relative to the ubiquity of computer usage.

The costs of computer systems to purchasers are easy to measure. Ignoring inflation, over the past three decades, supercomputers have uniformly been priced in the range of $10 million to $30 million. Meanwhile, through the development of PCs, the lowest-priced computers have dropped from supercomputer prices to the $1 thousand level. At a constant price, high-end users have benefited from an enormous performance growth (about 10X/7 years) over the decades, while the price of the low end systems has dropped by a factor of, perhaps, 10,000 in the same time period (and the lowest priced systems actually continue to provide increased performance at a constant price).

It is difficult to find any other technology that has had such large performance/price gains in the same era. By contrast, and probably at the opposite extreme of technology cost change for "constant performance," the 17-mile-long Century Freeway in Los Angeles opened in 1993 at a cost of $127 million/mile, whereas the Pasadena Freeway opened in 1940 at a cost of $1 million/mile [NYT93] (ignoring inflation again). Comparing apples to oranges, this hundred-fold increase in cost per construction mile is about a million times worse in cost per unit than that of the purchase price of the lowest performance computers over the same 50 years (ignoring inflation in both cases).

The computer industry itself is intrinsically valuable for the economy as a whole. MITI (the Japanese Ministry of International Trade and Industry), in *Vision for the Year 2000*, predicted in the late 1980s that by the end of this century, 22% of the new jobs created in Japan would be in the computer industry. Japan has long stressed the importance of the computer industry, and despite a late start, by 1987 the combined sales of the Japanese computer companies had equalled IBM's sales [DeLS89].

Although the benefits of computing appear everywhere in the world today, evidence of the importance of computing relative to other technologies may be seen in the first three awards of the biennial Charles Stark Draper Prize by the National Academy of Engineering. The Draper Prize is the world's largest ($375,000) and most prestigious prize for engineers; it was first awarded to Jack S. Kilby and Robert N. Noyce (1989) for the invention of the integrated circuit, upon which today's computers (and many other innovations) have been developed, then to Hans von Ohain and Sir Frank Whittle (1991) for the development of the jet engine, and to John Backus (1993) for developing FORTRAN, the first general-purpose, high-level programming language. Thus, fundamental computer technology has been recognized in two of the first three Draper Prizes.

1.1.3   Cycles Toward Progress

The progress of science and technology is based on cycles of cause and effect that are fueled by invention and utility. We all know that "necessity is the mother of invention" on the one hand, but we are reminded of a "solution in search of a problem" when an attractive technology has not yet been utilized commercially. As progress is made, every new idea first passes through phases where it poses problems to be solved, and then through phases where it has become a solution technique.

George Westinghouse and Thomas Edison pushed opposing techniques for electrification, and even though these techniques were based on approaches that were relatively easy to analyze mathematically, the AC (Westinghouse) vs. DC (Edison) debate over commercial utility went on for years. For some time, each was able to develop supporting markets, but experience in the field and new technology were required before the ultimate choices were made universally. In the midst of a difficult technology debate, it is crucial to distinguish open problems from solution techniques. Managers frequently leverage one with another, as when a computer company CEO tries to force machine designers to use technology that has been developed elsewhere in the firm. Sometimes this pays off handsomely; at other times it leads to a disaster. The point is that managers should not confuse problems with solutions. On other occasions, innovative solutions to new problems are developed, and then ignored by managers who are concerned with traditional problems, which results in the loss of major business opportunities, as in the case of Xerox PARC and interactive personal computer ideas [AlSm88].

In the computing world, there is only one valid business definition of a "solution" in the competitive marketplace: If real users are willing to pay for a system, it can be regarded as a computational solution for certain problems. Technologies that cannot compete in a free marketplace may be regarded as interesting technologies, solutions waiting for problems to solve, research activities, or merely as business problems yet to be solved. Academic- or industrial-research definitions of a solution can, of course, be much broader than the business definition, and this breadth also holds for government support of research.

From the beginning, academic leadership and government support have played a central role in the development and use of computer systems. ENIAC, the first U.S. electronic computer, was finished in 1946 by the University of Pennsylvania for the U.S. Army to compute ballistics tables, and many early computer projects in Europe had their roots in World War II military programs. Major investments have been made in computing over many decades by the Atomic Energy Commission (later the U.S. Department of Energy – DOE) for its weapons programs, the National Security Agency for its cryptography programs, and NASA for its space programs. Research efforts in universities have been broadly funded by the National Science Foundation since the 1950s, and the U.S. Department of Defense through its Advanced Research Projects Agency (ARPA/DARPA), has supported large university projects as well as industrial R & D efforts since about 1960.

Over the decades, computer system complexity has increased, and performance has come to depend more and more on concurrent system architecture and software – the simultaneous execution of various operations that traditional sequential computers executed one after the other – than on discovering the physical principles of faster circuits to enable faster sequential computers. Because of this shift, the fundamentals of system performance have become much more difficult to understand. Consequently, policy makers and decision makers in industry and government are faced with much more difficult issues now than they were in the past. Their need for cogent and accurate performance information about competing parallel systems and ideas has become acute. In the end, decisions about which technology to push and how to advance it require a substantial understanding of the utility and performance of competing candidate technologies. Without such information, the cycles toward progress become protracted, and the process becomes much more difficult and error prone than necessary.

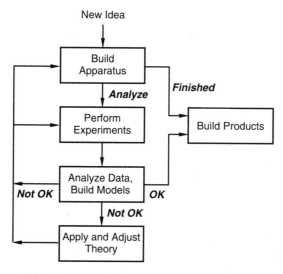

Figure 1.1. Process of Progress in Science and Technology

1.2 Technology Progress: Traditional Areas vs. Computer Systems

There are substantial differences between the processes by which progress is normally made in traditional science and technology [Kuhn70][Reyn91], and the way it occurs in high performance computer system design. Let us define **traditional science and technology** to include only areas that have foundations in the physical world. In science, examples are physics, chemistry, and biology. In technology, we have civil engineering, electrical engineering, and mechanical engineering; chemical engineering; and bioengineering, which have obvious correspondences with the sciences listed first. Although engineers often become involved with matters that are much more practical and empirical than scientists do, the traditional engineering areas each have their traditional equations to rely on.

It is indeed remarkable that modern engineers still can make innovations in products and processes by resorting to equations originally derived in past centuries by, for example, Newton, Maxwell, Navier, and Stokes. The process of traditional science and technology is sketched in Fig. 1.1. For ongoing fields this process becomes a perpetual cycle in which innovation leads to innovation. This is summarized in Sir Isaac Newton's famous observation:

"If I have seen further [than others] it is by standing upon the shoulders of giants."

Consider Fig. 1.1 in the technology setting, where designers begin with a prototype – or computational simulation – derived either from an existing product or theoretical concepts. Next, experiments are performed on the prototype and data is collected about the structure of the prototype and its performance at the micro and macro levels. If the prototype is acceptable, a product may be built; if not, the theory is reexamined, perhaps adjusted, and a new prototype is built or new experiments are performed on the old prototype.

1.2.1   Computer Circuits vs. Computer Systems

It is important to note here that the design and development of integrated circuits, which historically have provided most computer speed increases, are based on the above model. On the other hand, the computer system design process, which integrates hardware and software to realize a system architecture, differs in several ways from the model in Fig. 1.1:

1. In computer system design there are no fundamental physical equations to rely upon at the system level. There are logical equations to describe the functioning of various component circuits (e.g., the adder or multiplier) which can be simulated by solving complex equations (e.g., using SPICE), and this may be done for whole processors and memories using special-purpose, parallel computers (e.g., IBM's EVE systems), and there are behavioral models to describe the performance of subsystems (e.g., the cache memory or an interconnection network). With current technologies, however, the performance of the whole computer system when loaded with one program or another is only predictable by human intuition. This is also in contrast to mathematical equations whose computer solution can estimate the performance of a bridge, airplane, or chemical plant under a range of operating conditions. Of course, intuition can be quite powerful in all engineering disciplines in the form of "back of the envelope" system design estimations.

2. Many computer systems are not fully ready for end users when they go to market, in contrast with the results produced by builders of computer circuits, bridges, airplanes, or chemical plants. Until about 1980 most computers needed programming by end users (embedded and turnkey systems are exceptions), and except for the kinds of focused problem-solving environments introduced on PC's and workstations in the 1980s, that is still true today, a situation that is analogous to requiring a car buyer to provide his or her own engine and steering wheel.

3. The complexity of computer systems makes serious macroperformance analysis difficult, and parallelism exacerbates the difficulties. It is possible to use an existing computer to simulate a complete new computer system performing any particular computation, step by step, and of course this may

be carried out for many computations. If the range of studies is sufficiently broad, then reasonable insight may be obtained, but such detail is difficult to characterize in terms sufficiently abstract to communicate useful results to managers, marketers, and potential customers because there is so much variety in programs. This is in contrast to characterizations such as the load limit and expected lifetime estimates for a bridge, or the acceleration and gas mileage estimates available for an automobile. Supercomputer users typically are told a lot about peak speeds; however, the peak speed of a supercomputer is less relevant to most supercomputer users than the top speed of an Italian sports car is to most American drivers.

1.2.2   Progress in HPC

Fig. 1.2 illustrates these differences (the corresponding labels of Fig. 1.1 appear at the right). Computer systems are built and paid for in a variety of ways (as are new products in other fields). Computer systems are usually delivered to customers or potential customers for experimentation (as is frequently true with military systems, but less often true with commercial systems in other fields). The data analysis and model building step differs sharply from most other fields in that each user tends to focus on performance details that cannot be readily compared with other users' data or with manufacturer-supplied performance data. For certain user programs or classes of benchmark programs, this does indeed lead to new insights about how to improve the system. In many instances, however, the user is for the most part shown carefully selected, vendor-supplied performance information (the hype path), because the machine is so difficult to program that each of the user's real codes would require many months of expert effort to prepare them effectively for the system. Whereas military aircraft and other systems are built to (sometimes changing) detailed specifications, to fill their eventual roles, advanced computer systems require so much custom software that detailed performance specifications are often skipped.

Because HPC systems that reach the point of being deliverable to the customer usually find acceptance in *some* market segment, systems that reach the stage of running prototypes are seldom scrapped, unless they have been produced by large firms that can afford to take the loss and start over. Instead these systems are hyped, forced into the marketplace, and usually hold a niche until systems from other vendors overshadow them; in order to capture a new market share even large firms will produce machines of marginal long-term value if they see competitors successfully marketing similar products. Meanwhile, the engineers and marketers who produced the original system are scrambling to produce a successor system that performs better and will attract a wider customer class. The tragedy here is that the last step in this process replaces the "applying and adjusting theory" step (of Fig. 1.1) in many other fields. In fact, all businesses must adjust their products

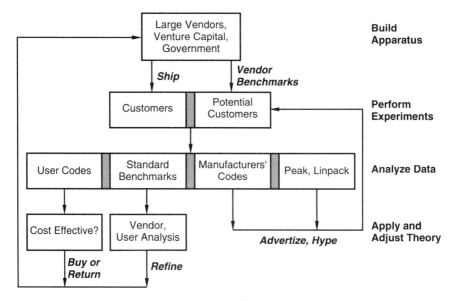

Figure 1.2.   Process of Progress in High Performance Computing

to suit market forces, weak products are sold in most fields, and in other fields most prototype failures do not cause adjustments to physical theories. However, in most other fields it is possible to make in-depth physical micro- and macro-analyses of why prototypes fail and then take steps toward major product improvements. Furthermore, in most fields, products that crash and burn lead to severe financial and legal consequences for the manufacturer, whereas in HPC, terrible performance may be dismissed as "incorrect use of the system," and the customer may be advised to try other algorithms or system software, or even other applications,.

In summary, computer science is a science of the artificial [Simo69], and computer engineering is an engineering of the synthetic. A new computer system is a synthesis of complex, evolved hardware and software artifacts that attempts to provide a system that is more useful and performs better than its predecessors. A computer system's usability is very subjective, and its system-level performance usually defies analysis. Because the finished product is often not fully ready for end users, each system competes in various end-user markets until the successful systems capture one or more of these markets. Although most of these statements also hold to some degree in other engineering fields, because of the differences outlined above, high performance computing is one of the clearest embodiments of the caveat emptor school of product distribution.

1.3 Computer System Performance and Technology

Great progress has been made in computer systems technology over the past 50 years, and this demonstrates what can be done without physical equations or detailed mathematical models to describe complete system behavior. The speed of sequential computer systems has increased by about 10X per seven years from the beginning of electronic computing in the late 1940s, mainly as a result of faster circuits but to some extent as the result of improved architectural designs. The usability of computer systems has been greatly enhanced by layers of system software, each of which provides something closer to what the user is comfortable with, but which, at the same time, incrementally slows down system performance. Various software libraries and utilities have been standardized and ported widely (e.g., upper layers of the Unix operating system) so that they need not be reimplemented on each new machine, (thereby speeding up system delivery schedules). Such software also provides machine-independent human interfaces (thereby enhancing human intersystem mobility). Problem-solving environments with "do-what-I-mean" and "what-you-see-is-what-you-get" capabilities have been available on inexpensive hardware platforms since the early 1980s, and this has truly revolutionized the computer industry. Some of this software speeds up user application programs, but most of it slows down the systems.

There have been performance clouds on the horizon for a decade. At the supercomputer level, from the Cray 1 of 1976 with its 12.5 ns clock period (one nanosecond is one billionth of a second), the Cray Research Inc. line was only able to push its clock speed down to 4 ns in 15 years, and subnanosecond clocks now seem to be in a receding distant future (see Sidebar 13, Chapter 4). This is due partly to electronic switching speeds, partly to speed-of-light limitations on signal propagation delays, and consequently partly to miniaturization and manufacturability difficulties. Thus, the growth in peak speeds of supercomputers has only been maintained recently by introducing parallelism into the system architectures. Instead of relying on the constant progress of hardware technology, as in the past, high performance computer systems have now come to rely on architectural innovations and on system software that allows users to exploit these architectural innovations.

1.3.1 Parallel Processing Potential

In principle parallel processors can speed up a computation architecturally by simultaneously performing operations that a sequential computer would perform serially. However, despite decades of research, today parallelism is used in a practical manner on relatively few types of computations. While researchers had merely hoped for major breakthroughs in past decades, during the 1980s the alarming falloff in the rate of sequential superprocessor speed increases forced designers as well as researchers to pursue the development of parallel supercomputers much more aggressively. By the early 1990s many people saw parallel supercomputers as a critical need for the near future, so a great deal of money and talent have recently been devoted to meeting this need .

A much more serious issue than how to build faster supercomputers is the matter of how to build faster computers generally – personal computers, workstations, and network servers – because so much of our day-to-day world depends on these machines. At present, there is very little discussion of the fact that by 2000, parallelism will probably be an essential need in *all* computer systems. Within their own community, microprocessor designers are all focussed on parallelism – within processors and between processors – as essential ingredients of next-generation systems. This is the same design community that in the past decade has borrowed substantially from the supercomputers of the 1960s and 1970s, ideas ranging from pipelining and operational parallelism to the need for very advanced software technology in compilers.

Currently, these designers seem to be assuming that the necessary architectural and compiler technology will trickle down from supercomputers when needed, as it has in the past. At the same time, many supercomputer designers have come to rely on the idea that supercomputers based on "killer" microprocessors will enable them to design ever faster systems. In a sense we now have designers at two ends of a spectrum, both expecting the appearance of a technological missing link, namely practical parallel software and architecture ideas.

1.4   System Component Changes Change Companies

In the 1980s, following a trend to exploit architecture for more performance, many serial microprocessors went to Reduced Instruction Set Computer (RISC) archi-tectures [HePa90]. These systems integrated compiler and VLSI ideas to produce high performance, but at the cost of a complex cache memory hierarchy whose ex-ploitation requires advanced compiler technology. This necessity to change from a performance reliance on semiconductor circuit speeds to a performance reliance on architecture and system software implied a concomitant reliance on open systems, primarily because the designers of complex systems must synthesize their systems from simpler elements designed by others. The consequences of this change have only partially been felt by the computer industry. To date it has allowed some startup companies effortlessly to enter the market with a big bang, but it has also led to serious confusion at such companies as IBM, Digital, and Cray, and has led to the destruction of Control Data, Burroughs, Honeywell, NCR, Univac, and other traditional companies in the forms in which they once existed. For computer center managers and end users in the supercomputer marketplace, the change has created a total blur of conflicting claims and undelivered promises that almost no one knows how to deal with except by trying everything.

People have been in agreement for years that "software is the real problem" in computing, in reference to its complexity and cost to write, debug, and modify, and because of its importance to the usability of computer systems. But most of this concern has ignored the fact that the same software that makes systems easier to use by raising the users many levels from the hardware has actually slowed down effective system speeds substantially. Put another way, it would not have been possible on a large mainframe of 25 years ago to run a window display system that today's PC users demand; neither the processor speed nor memory size of that time would have sufficed.

Now, we are faced with the unsettling fact that in addition to the many problems of producing high quality software, designers of modern high performance computing systems must *depend* on system software to deliver acceptable performance. For example, because the architectures of caches for individual processors, and parallel memories and interconnection networks for the whole system are so complex, compilers and libraries must be provided to make memory systems deliver high performance. The same is true for discovering parallel and vector operations to exploit architectural features.

The situation is summarized in Table 1.3, which shows that the basic technology components needed to build systems – hardware, architecture, and system software – contribute directly to increased machine performance, and at least indirectly to ease of use. On the other hand, user problem-solving environment (PSE) software, which enables users to do new things or at least makes old things easier to do, generally drags down system performance. As time passes, the focus of computer systems R&D moves upward in Table 1.3, because ease of use implies greater system effectiveness and better overall time-to-solution of users' problems. In the 1980s, computer speed increases became more dependent upon architecture and compiler enhancements, a trend that will become more pronounced in the 1990s, leading to the necessity of parallel processing to provide more speed. In the same time frame, problem-solving environments were introduced that allowed end users to exploit computers without custom progamming. Thus, in the future there will be more reliance on synthesized subsystems of great complexity and hence great cost in human effort to design. There will be less reliance on faster hardware devices, which are often difficult to design but have had a more solid physical and engineering base of support.

In summary, if users merely want the same levels of usability and problem-solving effectiveness that they have had in the past, but want to solve larger problems in the same amount of time, they will need more performance. Or, if they want to solve similar problems but do it more conveniently, they will need more complex PSE software whose support in turn requires higher performance systems.

System Component	Effect On	
	Machine Performance	Ease of use and effectiveness
User problem solving environment software	Down	Up via problem specification
Networking, file systems, and other operating system services	Down	Up via new services and flexibility
Compiler and library system software	Up	Up via optimization
Architecture	Up	Up via machine performance
Hardware	Up	Up via machine performance

Table 1.3.   System Component Effects

In either case the complexity of parallelism must be mastered. This will almost certainly require the sharing of technology and opening of performance information, changes comparable to the open sequential hardware and software changes that have seriously shaken IBM, DEC, and others in the recent past. Open performance information and standards are a key topic and recommendation throughout this book.

Sidebar 2: What Is High Performance Computing?

A crisp definition of high performance computing that will satisfy everyone is not given here, nor is it really possible. The "crisp" part is easy, but satisfying "everyone" is impossible. By contrast, it has always been possible to define a **supercomputer** as the fastest system available at any time, and to hedge by using peak performance to define "fastest," and then to extend this to some equivalence class of roughly equivalent peak-speed systems. Finally, having a large fast-access main memory helped clinch the case for certain machines in the past. This type of definition may lack a bit of crispness, but contrast it with the following.

To "the fastest machine with the biggest memory,"in practical machine selection one must add cost considerations. As microprocessor speeds have approached supercomputer speeds in the past decade, cost-performance has become a much fuzzier criterion. Furthermore, as software has advanced, ease of use and time to solution have become major considerations. Finally, as computer system architecture has advanced and multicomputer, networked systems have evolved, it has become more difficult to define something as simple as peak speed (which was to begin with, a highly flawed measure).

Today's computer buyers think of a **high performance computer** as one that will solve their own problems as quickly, conveniently, and inexpensively as possible. If the class of buyers ranges from national labs to home computer buyers, then this definition leads to serious problems in focussing on particular systems. But even if the class of buyers is carefully constrained, the types of problems to be solved and the constraints under which different organizations work may cause difficulties in using the definition. So it is indeed hard to satisfy everyone with a definition of high performance computing.

Nevertheless, the expression is in wide use today as a cliche' that leads people into talking about whatever they want to say. This book uses the expression in pretty much this way, although "performance" is generally used to mean "speed" on these pages. The reader is cautioned, here and elsewhere, to pay close attention to the context when these three words are encountered.

1.5   Attackers Run Amuck

In his book *Innovation: The Attacker's Advantage* [Fost86], Foster points out that in worldwide commerce and industry over the past century, old technologies and procedures have often been supported too long by old-line companies. Companies new to a field, the attackers, often have been able to move in quickly and displace the establishment. In the computer field, suppliers of the next-generation hardware components have done this repeatedly. For example, few vacuum tube companies made a serious transition to transistors for computer circuits in the early 1960s, and subsequent transitions, for example, from discrete transistors to integrated circuits, had similar consequences. In the computer industry, Route 128 and Silicon Valley have actually depended on technology leapfrogging to maintain their very innovative and important roles in the American computing industry (see, e.g. [Saxe94]).

But there are limits to everything. Suppose that an attacker has a product that is quite different from the attackee's product. If the attacker's product has one prominent feature that is very attractive relative to an attackee's comparable feature, the attacker will succeed, because the differences in the new product (which may initially appear attractive) are not comparable. The prominent comparable feature makes the sale. In high performance computers, the prominent comparable feature of each new system is almost exclusively peak speed, so many heads are turned by each new attacker, even though the machine may have crippling architectural problems that are not easily comparable with older products. Thus, if the incomparable features are not well correlated with overall delivered performance, the attacker's products will not have staying power. Just as automobile buyers of the 1950s tired of tail-fins and chrome after a few years, high performance computer buyers in the 1980s tired of the high peak performance products of many startup companies, which then collapsed.

Nevertheless, the scenario described above can lead to an attackers' frenzy in the otherwise rational model described by Foster. In high performance computing, such a frenzy has arisen because of several technological and cultural factors:

- Massively Parallel Processors (MPPs) are usually constructed with low to medium technology, so there are few technological and financial barriers to entering the business (see Section 4.1).

- Widely adopted open systems software has allowed easy porting of familiar programming environments to new machines.

- High performance computers have high obsolescence rates; typically systems are replaced after only three to five years, so managers are always shopping.

- In university and government lab research settings there is a large supply of (sometimes HPC-naive) people who are eager to try something new in hopes of finding a jewel, or at least of publishing a few papers.

In the 1990s this attackers' frenzy will end for several reasons. On the supply side:

- The attacks are basically incestuous, in that a few good people circulate from one company to the next, so the repackaging of old ideas eventually attenuates.

- The flow of money from venture capitalists to start new companies, and from the Federal government to develop or purchase new systems, slows down.

And on the demand side:

- The number of adventurous customers is limited, and having been burned once or twice, most of them will become very cautious. This is already occurring, for example, with MPPs in segments of the petroleum industry.

- Service and time-to-problem-solution are what customers ultimately are willing to pay for, but computer companies featuring peak speeds seldom feature service or software.

In the end, peak speeds can only be approached by end users through innovative systems and applications software, which today are crucial, largely missing components of service and time to problem solution. When the attackers' frenzy ends, it will be either because someone has solved the software problems or because the community (users, developers, and researchers) has given up on the software problems. The problems will only be solved by a large investment of high quality R & D time and money in HPC performance issues, not a characteristic of most companies participating in the current attackers' frenzy.

Companies participating in the attackers' frenzy thus appear to be succeeding because they do not focus on costly software and service, and thus are planting and cultivating the seeds of their own destruction. When software and service are included in the business model, we leave this attackers' frenzy singularity and return to the more rational business model described by Foster.

Because of the attacker's advantage, when practical parallelism becomes available, it will be possible for attackers to swiftly unseat established computer systems and even whole companies. The dream of being a successful attacker has motivated a number of startup companies in the past decade, and very limited successes have vaulted some of these companies into prominent positions in the supercomputer race. However, the race is still wide open, practical parallelism has not yet appeared, and the challenge to win still drives many people and companies. The attacker's advantage will motivate startups and unsettle established companies until practical parallel systems appear and the advantage is applied.

Sidebar 3: All the HPC News That's Fit to Print

Confusion within the technical community is reflected by confusion of the press, which in turn magnifies the confusion for public consumption. Because so many technical paths were being followed in the 1980s, performance claims and contradictory counterclaims were abundant. By 1990, for example, in a two month period the New York Times published the following four articles about four different HPC leaders:

1. March 16, 1990
Workstation Outperforms Supercomputer
IBM RS6000 performance announced on SPEC Benchmarks.
2. March 23, 1990
Cray Computer Still Fastest
The first Perfect benchmark results were reported.

3. May 1, 1990

Parallel Micros Overtaking the Fastest Computers

"Nobody will survive the attack of the killer micros."

4. May 25, 1990

Japanese Computer Rated the Fastest by One Measure

Discussed LINPACK results on NEC supercomputer.

Such articles have appeared in all of the major publications, including a *TIME* magazine cover story, front page *New York Times* and *Wall Street Journal* stories, and a *Business Week* article [BuWe93] entitled "In Supercomputing, Superconfusion." Even though no one really understands HPC performance, too many people have been willing to state opinions as facts. As a result, the credibility of the field has been diminished. Performance understanding is not much better today than in the past, but reporters have wisely reduced their coverage of non-events in the field.

1.6 A Comprehensive View of Designing Parallel Systems

1.6.1 Understanding and Improving Parallel System Performance

A simple and direct way of comparing parallel processing to sequential processing is by studying the speedup achieved over a sequential processor by using parallelism. Ideally, P processors would run any computation P times as fast as a single processor. While it is generally agreed that this is not a practically achievable goal, we still have no generally agreed-upon performance goals, and in fact there is little discussion of the level of performance that can be expected from practical, broadly acceptable parallel systems. One objective of this book is to focus attention on this simple issue and help promote an agreement on the goals of the parallel processing community, so that research and development efforts will know how far to push in various directions.

In this chapter we have discussed some differences between computer system design and most other engineering design. The key difference is that traditional engineering design is based on physical principles that give rise to equations, empirical data, and intuition about how engineering designs work.

Computer engineers likewise have intuition about how their systems work, and they have measurements of how various parts of their systems perform as well as overall running times for their systems on a limited range of real programs. However, there are no physical principles upon which this performance rests, so when their intuition fails, computer engineers are in a weaker position than most other engineers concerning what to do next.

To the computer engineers' credit, of course, is the fact that modern computer systems perform as well as they do. But the point here is that for parallel computing to become a practical reality, more empirical data is needed, models and simulators of performance must be strengthened, and rational ways of achieving higher performance must be developed. As the world's reliance on faster computers grows, and as high performance computer systems come to rely more on parallel processing, the need increases for rational methods for improving the performance of these complex systems.

Much of this book will explore the relationship between speedup, data size, and processor count, and we shall discuss macroperformance issues in these terms. To date, most parallel performance data has been incomplete (microperformance) and underanalyzed, and it is obvious that this has held the field back. The reason for the lack of completeness is that it is very time consuming and often difficult to collect macroperformance data. The under-analysis is due mainly to the shortage of data; ultimately, complete data sets will lead to complete models, detailed data analysis, and better systems.

1.6.2   Benchmarks and Metrics

The absurdity of past attempts to represent the relationships of speedup to data size and parallel processor count by a few numbers, and the naiveté of assuming that a single benchmark (e.g., Linpack or an FFT) could serve to represent a workload, are demonstrated by looking at such relationships for multiple codes, as we shall do in this book. And yet, the complexity of parallel performance is illustrated by the fact that even if we had plots of 3D surfaces representing such relationships, we would have to look much more deeply, and measure many more details than such surfaces reveal in order to isolate, understand, and repair serious system performance problems.

How many benchmarks and of what sizes must one use? The answer lies not in their number or size, but rather in the diversity of their structure. Because real codes may contain hundreds of thousands (or millions) of source program instructions and there are hundreds of important programs, the actual workload an HPC system faces may contain hundreds of millions of instructions. Thus, tens or hundreds of thousands of real instructions would be necessary, even if one were only attempting to span the set of all potential performance issues by sampling each field. In principle, one may stop adding new code samples to a benchmark suite when the point is reached at which new code samples do not reveal new performance issues, whether comparing multiple systems or isolating problems on a single system.

How many metrics must one use? The answer here lies in which performance

problems are being attacked. Again an overall principle is that we need enough
parameters to distinguish the performance among systems that have genuine differences in performance, or to isolate the performance problems of one system.
It is certainly true that it does not matter which codes are used as benchmarks or
which metrics are used as long as they meet basic criteria for solving performance
problems.

The number of metrics used must be sufficient to paint an overall performance
picture that is accurate in comparing two machines, but there are some loose ends
in this statement. First, one machine may not uniformly satisfy a set of tests better
than another machine. If this is the case, then other tests must be invoked – in
particular, various absolute measures (e.g., cost) are always used in real-world
situations. Secondly, the "accuracy" required of a performance picture depends on
one's goals. For machine selection, a rather superficial, relative metric comparison
(e.g., machine X beats machine Y on 80% of the benchmarks) combined with some
absolute value comparisons (e.g., actual megaflops on the most important codes),
may suffice. For designers, who want to isolate and repair system performance
problems, much more detail is necessary.

A major purpose of this book is to present ideas for achieving practical parallel
systems as quickly and inexpensively as possible. Thus it may seem that the allu-
sions above to machine comparison are off the point. However, today's accepted
wisdom is that machine selection has great practical importance, but that designing
better new systems is a completely different and much more difficult subject.

1.6.3   Comparative Machine Design

One theme of this book is that the localization, identification and mitigation of
system performance weaknesses can be done much more effectively in a setting of
multimachine comparison than by single machine analysis and design procedures
because:

1. Single machine analysis usually proceeds by boring deeper and deeper into
   the "generally accepted" bottleneck areas of a system, e.g. the cache. This
   consumes substantial resources and may give an unbalanced or non-system
   oriented result, e.g. an overdesigned and over-expensive cache memory.

2. Single machine analysis of a new system may completely overlook a crucial
   item or interaction that is novel and has not received much prior attention,
   e.g. a certain interaction of the compiler and the architecture. This can
   leave a "ticking bomb" bottleneck, or it can render a potentially important
   resource relatively useless.

3. Serious performance flaws may exist in the hardware, or software, or in their
   interaction. Thus a comparative study has the potential to localize problems

easily, whereas the hardware and software instrumentation of a single system to look for weaknesses is an unending process.

4. Multiple machine analysis that compares a potential (or existing) new system with several existing systems may expose major flaws in the new system immediately. Because of some remarkably strong feature in an existing system, that system may outperform the new system. Or the new system may have one or more serious weaknesses relative to the general existing state of the art.

Throughout the book we shall assume that our goal is to design the best parallel system and that comparative methods will be used to achieve the design goal. We have developed more details of comparative design methodology elsewhere [KiKu93], and there are a number of examples in what follows, of the use of comparative performance information (e.g., speedup scatter plots of machine A vs. machine B, as shown in Chapter 8).

1.7 From Technology Complexity to Mainstream Assimilation

The history of computer system design has been driven by the introduction of new ideas that enhance performance or usability, but which lead to complexities that can just barely be dealt with. Initial systems that use these ideas can raise great expectations and become successful attackers, but often exhibit serious shortcomings in other areas, compared to established systems; that is, gains in one area result in losses in others. Later systems improve the integration of the new ideas with the old; eventually the new ideas become completely assimilated, and designers go on to the next subject. Historical examples are the assimilation of floating-point arithmetic into fixed-point arithmetic systems, assimilating virtual memory and time-sharing into traditional monoprogrammed memory systems, and assimilating pipeline (vector) processing into scalar processing systems. Some transitions have failed – for example, associative memory systems and data-flow systems have drawn much research and development attention, but have never materialized in the marketplace as stand-alone system architectures. Parallel computing is in a transition phase, but its success is still not assured. However, it appears that if it is not successful by 2000 or so, there will be a major upheaval and shift in the computing world, because sequential machines will probably not get much faster, so users will have to lower their expectations about future growth of computer system capabilities or resign themselves to new programming difficulties to obtain more speed through parallelism.

People have made many attempts to introduce certain hardware or software complexities that support parallel computing, but to date few of these ideas have been universally accepted by the parallel computing community, and as a result, parallel computing has not become assimilated into the sequential computing community.

1.7.1   Shedding Complexity

Another aspect of technology evolution is the explicit shedding of the complexity that has resulted from an accumulated patchwork of system improvements. For example, after thirty years of evolution, by the late 1970s, the basic instruction sets that computers executed had become very complex, and the hardware necessary to execute the instructions had become inefficient. Thus, the accumulation of ideas that had originally been introduced to speed up performance were, in the end, actually slowing it down in what have come to be known as Complex Instruction Set Computers (CISC). At the same time, microprocessor chip sizes limited the amount of hardware that it was possible to use in a single processor, and compiler technology had made substantial advances. The Reduced Instruction Set Computer (RISC), in one sweep, simplified the instruction set and the control hardware needed to execute instructions, exploited compiler technology to handle some previously hardware-implemented issues about instruction stream processing, and squeezed powerful processors into fast single chips (or chip sets). As another decade has passed, manufacturable chip sizes have become much larger, and the new real estate allows designers to use more hardware. Some of this has gone into more cache memory, some into wider words, and some into more uniprocessor complexity by reassimilating certain CISC features. In the future we face a single chip trade-off between the use of more complex uniprocessors and the parallel use of simpler processors. The struggle between processing real estate and cache memory real estate remains in either case. The added complexity of designing and dealing with second-level, off-chip caches has arisen in this evolution and will remain for some time.

The point here is that complexity is sometimes in the eye and experience of the beholder. When such ideas are new and not well integrated into computer systems design, they are regarded as additional design difficulties that may not be worthwhile. As they become well understood and as their benefits become manifest, these once "complex" ideas become mainstream design techniques that are used everywhere. Other "complexities" are just that; after taking the plunge and using them in several systems, designers purge them from their repertoire or simplify them to the point of practicality for use in future systems.

Before exploring some details of where the parallel processing community is today, let us sketch a few historical examples that recall the difficulties of past assimilations of complexity.

1.7.2 Assimilation Examples

In the early 1960s, time-sharing and virtual memory appeared in many research computers to allow users easy access to large systems that had previously been available to one user at a time for fixed data size computations. By the early 1970s, MIT's Multics system had been developed jointly with General Electric and Bell Labs cooperation, and the system was sold commercially by G.E. (later Honeywell). Multics was a wonderful system for its users, but its complexity and cost made it a commercial failure for G.E. Meanwhile, Bell Labs' researchers developed a simplified operating system called Unix (a Multics pun), many manufacturers began to provide virtual memory hardware, and Bell Labs attacked the whole computer industry by licensing Unix very inexpensively to companies and universities. By the early 1980s, the desire for open, non-proprietary operating systems to provide users with the same interface from one machine to the next, the desire to share resources on networks, and the ubiquity of Unix due to Bell Labs' low cost licensing policy, started a trend to make Unix a universal operating system choice for all manufacturers. By the mid-1980s, with Unix, Sun displaced workstation innovator Apollo's proprietary Domain OS as the leader, while Alliant, Convex, Sequent (cf. Section 4.1), and others used Unix to cut into the dominant DEC VMS market share.

In the early and mid-1960s, pipelined and vector processors began to appear in various computer systems as a means of processor speedup in the supercomputers of the day. Control Data and IBM built such machines, as did Texas Instruments and others, but these systems never flourished in the marketplace. Because of their complexity and poor cost/performance ratio, they enjoyed limited customer acceptance. In the late 1970s, Cray Research, Inc. introduced the Cray 1 which became a marketplace supercomputer standard, and Floating Point Systems, Inc. introduced a minicomputer version that was usually attached as an accelerator to other computer systems. These machines were very popular in their marketplaces and produced many subsequent attackers. Today, virtual memory and pipelining are commonly used in microprocessors and are regarded as mainstream technologies.

Parallel computing has a history that reaches back to implementations in the 1960s, with an evolutionary path that has not yet led to the development of generally practical products. Because supercomputer clock speeds have already saturated due to the difficulties of increasing ECL circuit speeds, and because it appears that microprocessor clock speeds will saturate by 2000, parallel processing is currently a very prominent technology. This has been the case throughout the 1980s for parallel vector supercomputing and is increasingly becoming the case in the 1990s for parallel microprocessor MPPs. A goal of this book is to accelerate the progress of parallel processing toward its assimilation as a practical mainstream technology.

Sidebar 4: Tortoise and Hare Technologies

Just as the quarterback on the field and the reporter in the press box may have sharply different views of a developing play, so do technical insiders and marketplace observers have different views of technical innovation and product evolution. Controversy during the assimilation phase of a new technology is to be expected, and long time horizons are not unusual. For example, Multics began in 1963, but Unix did not appear until the mid-1970s and is only becoming a market-wide issue in the 1990s. Pipelined processor projects began on supercomputers in the mid-1960s, but pipelining became widely popular in the Cray-1 and Floating Point Systems machines in the mid-1970s, and found its way into microprocessors in the 1980s. Pressbox observers cannot be relied upon to make technical forecasts, nor can business and technology plans be based upon superficial speculation.

There have been many hare vs. tortoise contests in the technology arena. Outside observers seldom miss a hare, because hares quickly gain market share and often seem unstoppable. For example, RISC processors have made substantial practical performance gains in the 1980s, and the market for workstations and PCs has grown explosively. Meanwhile, supercomputing market size and hardware technology innovation have moved tortoise-like. In fact, gallium arsenide (GaAs) circuits have proved very difficult as high-speed devices (e.g., at Cray Computer Corp.), and emitter-coupled logic (ECL), which moved the field ahead for decades, seems doomed in view of CMOS and BiCMOS circuits. On the other hand, in the 1980s, workstations were introduced as a new product concept using open software (e.g., Unix), borrowing architecturally from HPC systems (e.g., pipelining), exploiting CMOS and BiCMOS circuits whose time had come, and incorporating several innovative ideas (e.g., reduced instruction and control complexity). Workstations were truly a hare relative to traditional vector supercomputers, which had to struggle with a losing technology and technical challenges in the unknown. Parallel architectural concepts (e.g., interconnection networks and cache coherency) and software (e.g., compilers and libraries) posed great difficulties.

Typical pressbox observations of these events are presented in a 1993 Congressional Budget Office (CBO) report [CoBO93] on HPCCI, which raises a number of questions about the value of the program. Overall, it does not make recommendations, but gives an analysis that seems to favor HPCCI expenditures on networking over HPC per se. The report cites the frequently stated fact that workstations have superior performance/cost on many computations. It also raises questions about the direction of idea flow in HPC. This book cites many examples of technology trickle-down from supercomputers to workstations and PCs, but the CBO report suggests that there is now a major idea flow in the opposite direction, because MPPs are now using RISC processors.

After admitting that there has been technology trickle-down from HPC to RISC processors in the past, and praising the hare-like RISC market growth relative to the tortoise-like HPC market in the 1980s, the authors state that "[M]uch, if not most, of the improvement in the performance of massively parallel supercomputers during the last decade can be attributed to the use of ever more sophisticated workstation RISC microprocessors" (p.58). In reality, when the report was written, Thinking Machines used one Sun microprocessor plus four custom Texas Instruments accelerator processors per processing node; Intel used its i860, which has not been used in workstations; Kendall Square and nCUBE used custom processors; and the Cray MPP used DEC alpha processors for which DEC had workstation plans; only IBM was using workstation processors (RS6000) in its MPPs, so the report's processor details were shaky. The fact that hundreds or thousands of processors are being used to get high performance, that they are effectively communicating with each other and memory, and are running parallel system and application software, seems forgotten in view of the hare-like workstation market growth!

A similar pressbox view of the situation is offered in *Computer Wars* [FeMo93], where after 100 pages of details and quotations about IBM's problems, the authors have a section entitled "The Role of Software and Design," that doesn't quote anyone. They note that for a decade, "microprocessor speeds have been roughly doubling every 12 to 18 months," which is true but due less to clock speed than architecture, and they then extrapolate "with no end in sight." Next a discussion of real processors, including the DEC Alpha at "100-200 mips," concludes that "a number of companies expect to introduce 1000-mips chips within the near future," which is explained by the wonders of RISC design. Even at the historical rates they quote, 1000 MIPS would take 3 to 4 years; in fact, a number of competitors have announced slower chips after DEC's initial Alpha deliveries, and no one has exceeded the Alpha clock speed in the 2 years following its introduction. The microprocessor RISC spurt of the 1980s will only be matched in the 1990s if parallelism can be tamed. The authors correctly note that "the newest chips pile on more and more intricate tricks" including "breaking up operations so they can be performed in parallel on the chip, and so on." Parallelism is hard, but the "and so on" part causes real problems!

Undeterred, the authors next explain the importance of MPPs and conclude that Thinking Machine's Connection Machine "routinely racks up victories over traditional supercomputers from America's Cray and Japan's Fujitsu and Hitachi." In fact, Thinking Machines was having as much trouble as everyone else in understanding and delivering practical MPP parallelism, and has now terminated manufacturing. Furthermore, we do not know how to deliver general purpose parallelism at the chip or system level, so extrapolations that breeze past this difficulty can be deeply flawed.

While the authors of both the CBO report and *Computer Wars* are evidently convinced that RISC technology can drive future MPPs, the CBO report suggests that MPPs do not have much of a future anyway, relative to workstations and vector supercomputers, so the HPCCI funds are being wasted. They totally miss the point that parallelism will soon be *necessary* at both ends of the spectrum, and therefore all of the resources available should be spent to solve the problems of practical parallelism. The RISC revolution in microprocessors has long since transitioned to an on-chip parallelism revolution, which is proving very difficult to complete. The crucial issue is how R & D funds should be spent, and the CBO report does correctly question massive government expenditures to design *and* purchase massively parallel systems.

Parallel processing is truly a tortoise technology, with beginnings that go back 30 years. But we must remember that the workstation hares have faced much easier technical challenges than the tortoise and have been able to borrow from the tortoise in the past; looking forward to 2000, the hare is again in need of the tortoise's technology to continue, but even the tortoise is having trouble proceeding as in the past. HPCCI and industrial funds must be preserved for parallel processing research as detailed in this book.

1.8   Financing HPC Developments

The competitive nature of the world has made the financing of high performance computing (HPC) easy, over time. In the early years, military competitiveness between the United States and its enemies fueled government expenditures; World War II and Cold War weapons design and intelligence processing are well-known examples that drove computing R & D. Later, as the practicality of computational science and engineering results became established, industry and academia became large HPC markets.

1.8.1   Industrial Funds

Before 1950, HPC efforts were financed by all computer companies. In fact, every early computer was a supercomputer by definition, but by the late 1950s, the Univac LARC and IBM STRETCH supercomputers were developed as separate, top-of-the-line systems. In the early 1960s, the computer market diversified with the introduction of DEC minicomputers and the IBM 360 line, which ranged from office-sized to super-sized computers. Into this setting CDC delivered the CDC 6600, which became *the* supercomputer standard and evolved into a sequence of machines that continues today. Many of the high-end systems lost money, but CDC based a very successful business on the 6600 and its successors.

While CDC is an example of a 1950s startup company, and Cray Research Inc. and Floating Point Systems are 1970s examples, there were few HPC startups until the 1980s. By then, parallel processing ideas were abundant, fast sequential computing faced a sequential speed squeeze, and venture capital money chased every entrepreneur. Even with costs ranging from a few tens of millions up to the $200 million range, these experiments to build parallel HPCs were abundant, due to the combination of venture capital excitement and large companies wanting the technology push and prestige of making the world's fastest computers.

This burst of activity was interpreted by many as a clear sign that some form of parallel processing was about to become a practical replacement for sequential speed growth. But it was the *competitive nature* of the business world that fueled this frenzy of HPC projects, rather than complete, solid solutions to the practical parallelism problems. So little was known about performance that charlatans and skilled innovators could be indistinguishable through multiyear design efforts. Even after systems were installed, because delivered performance was initially poor for most users on most systems, it was difficult to distinguish the good from the hopeless. Thus, many systems were produced, sold, and used, for which, in the overall evolution of better HPC systems, it was difficult to decide whether they presented new solutions or merely new problems.

Because there were so many activities, each new announcement of yet higher peak performance attracted new investment money and a new following, and diverted attention from the latest round of performance failures. In this attackers' frenzy, it did not even matter that a particular company would jump to a completely different architecture because its previous one was a performance failure; people believed that the new one would be much better, even though the manufacturer did not announce – or know in detail – why the old model had failed.

1.8.2   Federal Funds

The Federal government's HPCCI plan was, to some extent, intended to leverage these 1980s efforts and thus solve the problems of practical parallel processing. However, the HPCCI was launched despite the fact that not enough had been learned about the performance of prior systems. Since prior system performance was poorly understood, many participants still did not know precisely which problems needed to be solved and which were already adequately solved.

The Federal government has become confused about the distinction between problems and solutions on several occasions with respect to high performance computers. In the early 1980s the Lax report [Lax82] sounded alarms about the performance and availability of supercomputers. The National Science Board responded by establishing five supercomputer centers (with about enough NSF money for only three) while rejecting the notion that research in supercomputing systems per se was in need of a new initiative. Now, a decade later, we are seeing the consequences of this shortsighted decision to buy experimental systems, without funding sufficient crucial R & D before building them.

In the 1990s the FCCSET (Federal Coordinating Council for Science, Engineering, and Technology) reports have spurred Congress to action in passing the HPCC Initiative, but the Federal agencies passively organized themselves to focus on whichever systems ARPA and the industry agree to build. Little money is being allocated to the detailed performance measurement of each application on each machine, databases for the storage and comparison of performance results and codes, and new comparative performance analysis techniques for all machines. (For more details about this problem, see Section 10.5.2.)

Due to the complex nature of parallel processing, many industrial users and some manufacturers of supercomputers look to the government for guidance as well as financial support in HPC, and expect the HPCCI to provide major help. Rather than continuing the old process indefinitely, this book advocates some simple steps by which government, industry, and academia can work together toward achieving practical parallel processing.

Computer system design and the research use of computers are becoming more intertwined as the necessity of understanding and developing practical parallelism grows. Academic computational science and engineering (CSE) programs are becoming necessary to prepare for the future. The HPCCI has budgeted money to support academic CSE programs, which, if continued, will help accelerate the transition in tradition-bound academic institutions.

Sidebar 5: The High Performance Computing and Communications Initiative

The Federal government's HPCCI program attempted to reflect the attitudes of the parallel processing community in the early 1990s.

To announce its goals, an interagency report was produced in early 1991 [BBFY92], which we shall refer to as the FY 92 *Bluebook*, and from which we quote (italics added):

" Recent advances offer the potential for *a thousand-fold improvement in useful computing capability* and a hundred-fold improvement in available computer communications capability *by 1996."*

.... PROGRAM GOALS AND OVERVIEW, p.5

"... innovative systems ... will provide a one-hundred to one-thousand-fold increase of *sustained computing capability over machines that follow the more conventional design evolution path."*

.... HPCS, p.12

The first quotation is stunning in its italicized statement, against the background of 10x per 7 years throughout history; it refers to the potential for 1000x in 5 years, while the second quote hedges this with a 100x to 1000x increase. Regardless of whether one chooses 100x or 1000x, a remarkable jump over historical improvements is promised, and not just in peak or theoretical performance, but in "useful" and "sustained computing capability"

Early in calendar year 1992, the FY 93 *Bluebook* was released [BBFY93], containing the following (italics added):

"It will accelerate the development of *a thousand-fold improvement in useful computing capability* and a hundred-fold improvement in available communications capability by 1996, and it will *enhance the range of scientific and engineering disciplines that can effectively exploit this computational capability."*

.... PROGRAM GOALS AND OVERVIEW, p.5

"The program is designed to attack computational science problems by developing innovative systems that will provide *a one-hundred-to one-thousand-fold increase of sustained computing capability over machines that were in conventional use at the start of the program."*

.... HPCS, p.13

The first and third quotations are similar in the two *Bluebooks*, except that in 1993 the range of applicable disciplines is enhanced, thus expanding the practicality and usability of the program's results. However, the fourth quotation ends with a subtle retreat. Whereas the 1992 *Bluebook* appeared to compare future HPCCI increases to future increases along "the conventional design evolution path," presumably vector supercomputers, by 1993 this became a comparison with machines that "were in conventional use at the start of the program." Thus if Cray systems gained, say 10x during the 5 year program, the HPCCI machines would only have to provide 10x to 100x gains during the 5 years. Even with this hedge, the program promises remarkable results. It is no wonder that President Bush was moved to say (italics added):

"The development of *high performance computing and communications technology* offers the potential to transform radically the way in which all Americans will work, learn, and communicate in the future. It *holds the promise of changing society as much as* the other great inventions of the 20th century, including *the telephone, air travel and radio and TV.*"

.... President George Bush at signing of HPC Act of 1991, FY1993 *Bluebook*, p.5.

Taken at face value, the HPCCI promised extremely important and exciting results. Under some scrutiny, however, the second *Bluebook* indicates a retreat from the promises of the first *Bluebook*. To many experienced in the field, both of these *Bluebooks* were very optimistic, and to some they offered only impossible dreams. The FY 1994 *Bluebook* [BBFY94] has a new title introducing the National Information Infrastructure, is greatly expanded, focusses on applications, and appears not to mention performance in quantitative terms.

1.9   Conclusion

The advent of commercially available parallel computer systems in the 1980s must be regarded as a major milestone in the history of computing. However, despite the great strides made in parallel processing in the past 20 years, the technology still has a long way to go before practical parallelism emerges. Of course, we can now build on the many successful ideas of sequential computing, but parallel computing also presents a number of new problems, which have to date proven very difficult to solve.

Historically, computer manufacturers, computer users, academic researchers, and government policy makers have each played important roles in advancing high speed computation as a field. As the problems to be solved in producing high performance systems become more complex, however, it is not obvious that the processes of the past will serve us as well as they have to date. There is ample evidence that no individual, company, or agency knows how to improve the process. Moreover, there is little data available to support manufacturers' claims about current computer systems or to allow outside observers to make rational decisions. The reasons for a lack of data are that it is difficult to make measurements and there is no consensus about what to measure; in fact it seems clear that in some quarters such data is feared because of its possible implications. Thus some changes in the process are needed.

Today, to achieve high performance, parallel systems are being built of necessity; because the fastest clock speeds have improved very little in the past decade, parallelism is the architect's only hope. This means that for the first time in history, computer architecture is not just an interesting and potentially useful subject, but rather the future of high speed computing seems to depend on it. Furthermore, compiling for parallel machines is a major challenge. Whereas compiler research for sequential machines was pretty much a closed subject by the early 1980s, parallel compilation has blossomed in the past decade and is currently a very important subject. Finally, parallel algorithms need substantial development and implementation in useful libraries. As architectures become more complex, algorithms to exploit them become more difficult to understand.

This chapter has outlined four problem areas whose solutions are the main topic of this book:

1. **Open Performance** is discussed in Section 1.4 as a complement to the open hardware and software standards of the 1980s and as a solution to the remaining difficulties of assembling facts for users and designers of future generations of high performance computer systems.

2. **Comparative System Development** is discussed in Section 1.6 as a methodology for obtaining new levels of insight into system performance and performance improvement.

3. **Practical Parallel Processing** is discussed in Section 1.7 as the goal toward which the whole community must work in the 1990s.

4. **Computational Science and Engineering** as a new academic discipline may be the main benefit of the Federal government's HPCCI, as discussed in Section 1.8.

These ideas are discussed throughout the remainder of the book.

CHAPTER 2

HISTORY AND PRESENT STATE OF PARALLEL COMPUTING

2.1 Parallel Computing Today

Today, the parallel computing field is in a state of turmoil as various competing architectures struggle for market share and users are presented with a wide range of programming models, new languages, and compilers. In the midst of this, system designers must be constantly aware that the ultimate competition is not with some other parallel architecture or new parallel language; the competition is with sequential computing as it has evolved since the mid-1940s. Inexpensive personal computers that can be used without programming for a wide range of applications, make sequential computing a formidable competitor for emerging parallel systems, as do other systems, ranging from workstations to vector supercomputers, which offer users relatively friendly and powerful environments for problem-solving.

However, sequential clock speeds will not increase forever. The fastest liquid-cooled supercomputers' clock speeds have dropped from 12.5 ns (one nanosecond is one billionth of a second) in the Cray 1 of 1976 to about 2 ns today, but this is a tremendous letdown from the improvement of tenfold increases per seven years over the years since the inception of electronic computing. Meanwhile, microprocessors are now operating in the sub-10-nanosecond regime, and the killer microprocessor image is based on the fact that they seem to be closing ranks quickly with the fastest liquid-cooled superprocessors. Nevertheless, even though there are 5 ns microprocessors today, as the gap with superprocessors closes, one cannot expect to attain subnanosecond clocks easily on any system. Thus we are witnessing a squeeze on the perpetual speed increases that everyone has come to rely upon since the invention of the transistor. This sequential speed squeeze may have far-reaching effects in the next century.

A parallel processing imperative arises from this sequential speed squeeze, and because greater speed either allows problems to be solved more rapidly or provides more software functionality in a fixed amount of time, it is universally desired. Even though much is known about parallel processing, we do not yet know

41

how to build practical parallel systems, and this has led to the turmoil mentioned earlier. The challenge before our field is to solve the problems of practical parallel processing before the sequential speed squeeze becomes disastrous.

To understand the potential consequences of not solving these problems, suppose that by 2000 there is general agreement that there is no practical way to increase affordable computer clock speeds beyond the currently existing speeds at that time, say in the range of 1 ns to .1 ns. We would have four choices:

1. We could agree that the current computer speeds are fast enough and forgo the possibilities of running larger, more complex computations and system software in the future.

2. We could develop a massive crash program to discover alternate low-cost hardware technologies for sequential computing.

3. We could develop a massive crash program to solve the architecture and software problems that would enable parallel computing to replace easy-to-use, general purpose sequential computing.

4. We could agree that future computer speed enhancements will be available only for certain types of computations, and then only with a substantially greater programming effort; that is, we could agree that parallel processing is a special-purpose technique.

It is unlikely that the first choice would be acceptable to many people; for example, even now those with minor computation jobs crave faster clocks to support more elegant windows on their screens. Since by 2000 we would have already invested 50 years of intense worldwide hardware research and development, chances of success with the second choice are small. Thus, we are left with a choice between points 3 and 4, which essentially is the issue of whether parallel processing is a general-purpose or special-purpose technique. Although observers may believe that the basic issues of parallel processing have been receiving sufficient attention from the R & D community, one thesis of this book is that they have not, despite the availability of substantial funds.

The key questions to be addressed in developing practical parallel processing are:

I) Can parallel processing be used in general purpose computer systems?

II) Will parallel systems be sufficiently easy to use?

III) How much future speed increase can parallelism provide?

Judging from today's best systems, we can see that parallel computing R & D still has a long way to go before affirmative answers can be given to the first two questions. Chapter 1 presented some serious differences and resulting difficulties between computer system design and most other engineering design, including that of computer hardware circuits, which have been the prime movers in advancing computer speeds in the past. Thus, this book is not a plea for additional R & D funds, nor an attack on inflated spending, but rather a statement that some funds have been misdirected (e.g., in pursuit of faster peak speeds), that certain important, unexplored areas need attention, and that the computer system R & D process itself needs examination and improvement. In this chapter we will sort out the basic issues, give examples of the current state of the art, and indicate what still remains to be done to make parallel processing a practical success.

2.2   Two Eras

Fig. 2.1 presents a century-long view of computing technology divided into two eras: the Sequential Computing Era and the Parallel Computing Era. Each era is further subdivided into four phases that are oriented toward usability and the user's view of systems. The **architecture** phase refers to the hardware systems alone, and to this are added three software phases: **compilers**, which translate high level languages and optimize user-written programs for machine execution; **applications software packages**, which free users from writing certain standard pieces of code; and **problem-solving environments**, which integrate compilers, applications packages, and other software into "Do what I mean" software systems that free users from most programming chores. Finally, each of these phases is broken into three segments: the first (denoted by a broken line) refers to a period of research and development efforts (**R & D** segment); the second (denoted by a solid line), refers to the release of commercial products (**commercialization** segment); and the third (denoted by a broken line), refers to a period when, although there remain a number of open questions, the topic is no longer regarded as a hot research area, products are easy to manufacture, and prices and advertising direct the market (**commodity** segment).

The Sequential Computing Era began in the mid-1940s with the construction of a number of computer systems in research settings, as shown by the dotted architecture line in Fig. 2.1. By about 1950, computers were available commercially, as denoted by the solid architecture line. Compiler research and development began in the early 1950s, and commercial Fortran and Cobol compilers became available by the late 1950s. By the late 1980s, we show the solid architecture and compiler lines giving way to broken lines as the merger of uniprocessor architecture and compiler ideas in RISC systems reached wide commercial acceptance.

In the early 1970s, commercial applications software became available on

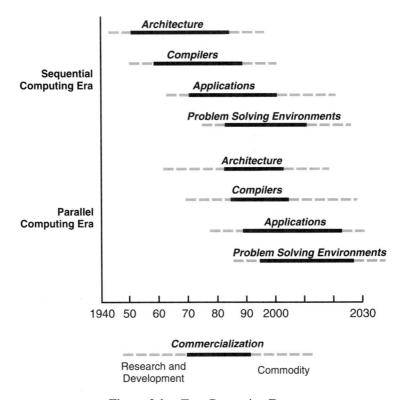

Figure 2.1. Two Computing Eras

uniprocessors, and by the early 1980s complete problem-solving environments (PSEs) emerged in the form of word-processing and spread-sheet software. In fact, the low cost of microprocessor system hardware and the convenience of PSE software led to the personal computer and workstation revolutions of the 1980s. Note that we project the research phases of applications and PSE software to extend beyond the year 2000 for uniprocessors.

Computing in the 1980s was made tremendously exciting for laymen and computer professionals alike by the development of low-cost personal uniprocessors as well as the introduction of commercial parallel systems. Fig. 2.1 shows that the Parallel Computing Era began at just about the same time that uniprocessor PSEs made sequential computing affordable by the general public. The same four phases are shown unfolding for the Parallel Computing Era in the 1980s and through the mid-1990s.

The phase shift between the introduction of each of the four phases of the Sequential Computing Era was about ten years, and we estimate that assimilation, the co-occurrence of each of the commercial and research segments, took about thirty years. This leads to two key questions for parallel computing:

How great a time delay will there be between each of the four phases in the Parallel Computing Era, and how long will the R & D segment of each phase last before it becomes easy to produce high quality commercial products?

The optimistic answer is that because we have learned so much from the past fifty years of sequential computing, the phase shift will be reduced to, say, five years, and each research phase will drop to ten or fifteen years. The pessimistic answer, however, is that parallel computing is so much more difficult to understand and the design problems are so much more challenging, that these numbers will be much higher, perhaps exceeding the corresponding times for developing the Sequential Computing Era. There are important policy issues for government, industry and academia here, which we will discuss throughout the book.

The answer to these questions will be revealed over time as research and development efforts advance parallel computing and sequential computing speeds run their course. In the next decade it seems obvious that the rate of speed increase of microprocessors will continue to decline, as it has for micros and superprocessors in the past decade (see Sidebar 13, Chapter 4). Thus, users' attention may be further torn between the potential speed advantages of parallel systems and the existing usability advantages of sequential systems. In any case, it appears that computer system design will continue to be an important and exciting field well into the 21st century.

Sidebar 6: Is Parallel or Sequential Computing More Natural?

Real world examples abound of parallel control and the independent operation of multiple subsystems. At the level of synthetic systems, supermarkets have parallel checkout queues and farmers plow parallel furrows, while at more fundamental levels, all of nature acts simultaneously at each time instant. The neurons in our brains fire simultaneously, so we basically think in parallel. Thus, while time appears to flow sequentially, the rest of our world seems to work in parallel.

On the other hand, a person cannot listen to a radio newscast, balance a checkbook, and hold a conversation simultaneously, even though distinct human I/O devices are used for each of these, so individual human parallelism is limited. If a family were going to the grocery store and each family member simultaneously wrote down a shopping list, chaos would result without the global control or sharing of ideas. Similarly, to be effective, the parallelism of synthetic systems requires careful coordination.

The idea that thinking about parallel processing is more natural than the sequential counterpart is frequently presented in support of parallel processing. The human mind easily grasps the notion of a large collection of data elements in a matrix or tree as a single data structure object, and can therefore easily formulate ideas about parallel operations on all of the elements in these objects.

Parallel algorithms for adding matrices, sorting lists, or comparing trees can easily be thought of as single conceptual steps, and hence as individual tasks executed in parallel on many data elements, whereas sequential algorithms to carry out these processes may contain many individual computer steps. However, when we try to invent or describe a complete computational process, we must break the overall process into manageable parts and deal with limited aspects of the process at each conceptual step. Furthermore, to plan a program that contains a number of conceptual steps, each with the complexity of the algorithms above, forces the human mind to deal with one algorithm (or two) at a time, which is rather like listening to the radio, followed by balancing the checkbook, and then conversing. Even if the conceptual steps allow simultaneous consideration and their computer execution can be overlapped, any interactions that exist between them must be coordinated in the manner of multiple shopping lists.

While formulating concepts in parallel is often easy and natural, developing parallel algorithms that are correct and run fast can be very difficult and require intricate sequential thinking. Confusion about whether it is more natural to think about sequential or parallel computation is analogous to the ambiguities caused by human inabilities to move from focussing on individual details to abstracting details away to understand the overall picture of any real world subject.

2.3   The Practicality of Parallel Computing

In Section 2.1, three questions were raised concerning the practicality of parallel computing. The first two, which are discussed below, are qualitative and closely linked; the third concerns the speed potential of parallelism and is discussed throughout the book.

General Purpose Computing

It was shown long ago (see, e.g. [Kuck78]) that the use of parallel computers could be **practical** for certain specific purposes. For the past 20 years we have been debating whether they can become general-purpose machines.

However, a rigorous definition of "general purpose" is impossible, and intuitive definitions are time-varying as the effectiveness of sequential machines evolves toward non-programmed, "Do what I mean" systems.

It is easy to argue that we have not really had general purpose machines since the early 1960s, when the IBM 360 introduced a family of machines with equivalent instruction sets, and Digital Equipment minicomputers became popular. But there are more fundamental issues than a machine's price and market segment utility. We can characterize the issues using three technical points:

1. Program structures,

2. Data structures, and

3. Data sizes.

We assume that a **general-purpose computer** should deal with each of these across a universal range, although it is even acceptable to allow certain program modifications from machine to machine. The important distinction is: How does the performance vary? We say that a machine's performance is stable if it does not vary too much over a certain set of computations (see Section 6.7). If this set of computations is sufficiently broad, the community intuitively agrees that the machine is a general purpose one. Thus we must deal with two questions:

A. Is the collection of applications sufficiently broad?

and

B. What performance range should be called stable?

Without rigorously defining a general-purpose machine, we can clarify the progress being made over time toward general-purpose parallelism by systematically examining the three technical points above relative to these two questions.

Ease of Use

The second issue to be addressed in demonstrating that parallel computing can replace sequential computing is **ease of use**. This issue is even harder to define than distinguishing whether a system is a general purpose one, because it involves the opinions of users. The simplest indicator of parallel ease of use is to observe the extent to which users are unaware of whether they are using a sequential or parallel system; in other words, requiring that parallel systems be as easy to use as sequential ones (see Section 3.8), but most people would agree that this is too severe a requirement for the next few years. Furthermore, it is reasonable to require of users certain behavioral changes in adopting parallel processing; whole communities of users have

		Relative to era		
		Peak Speed	Hardware Technology Level	Software Quality
1960s	U. of Illinois Illiac 4 Bell Labs PEPE	high	high	low
1970s	Goodyear Aerospace STARAN ICL DAP, Goodyear MPP	high	medium	low
1980s	Hypercubes SIMDs	high	low	low

Table 2.1.   Brief History of Massively Parallel Machines

regularly made shifts that approximately held ease of use constant while increasing portability and openness (e.g., Unix) or reduced cost (e.g., new third party software).

Our discussion of practical parallelism will focus on developing effective, scalable architectures, providing powerful compilers for languages that are similar to existing languages, and embedding them in familiar programming environments and operating systems. Chapter 5 presents this subject and concludes with five tests for practical parallelism which are expanded in the remainder of the book.

2.4   A Brief History of Parallelism

Table 2.1 gives a brief history of massively parallel computing in terms of performance and technology levels. For each of three decades, parallel computing has offered the highest performance levels available, compared with other systems of the era.

Furthermore, the hardware technology has changed dramatically over these three decades. In the 1960s, parallel systems used the highest level of technology available, so the systems were difficult to manufacture, expensive, and hence, rare. In the 1970s, a second generation of parallel systems appeared that used simpler technology (e.g., bit-serial processors) and so were easier to manufacture, less expensive, and more commonly available. By the 1980s, with the advent of standard microprocessors and busses, and increasingly larger memory chips, the hardware aspects of parallel processing had become low tech, and many companies as well as university research projects were able to build parallel systems. On the other hand, in each period, it was difficult to exploit the parallelism fully and achieve the high potential performance levels because the software remained a very high technology item: that is, it did not perform as well as was hoped and was difficult to use.

Thus, the history of parallel computing systems can be viewed as one in which the building of larger and larger systems has become easier and easier in practice (cf. Section 5.3). But as their size increases and, to some extent, their architectures have been weakened by lower-tech hardware approaches, the software challenges have remained enormous. So the appeal of peak speed remains high, the appeal of low cost has grown (relative to fast scalar supercomputer processors), but the software appeal has remained low. In this climate entrepreneurial companies have introduced all manner of new products, but to date few end users have achieved production-level practical results from parallel computing.

Sidebar 7: Massively Parallel Processing History

The history of parallelism and simultaneity in computing is as old as the history of computing itself. Charles Babbage, who built the first major mechanical computer before 1850, was proud of his ideas about parallel arithmetic, and one can infer from his writings that he also considered parallel processing of some type. In the 1920s, Lewis F. Richardson proposed that computational meteorology for weather forecasting be done in parallel by a large roomful of people with mechanical calculators, under the control of a leader who would call out orders. In the 1950s, John von Neumann considered the analogies between computers and the brain, and put forth parallel computing models.

Most 1950s computers used parallelism within arithmetic operations; some had multiple functional units, and a few had multiple processors. Compagnie des Machines Bull began the Gamma 60 project in 1956 under the direction of Philippe Dreyfus, and eventually delivered 20 multifunction/multiprocessor systems. Konrad Zuse, who had built a series of early machines in Germany – his general purpose Z3 was built between 1934 and 1941 – filed a patent application in 1956 for an array of processors sharing the memory of a magnetic drum. In 1958, Stephen Unger of Columbia University proposed a 2D array of bit-serial processors for picture processing; in 1959 John Holland at the University of Michigan proposed an array of processors together with a number of uses. At the time, all computers were built from vacuum tubes. The first transistorized machines came in about 1960, and integrated circuits still lay in the future.

In the early 1960s, Westinghouse Electric built Solomon, a bit-serial parallel system, under the direction of Dan Slotnick, who moved to the University of Illinois in 1965 where he initiated the Illiac IV project. Illiac III, a special-purpose, parallel bit-serial machine for image processing was already under way at Illinois under the direction of Bruce McCormick. When it was completed, Illiac IV consisted of 64 high-speed processors and was installed at NASA Ames Research Center in California, where it served through the 1970s as a research facility.

From the late 1960s to the early 1970s, there were several other parallel system projects of importance. Bell Labs designed the PEPE system, in a project led by Jack Githens, for the Defense Department's anti-ballistic missle defense program, to do radar signal processing. This was a very specialized application requiring infrequent interaction between independent processing threads; a central computer controlled the parallel processing array. Goodyear Aerospace in Akron, Ohio built a series of bit-serial parallel systems for special purposes, including air-traffic control and radar signal processing, under the leadership of Jack Rudolph. A number of parallel Staran systems were eventually deployed in airborne military radar systems. Major intellectual leadership for these projects came from Ken Batcher, who in 1968 demonstrated a remarkably fast parallel sorting system design. In England in the early 1970s ICL designed and built the DAP system which they sold as an associative memory attachment to other ICL systems. The DAP design work was led by Stuart Reddaway.

In addition to these parallel systems that were built for speed, multiprocessors have long been used for reliability. George Stibitz built several systems at Bell Labs in the 1940s that had self-checking hardware, including a second processor that could be used to check the first. In the 1970s, Tandem made a commercial success of multiprocessor computing to provide "nonstop" capabilities in settings that are extremely fault sensitive, for example, real-time banking operations.

Parallelism has been part of the computing scene from the beginning, but in the second half-century of modern computing, it appears destined to become the central architectural feature.

2.5   Past Parallel Processing Successes

Over the past 25 years the supercomputing community has had mixed success in delivering effective parallel processing to users. We shall divide the successes into three categories: true successes, special-purpose successes, and false successes.

Machine (years)	Basic Architectural Feature	Architectural Bonuses	Relative Price	Software View	Overall Weaknesses	Market Appeal	Profitability (early)
CDC STAR 100 Cyber 205 1960s-70s	Fast Pipelined Vector Operations	Memory-to-Memory Programming	High	Fortran plus Vector Instructions	Slow Scalar	Vector Instructions and Speed	Low
Cray 1 1970s-80s	Fastest Scalar Processor	Pipelined Vector	High	Fortran plus Assembler	Software Weak	High Speed	High
Cray X-MP, Y-MP, C-90 1980s-90s	Fastest Scalar Processor	Parallelism	High	Fortran Directives	Cost vs. Workstations	High Speed	Medium
Massively Parallel 1980s-90s	Many Microprocessors	Massive Parallelism	High	Fortran plus Libraries	Software Weak, Microprocessor Performance Low	Exciting Peak Speed	Low

Table 2.2.   Key Supercomputer Overview

2.5.1   Supercomputer Successes

The computer systems discussed in this book have been built because of their performance potential. They have succeeded in the marketplace because of their delivered performance, but their marketplace acceptance has also depended upon their usability. Each machine's success can be judged on two scales: its technical innovation and influence, and its financial success and market staying power. It should be obvious that these two scales measure quite different attributes; in fact it is fair to say that few machines do well on both scales. A truly innovative machine usually has noticeable weaknesses, and if another company can copy the innovations and improve the overall system, that is, better assimilate the innovations to the mainstream, then it has the attacker's advantages (cf. Chapter 1) and may well succeed in the marketplace. As we shall see below, this technology leap frogging has been repeated many times in the history of high performance computing. In fact, over the past 50 years the entire progression of machines has been built by this process, each new system building upon the preceding few, often by the same people in a new organization.

Table 2.2 lists a number of supercomputer systems from the past 30 years. It characterizes these systems in several ways that explain why the systems made it to the marketplace, but also why they were superceded. We begin with supercomputer product lines, from the past three decades.

Control Data Corporation began work on the CDC STAR 100 system in the mid-1960s, and this product line carried through the CDC Cyber 205 in the 1970s and finally ended with the ETA Systems effort, which collapsed in the late 1980s. These machines were based on a memory-to-memory vector instruction set and multiple pipelined functional units. They offered a powerful set of vector instructions that were easy to use, nicely matched the users' mathematical notation, and gave relatively high performance. However, because their scalar performance was relatively slow and vectorization was often hard to do, manually or by compiler, their peak performance far exceeded their delivered performance. Nevertheless, this line of systems attracted many satisfied users for almost 20 years.

By the mid-1970s, Cray Research Inc.(CRI) released the Cray 1, which had vector instructions that operated only on 64-word vectors that fit into vector registers (not main-memory sized vectors as in the STAR 100 and Cyber 205), and thus presented a number of programming difficulties which Cray compilers did little to hide from the users. While it was harder to program and had no better software than the Cyber 205, the Cray 1 had the fastest scalar performance available, based upon its pipelined arithmetic units with a 12.5 ns. clock period. Thus, the system was a winner even when its key feature – vector processing – could not be programmed into an application. The Cray 1 sold very well and survived in the marketplace into the mid-1980s, by which time the CRI Cray X-MP, Cray Y-MP series had succeeded it. These machines improved upon the Cray 1 single processor architecture by providing additional memory bandwidth, handled sparse vectors better, and through evolution had better software than the Cray 1. Thus the vector uniprocessing abilities of these systems was maturing so that programmers could automatically achieve vector performance that was better than scalar performance. However, the new line added the excitement of parallel processing by offering first two-processor, then four- and eight-processor shared memory systems. The performance benefits of this parallelism were, like the vector benefits of the Cray 1, not available to the faint of heart; however, the software for exploiting parallelism has improved and continues to evolve to the present. A difficulty began to appear by the mid-1980s: for programs that vectorized poorly, some workstations produced performance that was only 2 to 5 times slower than the Crays. While they lacked the large memory capabilities and peak speed potential of supercomputers, these workstations cost only several tens of thousands of dollars, whereas supercomputers cost several tens of millions. Most Crays have long job queues, so that overnight batch processing of a one-hour Cray job appeared much worse than half day (or few hour) computations on a workstation in one's own office. Furthermore, users pay by the hour for Cray time, whereas the desktop workstation is "free" after the initial investment, although a workstation user must become one's own system manager, whereas most supercomputers are managed by large technical staffs.

In the late 1980s massively parallel processor (MPP) systems from Intel, Thinking Machines, nCUBE, and others [Hwan93],[Bell92], appeared as a serious threat to Crays and other vector or parallel-vector traditional supercomputers. As indicated in Table 2.1, these machines promised top peak speeds and so appeared to be the natural successors to vector supercomputers, especially when one realized that they were based upon $1,000 microprocessors rather than $10 million vector processors. The downside included the fact that the software was very weak, requiring much more user effort than traditional supercomputers had for many practical applications, and the cost was higher than expected. By the time a system was fully configured with memory and disk, and sufficient margins were added to cover software development and system research and development, some MPP system consumers were experiencing supercomputer-level sticker shock. The major difficulty however is that when the Cray 1 ran in its degenerate scalar mode, it was the world's fastest computer, but if an MPP runs a job on a single processor, the user effectively has a $10 million workstation. In other words, everything must go exactly right with the software to get cost-effective MPP computations, whereas a Cray 1 was the world's fastest even when everything went wrong. Thus, although the MPP market appeal has been exciting to research users, general-purpose production-oriented customers have largely shied away from these systems.

Special-purpose success can be achieved for various types of parallel computation. For example, parallelism *can* decrease one user's time to solution if, say, a set of totally independent runs is being made back to back. This is an example of a so-called embarrassingly parallel computation, which includes anything that contains large independent data sets for one program or a collection of whole codes that are independent but are considered by a user to be a single job.

More broadly, any code that had been regarded as a single sequential computation and has a structure which it is trivial to parallelize can be regarded as embarrassingly parallel. Other codes that are more difficult to parallelize also deliver good performance on the right architecture; most examples of these are in the scientific and engineering domain. Section 3.4 expands on the details of various application areas.

There are many successful examples of special-purpose transaction processing and database applications that have high degrees of parallelism. Teradata created a major business in this domain in the 1980s, and other recent examples include Oracle on nCUBE, various commercial database applications on Sequent, and the use of MPPs as associative memory junk-mailing engines. In 1994, in attempts to attract and penetrate the commercial market, Cray Research purchased Savant Systems, IBM announced a unification of microprocessor technology across its traditional mainframe and desktop systems, and Intel renamed its Supercomputer Systems Division the Scalable Systems Division and launched a new commercial project.

While MPPs are not yet demonstrated successes, they have recently been introduced as video and data servers in two-way cable TV networks, which has attracted a number of manufacturers on the "multimedia superhighway." Intel MPPs are being offered by Univac and Intel Scalable Systems Division for the commercial market. ATT and Silicon Graphics have formed a company to design and build two-way video and data servers for cable TV and telephone company use.

In summary, historical supercomputers have been economic successes to varying degrees. They have also found varying degrees of market penetration. In recent history, the Cray 1, X-MP and Y-MP might be called general-purpose supercomputers compared to the MPPs we have seen to date, which have at best achieved special-purpose success in multiple marketplaces. Some vector supercomputers, parallel minis, and MPPs have been economic successes, simply because they can simultaneously run independent users' jobs. The next section dismisses this technically as multiprocessing and not parallelism.

Sidebar 8: Supercomputing People

In the early 1950s, University of Minnesota electrical engineering graduates Seymour Cray and James Thornton first joined Electronics Research Associates (ERA) and later Univac, where they learned to design computers; in the late 1950s they joined the new Control Data Corporation. There they teamed up to design the CDC 1604 and later the highly successful CDC 6600, which may be regarded as the first mass produced supercomputer. That system evolved into the CDC 7600, and they began to work on vector processing systems. Thornton initiated the CDC STAR 100 vector supercomputer project in Minneapolis in 1965, while Cray, who had formed the CDC Chippewa Lab in Chippewa Falls, WI, pursued an 8600 system, which never made it to the marketplace. The STAR 100 was delivered but had performance problems; it later evolved into the CDC Cyber 205 family under Neil Lincoln. In 1974 Thornton left CDC to form Network Systems Corp., the first company dedicated to providing high speed system interconnection technology. Meanwhile, Cray left CDC to form Cray Research Inc.(CRI), and by 1976 CRI delivered the first Cray 1 system. Seymour Cray went on to develop the Cray 2 system in the 1980s. Because the Cyber 205 was losing to the Cray 1 and CDC had diversified so much, William Norris (CDC Chairman and founder) decided to spin out ETA Systems in 1983 as a separate firm to focus on supercomputers, and Neil Lincoln led the design of the ETA 10. ETA delivered some systems but collapsed in 1989.

Steve Chen, who had studied in the author's group at Illinois and worked on the Burroughs Scientific Processor (BSP), brought a broad architectural perspective to Cray Research in 1980. He refined the Cray 1 architecture and added parallelism, producing the Cray X-MP and Cray Y-MP systems. These system lines, with up to 16 processors, far outsold the Cray 2, which CRI eventually produced to compete with itself. Because it had not fixed some of the original Cray 1 problems, the Cray 2 only sold about 20 copies after it appeared in the mid-1980s. By 1987, Chen left to form Supercomputer Systems Inc.(SSI), with broad IBM support; in 1988 Cray left CRI to form Cray Computer Corp.(CCC) and develop the Cray 3, with major initial CRI support. In 1993, after developing a prototype, SSI failed, in part because of IBM's enormous financial and management problems. After several technical and business reversals, CCC survived on additional public financing, but without a Cray 3 sale (the National Center for Atmospheric Research was delivered a 4-processor "loaner" system in May 1993) failed in 1995. Traditional hardware technology has been a major problem in both cases; SSI's costs escalated greatly due to ECL's loss of favor and CCC had major problems with gallium arsenide and manufacturing. With Les Davis – who actually produced manufacturable products for both Seymour Cray's and Steve Chen's designs – as its technical leader, CRI evolved the Y-MP into the C90 in 1991, and continued to develop the vector/parallel system line as well as a CMOS version (the J series) and the massively parallel T3D system (based on DEC Alpha microprocessors).

These machines have been the supercomputer workhorses of the world for the past 30 years. They were developed by a very small group of people who pushed technology to the limits and innovated many of the architectural ideas used in today's fastest systems. That tradition is now threatened by technology trends and the great complexity of developing practical parallelism.

2.5.2 False Successes

These fall into several cases. First we include all uses of parallel machines as multiprocessors running independent jobs. These are indeed productive uses of the machines, but they simply do not qualify as parallel computing because multiple jobs are assigned to multiple processors while the memory hierarchy is shared to some degree. Multiprocessing does increase system throughput, but it does not increase the speed (or decrease the turnaround time) of a *single* computation. Little technical innovation or influence can be claimed for such uses because multiprocessors have been successfully used in this way since the 1960s. Modern examples include almost all production codes run on Cray X-MP and Y- MP systems and many uses of superminicomputers like Sequent and Encore. Some MPP victories have come down to providing a massive collection of workstation servers in a single box for the separate use of remote, individual users.

Other categories of computation are often economic successes for system manufacturers but "false successes" economically or technically for the purchaser:

1. The machine is purchased, set among a collection of other, more useful systems and simply regarded as an exotic item in a broad collection, like a panda in a zoo.

2. The machine is used by only a small group of aficionados to develop some test programs whose successful running and future potential is written up

in technical papers and widely discussed. The difficulties that make this an economic failure for the purchaser include:

a. The programs developed do not have the same functionality or utility as those normally run, and so are generally regarded as useless in practice.

b. The programs developed do not run substantially faster than they did on previous equipment, but a great challenge was met, a great success was achieved, even though the programs are generally regarded as useless in practice. Sometimes the new programs are not tried on the old equipment, thus leading to a false performance success. On other occasions the new programs have been ported back to the previous equipment and are found to run even faster there than on the new MPP [CyKu92].

c. The programs developed are useful but require much highly talented human effort that could be used more profitably elsewhere. Furthermore, little is learned in the process that can be generalized to the next problem.

d. The programs developed are useful but are not portable to other parallel systems or even to sequential workstations, which reduces both their breadth of use and maintainability, respectively.

3. One group in an organization has a truly great success: a code is developed quickly, and new results are achieved. This causes wide interest within the organization but leads to many later type 2 (above) failures.

2.6   Parallel System Quality

Traditional computer system quality is measured in terms of cost and performance metrics that include clock speed, computational rates (megaflops, mips), and times to run particular benchmarks. Other qualities advertised include a machine's physical characteristics, such as various memory unit sizes, system weight, and power and noise level, as well as ease of use and other qualitative issues. These metrics are valid for sequential or parallel machines, but parallel machines require additional metrics.

Most obviously, parallel system performance analysis must include the processor count and various other metrics related to the speed gained by adding processors to a system. In addition the performance of parallel systems is much more sensitive than that of sequential machines to the characteristics of the programs being run. Data size, data structures, and program structures can all affect parallel performance in major ways, and these issues are of central concern to parallel system designers.

The performance irony here is that this forces us to examine these same issues for sequential machines, before we can state how well parallel machines are really doing. In other words, parallel machines will be judged against sequential machines in terms of every quality on which sequential machines have ever been judged, including those that are so obvious that they were never discussed for sequential machines. This is an observation that computer manufacturers have found difficult to accept [PeZo89] and that we will develop throughout this book (cf. stability, data size scalability). For example, after programmers choose basic algorithms, with their major effects on performance, they always have a number of options about how to write a program and choose data structures. Even though usually minor performance differences did result from the particular choices made for sequential computers, those differences were so small that human understandability and similar factors dictated programming style. Parallel computer performance is much more sensitive to these choices, and this causes the developers of production systems to experience many of the parallel software problems that have been faced for years in R & D efforts. The point here is that parallel system designers must now be aware of what performance-swing tolerances there have been in sequential machines, and they must develop an understanding of how far these tolerances can be pushed in the parallel computing era. This idea is formalized and expanded in PPT2 in Sections 5.6 and 6.7.

As mentioned above, computers can be described in quantitative terms, but are frequently compared in qualitative terms, as well, such as the ease of use of an editor or the expressiveness of a language. In this book we emphasize quantifiable issues, although we also address certain qualitative aspects of performance numbers. In other contexts, people say, for example, "It is below freezing outdoors and too cold to..." with no real concern about the issue of water changing state; fast drivers back off from the tachometer's red line without detailed understanding or concern about the state of their engines; and some investors are thrilled when the Dow Jones Industrial Average reaches a new high without knowledge of how or why it hit the previous high. In other words, for quantitative data in many areas – physical constants, engineering safety factors, or financial indices – humans have intuitive, qualitative feelings.

For the quantitative data presented concerning relative metrics, we shall introduce qualitative, value judgements. For example, "acceptable" performance levels are discussed, based partly on the author's perception of what the community believes today, and partly on what appears necessary to make parallel processing practical. The positions presented are expected to open a discussion of these topics, which will reflect quality as it changes over time.

Sidebar 9: Parallel Program Example

Parallel processing allows two processors to execute a program twice as fast as one processor, by doing half of the computations on each processor. Given the right program, using the right algorithms, compiling with the right compiler for the right system, a speedup of two is possible in theory; otherwise a lower speedup will result. For example, the sequential program:

do for i=1 **to** 100
a[i]=b[i]+c[i];
enddo

would require the time of 100 additions using one processor, whereas the parallel program:

do parallel
for i=1 **to** 50
a[i]=b[i]+c[i];
for i=51 **to** 100
a[i]=b[i]+c[i];
enddo parallel

would require only the time of 50 additions using two processors. In principle, 100 processors could carry out the computation in just one addition time, although in practice, overhead time to control parallel computations and move data degrade these ideal speedup bounds. In reality more than 1000 operations may be necessary to overcome the overhead and to achieve any performance gain, even on two-processor current systems (cf. Chapter 5 for architectural constraints).

2.7 What Do Users Want, What Do They Need, What Are They Getting?

Ultimately, to be competitive in a free-market economy, it seems clear that parallel computing must compete on equal terms with sequential computing. That is, for the parallel era to be realized, parallel computers must provide users with an image that is similar to that of sequential computers. Because there have been a variety of special-purpose machines in use for many years – perhaps since the introduction of the IBM 360 family and the DEC minicomputers in the early 1960s – and because modern problem-solving environments make sequential computers usable without programming them, the sequential computer image is not simple to delineate.

Nevertheless, we list below several characteristics that are necessary constituents of a user's computer image. (The following ignores issues of cost, physical size, portability, and ownership, focussing instead on performance and ease of use.)

1. Programming Familiarity

Programs must be written in familiar, traditional languages or in easy-to-understand variations of such languages. Similarly, the use of the problem-solving environment must have a familiar or improved look and feel from system to system.

2. Performance Stability

Performance must be stable; from one computation to the next, the computational rate cannot vary much more than it does on currently used systems.

3. Performance Portability

Codes must be easily moved between machines, and performance must remain stable for these codes.

The difficult task of producing good software for parallel systems should be viewed from the perspective of the past effort expended to bring sequential system software, and thus computer usefulness, to its present state. In Fig. 2.1 we presented two computing eras that span a century. Sequential computers did not come into widespread use until compilers were invented in the late 1950s. The commercial availability of applications software accelerated their use in the 1970s, but in the 1990s applications software is still under intense development for sequential machines. In the 1980s, computers became a commodity item with the availability of low-cost microprocessors, but they became widely usable only through the invention of software problem-solving environments, which enabled users to have spreadsheets or engineering CAD without programming. Only input from the user's problem domain was required. Thus, about 25 years were required after the invention of the compiler to transform computer usage from a process that required technical expertise, to a process that anyone could learn. We do not yet have high performance compilers for MPP systems, and although parallel processing can achieve reasonable acceptance without problem-solving environments, the complexity of parallel systems may eventually *require* PSEs for their universal acceptance.

Some optimists feel that a better system will make its own market regardless of other factors. This seldom happens unless there is a tremendous performance advantage, the system enables the user to do something that has not been possible in the past, or there is a captive market, for example, another part of a computer system company or a set of government contractors who buy the systems with earmarked money.

Despite the above, there has been and will undoubtedly continue to be a good market for parallel systems as they evolve. Some compelling arguments are offered by the industry for initiating parallel processing efforts:

A. The sooner, the better

This view is predicated on the eventual necessity for users to embrace parallel processing and simply argues that any effort devoted to current machines will eventually be rewarded. It has at least a grain of irrefutable truth, but in the worst case it ignores the practical difficulties mentioned earlier. It also ignores the fact that from model to model many MPP vendors have made major changes in their architectures and programming styles and thus have demonstrated to any rational customer that the manufacturers themselves are confused about where their own products, as well as the field, are going. An example of this type of failure was the decision by the National Center for Supercomputer Applications, a National Science Foundation supercomputer site, to move all of its users into the future by replacing its Cray with a Thinking Machines CM-5. The result was that many users simply used the network to access Cray machines at San Diego and Pittsburgh NSF Centers; they were not willing to have administrators impose new computer performance struggles on them.

B. Naiveté succeeds best

This approach presumes that people with extensive backgrounds in sequential computing are in some way crippled by their background, (item 1, above) and find parallel programming difficulties where none exist, in part because the real world (including peoples' minds) actually works in parallel (see Sidebar 6). Proponents of this view observe that computer-naive people (e.g., groups of high school students visiting a supercomputing center for a two-week summer program, as are frequently reported in these centers' newsletters) can often learn to obtain high performance from parallel systems, and therefore anyone else should be able to do so. There are several weaknesses here. In the light of performance stability and portability (see 2. and 3. above), such claims must be scrutinized for their definition of high performance, and for which codes and which architectures the claims are made.

C. The stronger, the better

This argument admits that the subject is difficult and the time frame for practical parallelism may be a big unknown, but (contradicting B) invokes the macho-programmer-scientist panacea. The fallacy here is that in the past some of the world's top scientists and engineers have devoted major portions of their careers to parallel processing without achieving anything near the success for which they had hoped. It is important to understand that today there are very few production codes running successfully on parallel systems, including even the modest parallelism of 8-to-16 processor Cray systems.

2.7.1   User's View of HPCC Initiative

For more than a decade leading-edge scientists and engineers have been confronted with a sequence of parallel machines, most of which supported different software and programming models of parallelism. Initially, users are excited and challenged by these systems, and sometimes they are very successful in using them, but often they are eventually frustrated by the difficulties of obtaining good results. When pressured by their organizations to use these machines, some do; others continue to use earlier supercomputers and minisupercomputers; others strongly endorse workstations, which are usually much more cost-effective (but slower, absolutely); and still others try to design their own parallel machines. Some feel (privately) insecure about their inability to use these machines that "everyone else" likes, and others feel like unwilling guinea pigs in a grand experiment that is of no benefit to them. Of course, some have achieved genuine successes and enthusiastically press forward with new problems on new machines.

Sidebar 10: Parallel Algorithm Complexity

Sequential algorithms – precise specifications of a series of steps that solve given problems – have been in use for thousands of years; the name *algorithm* itself is traceable to a 9th-century Muslim mathematician (al Khuwarizmi). Some would say that all parallel algorithms are mere adaptations of sequential algorithms. Others would reply that because of their added complexity, parallel algorithms are a more difficult subject than sequential ones (cf. 2.2).

In the sense that any sequential algorithm can be regarded as a degenerate parallel algorithm, there are *more* parallel algorithms than sequential ones (which makes the subject of parallelism more complex). However, in that only a limited number of sequential algorithms have useful parallel versions, and that, roughly speaking, any useful parallel algorithm can be mapped to a sequential form, there are more basically distinct sequential algorithms than parallel ones.

Because the data structures and control of a parallel algorithm usually have additional complexity beyond those of the sequential version, and assuming that all parallel algorithms have sequential algorithm bases, each parallel algorithm version has added difficulties in logic and implementation.

This philosophical discussion may be of little practical interest. However, a major practical issue arises in the use of algorithm libraries in real computing. In sequential computing, one decides which algorithm to use on the basis of the number of steps each candidate requires, as well as the nature of the problem to be solved. But in parallel computing, in addition to these criteria, the data size and processor count may determine which library algorithm to use. For example, the part of an algorithm that dominates overall running time when one or a few processors are used may be completely different from the part that dominates when thousands of processors are used.

A library that allows selection of data structures and algorithms to match a given program logic, data size, and processor count will provide major parallel performance benefits (cf. Section 10.2.1). Because of these complexities and the long-term tendency to bring computers to the users' level, libraries for practical parallel systems will reach new levels of power and importance.

2.8   Current and Future HPC Policy

As a nation and throughout the international community we are moving toward broader use of parallel computing, so an important question is: What policy changes can be made by industry, government and academia to expedite this move? Consider the fact that companies introduce new products or services in one of three basic ways:

- Tradition Driven: Sustain corporate tradition by evolving new products from old ones,

- Demand Driven: Find out what customers want and then try to provide it, or

- Supply Driven: Develop something very innovative and then try to sell it.

The computer industry follows all three paths but is largely demand-driven and evolutionary (Section 4.1 refines these ideas). Small improvements are generated here and there to satisfy particular customers and then sold to everyone. Occasionally a breakthrough occurs which causes changes in directions in the supply-driven mode, and may be thought of as revolutionary. From the demand side, the problem with parallel processing is that users know that they want more speed for certain programs, but they cannot usually say much else that designers can act upon. On the supply side, parallel architectural innovations often do not meet user desires, so progress has been difficult. However, there are some simple policy changes that should help to correct this situation.

Throughout this book we discuss policy matters in various contexts, criticizing certain existing policy and advocating some new ideas. The old policy, on average, has served us well but is easily criticized and vulnerable because progress toward practical parallel processing is stumbling and money is limited. The policy changes are essential if we are to succeed in developing parallel computing in a reasonable time frame and cost. The recommended changes in thinking and budgeting are relatively minor but should have major, self-correcting effects on our overall HPC efforts.

2.8.1 Spread of the Parallelism Idea

As an idea, parallel processing dates back to the beginning of human computation [Bail92] and the beginning of machine computation [Kuck78]. The promise of parallel computing came to the foreground for users in the 1980s as many companies offered parallel system products. As we have seen, there were two reasons for this: the increasing difficulty in building faster supercomputers based on faster circuits alone, and the wide availability of rather fast, but commodity priced microprocessors.

The 1980s were a decade of divergence in computer systems: almost every previously imagined architecture was built or attempted. The awareness and expectations of the user community have now been raised to a very high level. For example, we have reached a point where the achievability of massively parallel systems with teraflops performance is an article of faith with many people. Unfortunately, there is little discussion of what is really meant by teraflops performance, and there is essentially no evidence that ordinary users will be able to achieve teraflops performance on real codes in the foreseeable future. "Scalable teraflops performance" has become a mere slogan. What has happened historically was summarized in Table 2.1 which pointed out that parallel machines have always demonstrated peak speeds that are very high relative to any era, and have had uniformly low software quality. What has changed over several decades is that the hardware technology has caught up with the architectural needs, so it is now easy to produce parallel machines.

2.8.2 The 1990s

The 1990s seem to present users with a parallel processing imperative: Go ahead with parallel computing, or fall behind in R & D. This is a natural progression, but the validity at this time of the parallel processing imperative in free-market economic terms is open to question. The central question seems to be: When should one make a serious investment in parallel computing? Fig. 2.1 implies the secondary question: When will parallel software quality improve?

It seems inevitable that the 1990s will be a decade of convergence in parallel processing, and there are two possible outcomes. One is a convergence on nothing, that is, a failure of the field to deliver anything that is very useful to more than a handful of zealots. The other is a convergence on practical high-performance parallel systems, and this implies easy programmability, performance portability between systems, and stability of performance from computation to computation.

In the long run, many believe that parallel processing will prevail. There are a few architectural issues and many software issues that remain to be resolved, but from many purchasers' and users' points of view it is just a matter of time until parallel computing provides solid, cost-effective results.

We use the term *Practical Parallel Processing Policy* (P^4) to encompass the worldwide effort to develop practical parallel systems by 2000. Worldwide industrial efforts are being organized to develop parallel system products: the U.S. government's HPCCI, Europe's High Performance Computing and Networking (HPCN) Esprit initiative, and scattered Japanese government efforts. The importance of parallel processing is widely recognized, but the focus and specifics are in a shambles, despite the past worldwide expenditure of billions of dollars on parallel processing R & D.

2.8.3 Industry

It is obviously impossible for any person, book, or committee to have much effect on the worldwide computer industry by announcing ideas to the industry about what kind of systems they should build. This is true partly because no one knows exactly what to do, but even if someone did, it would be impossible to make the argument convincingly without demonstrating a working system. Nevertheless, some simple steps are recommended in this book that would make major improvements to the current *process* and increase our HPC success potential for future systems.

At the core of the difficulty in understanding any computer system's performance is the lack of performance information. We have performance information about parts of systems, but not about whole systems. Without quantitative data about the overall structure of any engineering system as well as its parts, most engineering progress would be impossible. In Chapters 3 and 4 steps are proposed that will make it possible to obtain and analyze such data, and base design improvements upon it. These steps must be carried out by system manufacturers, but they require the cooperation of system users.

2.8.4 HPCCI

As a number of computer manufacturers are building massively parallel systems, and many scientists and engineers are contemplating more use of such systems, the U.S. government has launched the High Performance Computer and Communications Initiative (HPCCI). There are two aspects of HPCCI which arose in two related communities: High performance computing (HPC) and the National Research and Education Network (NREN). The NREN project, which evolved from dozens of previous commercial and research wide-area communication networks, is billed as "the 1990's answer to the 1950's interstate highway program" and was long advocated by then Sen. Albert Gore, Jr. Currently, the information superhighway involves most of the telecommunications industry, and the government's role in moving so broad a field ahead is questionable. This book says little about NREN.

A number of analogies have been proposed to explain or justify HPCCI. We use the 1960s decision to put a man on the moon to explain two points about the HPC part of HPCCI.

I. It was clear to everyone what putting a man on the moon meant. To build a teraflops computer by 1996 (or later) is a much less clear concept. The main difficulty is that to deliver teraflops performance in all applications areas will be impossible, to deliver it in some may be possible, and to reach peak teraflops performance will happen without government subsidy. The only useful program is the middle path, but HPCCI has launched so broad a program that we appear to be trying all areas with the hope of hitting a few. Such an approach wastes money on many areas that should be spent instead to ensure the success of a few.

II. The intrinsic scientific and technical reasons for putting a man on the moon were unclear before we achieved success and still remain unclear to some people. The intrinsic merits of faster and faster computers and the cost of their development can be debated, but past successes with high performance computers in scientific research and engineering design make the payoff much easier to understand for future computational grand challenges (see Chapter 3).

If the HPCCI program is to survive budget cuts and make a significant contribution to our quest for practical parallelism, it will have to sharpen its focus. This book attempts to sketch some of the important P^4 foci. The largest gap in HPCCI is its lack of a coherent plan to measure, analyze, explain, and improve parallel system performance. Correcting this problem would have far-reaching benefits.

There is much discussion of computational grand challenges through which parallel computing could make major contributions to solving the world's technical problems, and it is important for the community to have a better focus on some of these golden eggs. However, a major goal of this book is to raise everyone's awareness of the Greatest Grand Challenge, namely the development of practical parallel processing through which the world would forevermore be able to increase computer performance, without the need for faster circuits. This book advocates solving the problems of designing the goose; the golden eggs will then follow naturally.

2.9 Summary

Chapter 2 presents the current state of high-performance computing in nontechnical terms. It also sketches an historical outline of the paths taken and machines built that led up to the present, and presents some possible future scenarios. Some alarms are sounded concerning the future, that are based on historical experiences and today's understanding of the problems of high-performance computing.

The message of Chapter 2 is straightforward. Faster and faster computers have come about like clockwork since the late 1940s, and today the whole world relies on computers. However, faster hardware cannot keep on appearing forever, and there have been signs for some time that alternatives must be found. There is an expectation among computer users today that parallel computing can fill any gaps in performance left by difficulties in producing faster hardware circuits. Computer system designers, on the other hand, are finding that it is extremely difficult to fill these gaps. In summary, two key technical points are raised above: We must deliver performance to a wide range of users and we need cost-effective software and programming techniques to access the performance. Throughout this book we deal with these two aspects of making parallel processing a practical technology.

Chapters 1 and 2 outline the problems of HPC and the difficulties in solving them, and indicate some directions that will help in their solution. In Chapter 3 we outline a number of software issues as well as specific HPCCI recommendations that affect the research and user community. Chapter 4 explores parallel system architecture and Chapter 5 gives an overview of parallel performance.

CHAPTER 3

PARALLEL COMPUTER SYSTEM SOFTWARE AND WORKLOADS

In this chapter and the next we shall outline in layman's terms the structure of parallel computer systems, the workloads that users expect them to carry, and the results they produce. The discussion is intended to be analogous to describing bridges by showing photos and diagrams of several and then enumerating the types of traffic, wind, and waves that one would expect as loads on the bridges. As a bridge must be designed to withstand certain extreme loads—an earthquake or barge collision—so must a high-performance computer withstand extreme loads. Important but difficult issues arise first in defining these loads and then in agreeing on how the system should perform in response to them. Traditional engineering designs (e.g., bridges, airplanes, or computer circuits) are subjected to extreme loads generated by nature (e.g., earthquakes, severe atmospheric conditions, bursts of electromagnetic radiation, respectively), but high-performance computer systems are subjected to a wide range of specific users' programs, which leads to

The central problem of parallel computer system design:

Users can develop programs with infinite variety, and many types of programs lead to disastrous performance degradation on any particular system.

Manufacturers' representations of parallel systems vary widely, and much of the confusion about parallel computing has arisen from the differing points of view and expectations created by manufacturers and other boosters, and sustained by the press. The image of high-performance parallel computing among end users and their management is based on historical performance-increase expectations, and is enhanced by marketing hype. But the performance realities may differ sharply from the historical clock-speed driven image, because parallel systems have performance instabilities that depend on the infinite variety in users' program details.

At one extreme, programs that perform poorly can be regarded as standard workload examples, or at the other extreme, as anomalies that can be defined away by keeping users of such programs away from the system. The "central problem" of *high-performance computer marketing hype* is to sidestep poorly performing programs and market segments without frightening away other potential users. From the users' perspective, each code may perform quite differently on a variety of current systems. Thus, we are again led back to the question of whether particular high-performance systems are general purpose or special purpose.

A major objective of this chapter is to discuss how designers and users can characterize high performance computer (HPC) workloads and performance in sufficient detail, and communicate with one another in order to make rational decisions about how to improve system performance.

3.1   High Costs and Diverse Benefits of Computing Research

The development of highperformance parallel computers is a major engineering undertaking. Individual projects can consume hundreds of millions of dollars; collectively the nation has already spent billions of industrial dollars on parallel computing. In the 1990s, the HPCCI (Section 2.6) has spent up to $1 billion annually of public money. Obviously, our first question must be:

"Are the high performance computing expenditures worthwhile?"

One can compare high performance computing with technological innovations of the past in terms of expense, complexity, importance, and probability of success (recall Section 1.1). The point here is simply that because of the world's total dependence on computing and apparently insatiable desire for more speed, the present exploration of parallelism will, without question, continue to its logical conclusion – whether it is success or failure. How urgently it should be pursued and hence at what rate money should be spent are arguable issues. But it is clear that because of the ubiquity and flexibility of computer usage, we can predict paybacks that are focused with respect to application areas. That is, we can say that an automobile engine with higher fuel efficiency and better emission control *can be produced* in some measure by computationally analyzing and solving certain problems in computational combustion and in the mechanical and materials aspects of engine design. The specifics of what will happen are as uncertain today as they were in the 1960s about whether the Apollo program would produce Tang or Teflon first, or a century earlier about whether AC or DC would prevail in the electrification contest. Nevertheless we can be sure that a deeper computational understanding of these problems is certain to produce some improvements in auto engines. Furthermore, there are fail-safe aspects to computing. Even in the case where the resulting improvements are smaller than expected, it is arguably true in many fields that have been subjected to extensive computational modeling in the past, that using computational methods to solve a problem is more cost effective than using traditional engineering methods.

The clinching argument here lies in the additional benefits of being able to use computer programs in quite disparate fields. For example, even if we fail to solve the automobile engine problem because the improvements obtained are too small, we may later be able to solve an important *aircraft* engine problem with the same software. Or we may be able to solve problems about the cost of home heating or the useful lifetime of concrete structures, by using exactly the ideas and software generated in the automobile engine problem.

As an example, Electricité de France spent an enormous amount of time and money to develop the highly successful N3S code for nuclear reactor design. This code has helped France to become largely independent of fossil fuel and hydroelectric power. The surprising dividend is that N3S has also been used in the French aerospace industry for airplane design.

In summary, if we focus on some set of priorities high performance computing can be guaranteed to produce important results. The Grand Challenge computational applications (Section 3.3) should not be regarded as problems that can be "solved". Instead they should be regarded as focus areas in which improved products, new products, and new engineering or scientific insights can be generated. Additionally, we can guarantee that eventually fallout will occur in other computational science and engineering areas.

3.2 Crunching And Simulating Styles

Computers possess a universality which makes them remarkably powerful, but at the same time makes it difficult to categorize and explain their methods of use. This might cause one to wonder about the limits of what can be computed and about the power of various hardware and software systems. Philosophers, logicians, and mathematicians struggled for decades with questions about what could and could not be proven and what could and could not be computed using specific techniques. There is a great similarity between a mathematical proof and the execution of a digital computer program, in that each is a series of relatively simple steps that leads to a final and sometimes surprising result.

In the 1920s, Kurt Gödel, in a profound and startling result, showed that there are limits to what can be proven in any kind of mathematical setting, and before 1940 Alan Turing demonstrated a simple abstract computer (the Universal Turing Machine, UTM) which can compute anything that can be computed at all by a digital computer (the Church-Turing thesis). Turing's result shows that a universal computer architecture can be very simple; more architectural complexity can gain more speed but not more logical power. It also shows that the UTM can be programmed with very simple instructions to compute anything that is computable. Like Gödel, Turing also showed that some problems are "uncomputable"; for example, we cannot write a program that can decide whether any program presented to it will ever stop running!

Thus, when modern computer research began in the 1940s, there was a firm foundation concerning the ultimate power of computer systems, but no clear ideas about how to build good computers or how best to program them. As the field has evolved, larger memory, more parallelism, and better algorithms have been used to make computers run faster, but these factors cannot affect the fundamental nature of the kinds of problems computers can solve.

Over the past 50 years various styles of computing have emerged, which we summarize broadly in two categories: crunching and simulating. These two categories describe what home computer users can do without even modifying the programs provided with their systems, as well as what the most advanced supercomputer users can accomplish with state-of-the-art programming techniques.

In **crunching**, a computer processes input data and the computation leads to a single, perhaps complex, result of value to the user. One example of crunching is typing in a sequence of words which the computer processes to produce a well-formatted letter, free of spelling and syntax errors. Another example would be a program that processes census data in order to determine which state has, for example, the highest per-capita income among computer programmers who are married and childless.

In **simulating**, a computer processes input data to produce a set of results that are collectively of interest to the user. Usually, more than one aspect of a simulation result produces entertainment or insight for the user. One example is a computer game to which a user initially provides merely a "go" signal, and the computer responds with a series of images that interact with additional user inputs over time. In another example, an engineer designs a building, subjects it to a variety of simulated earthquakes, and observes the deformation of the building's foundation over time.

A major distinction between the simulating and crunching styles is that simulation results are much more computationally dependent on the user's choices of parameters for initial conditions and for intermediate steps than are crunching results. Thus, by making choices the user can strongly influence the initial type and the course of a simulation, and in the process be more amused by a game or learn more about cause and effect in an engineering design. In crunching, there are usually fewer computational choices: the text of a letter is predetermined, and the census data comes from field workers while queries come from analysts; the computer user specifies which processes to apply to which data, and the rest is more or less automatic. Another distinction may be made by comparing the complexity of the computational model with the quantity of data involved in a computation. Generally, simulations have greater model-complexity per unit of data processed (e.g., engineering and scientific computations) than do crunches (e.g., database and text-processing applications).

Computational Style	User Classes		
	Home, Clerical Office	Business, Government	Science/Engineering R & D
Crunching			
Symbols	Word Processing (Spelling,Style Checking)	Legal, Medical Text Retrieval	Literary Authorship (e.g. Dead Sea Scrolls)
Combination	Desktop Publishing (Text, Tables, Figures)	Census Data Analysis	Climate Data Analysis
Numbers	Financial Spreadsheets	Bank Transaction Processing	Seismic Oil Exploration, Experimental Data Analysis
Simulating			
Space	Chess	Computational Aging of FBI Photos, Architectural Design	Thermal Gradients in Automobile Engine, PC Board Layout
Space/ Time	Action Games	Daily Weather Forecasting, Flight Scheduling, Highway Traffic Flow	Long Range Weather Forecasting, Aircraft Structural Design

Table 3.1. Crunching and Simulating Applications

It should be realized that both computational styles can offer equivalent challenges in terms of the complexity of algorithms or the difficulty of developing codes. Any of the computation types of Section 3.4.3 could apply to either style.

There are ambiguities in these definitions of crunching and simulation, in that a series of number crunching calculations may easily be interpreted as a simulation, or on the other hand a simulation process may produce no intermediate information and lead to a final state which provides a "yes" or "no" answer to the user's original question. Nevertheless, crunching for a final result and simulating for a sequence of related results are the two styles that provide a generally clear distinction in practice.

In Table 3.1 we expand the ideas into several styles of computations for three broad classes of users. The user class columns are intended merely to represent three general levels of user expertise and system power. Although all data is stored in binary form inside computers, any item can represent a number or a symbol, so we divide crunching into these two rows, plus a combination row, and give examples of each. Simulations can be regarded as spatial in nature (e.g., a chess board in which time is of secondary importance), or as a space-time continuum (e.g. an engineering simulation or an action computer game).

A traditional characterization divides computing applications into engineering and scientific computing vs. transaction, database, and text processing. Whereas engineering and scientific computing are major consumers of computing resources, by various cost and volume measures, transaction and database processing exceed engineering and scientific computing. Many of these are crunching-style computations, in that large masses of data are processed in routine ways to produce outputs. Examples abound in banking, insurance, airline reservations, and accounting, which fit the crunching style and for which the programs are never changed by users. Many of these applications possess substantial parallelism, and because the programming is done by expert applications programmers, efficient parallel codes have been developed for specialized computations. The Teradata systems have been very successful in this area. Recently, financial planning, risk analysis, and portfolio selection, for example, have adopted complex new computational models, so whole new industries are now embracing the simulation computational style.

Engineering and scientific computing, the traditional workload of supercomputers, more often produces simulation-style computations. Although there is much application software available for these purposes, end users often modify and extend programs themselves because particular simulations demand it. For a variety of reasons, this kind of code is harder to parallelize than that in the transaction and database area. Recently, MPP vendors have been trying to span both areas with their systems, but problems of reliability and software maturity must be resolved if business applications are to be truly successful.

The parallelization of production codes in any application area is a major intellectual and business achievement. However, it would be shortsighted to think that a tour de force in this regard guarantees success over time. The problem is that good programming tools are necessary to keep codes updated, and as applications evolve over time, the *relative balance* between the times required by various parts of a code changes. Some have argued that their success in parallelizing a particular application is a breakthrough because as time passes, the data size will grow forever in just the areas that parallelize well (cf. Section 5.3). Although this may be true in certain instances, it is best kept as a hope or dream, because the dynamics of the computing world frequently demand unanticipated changes, and as we shall see in Chapter 4 and beyond, small bottlenecks can wreak havoc on whole computations, a circumstance that has led to the ultimate downfall of some MPPs and their manufacturers.

3.3 Describing the Workload

To focus attention on computational science and engineering (CSE) as a discipline, in the mid-1980s, Kenneth Wilson, a theoretical and computational physicist and Nobel Laureate in Physics, coined the expression, **Computational Grand Challenges**. He also proposed a series of meetings in which the nation would sort out important applications and focus attention on the resulting Grand Challenges.

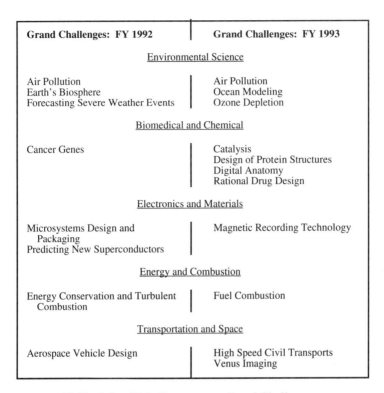

Grand Challenges: FY 1992	Grand Challenges: FY 1993
Environmental Science	
Air Pollution	Air Pollution
Earth's Biosphere	Ocean Modeling
Forecasting Severe Weather Events	Ozone Depletion
Biomedical and Chemical	
Cancer Genes	Catalysis
	Design of Protein Structures
	Digital Anatomy
	Rational Drug Design
Electronics and Materials	
Microsystems Design and Packaging	Magnetic Recording Technology
Predicting New Superconductors	
Energy and Combustion	
Energy Conservation and Turbulent Combustion	Fuel Combustion
Transportation and Space	
Aerospace Vehicle Design	High Speed Civil Transports
	Venus Imaging

Table 3.2. U.S. Government Grand Challenges

Despite considerable efforts on the part of Wilson and others, no list of Grand Challenges has ever survived for more than one fiscal year. Table 3.2 shows lists of the Grand Challenge computations for two fiscal years taken from [BBFY92] and [BBFY93]. The lists have been reordered here in an attempt to show some relationships between their content, although the reports indicate that the lists are samples and that many other important areas exist. However, the attention of many scientists and engineers has been directed to CSE in the past decade by the ongoing discussion of Grand Challenges. In Chapter 10 we discuss the academic role in developing CSE as a discipline. Today Grand Challenge Computation has become a cliche that is too often applied to anything that has run successfully on an MPP. However, the notion has also focussed the attention of users, policymakers, and some academics on the importance of CSE [HaLi92].

To reiterate, program and data structures are important determinants of system performance. The other half of the puzzle is the architectural structure of a system. If the software and the hardware fit together properly, the whole system performs as desired. Although this may imply that computer architects are obliged to design systems that match their customers' software, an obvious problem is that the software is being modified continually, so the architects do not have a fixed target. As a nation, we cannot decide on a fixed set of Grand Challenges, each field cannot agree on which key problems to solve, and advocates of each contending key problem area disagree about what computational methods to use. Thus, in the end it is no surprise that compromises are needed, and design decisions must be made under uncertainty.

It is clear that to achieve practical parallel systems requires new developments in software as well as architecture. We will discuss the architectural issues below, but here we examine how users can communicate their applications needs to system designers. It is easy to enumerate a list of possible applications that system designers should study, and then to think of reasons for rejecting each one. For example, we could consider all of the major scientific and engineering codes in use today—but that is too much code, much of it is proprietary and hence unavailable for study, and the code represents yesterday's thinking. Or, we could consider a set of Grand Challenge Codes that represent future thinking—but there has been no agreement on a fixed set of such codes, and if there were agreement, it would be on a very large code set. Why not, as a compromise, have a group of users draw sample codes from various fields that are currently in use in industry or under development by researchers? This motivation led to the Perfect Benchmarks, which have been in use for high-performance systems since the late 1980s. Similar motivation led to the development of the SPEC Benchmarks for workstations in the late 1980s. In Section 3.6 we extend the discussion of these benchmarks.

Sidebar 11: Wilson and the Grand Challenges

Having helped invent the theory of quantum chromodynamics in the 1970s, Kenneth Wilson of Cornell University realized that to test and exploit the theory fully would require substantially more computing power than was available. Like many other physical scientists and engineers, he had relied on Floating Point Systems (FPS) machines for cost-effective computing power. Unlike most others, Wilson began to push FPS to build faster systems through parallelism. After receiving the Nobel Prize in Physics in 1982, Wilson became an indefatigable advocate and spokesman for HPC and the challenging problems that HPC systems could potentially solve. His FPS relationship led to the ambitious Tesseract system project at FPS, which ultimately was a failure. Wilson's efforts did have significant effects in Washington, in academia, and in industry, raising everyone's awareness of the importance of computational science as an equal partner with traditional theory and experimental work. As a direct result of Wilson's efforts, together with prior reports, including the comprehensive Lax report

[Lax82], the NSF supercomputer centers were established in 1985. Later the HPCCI evolved to build and provide wide-ranging access to high-performance computers, for what Wilson had named Grand Challenge Computations.

3.4   Program Structures vs. Architectures

In this section we define some terms that are used throughout the book. Some of these are in general use without clear definitions. Because there are many kinds of computations, it is obvious that they are not all of equal importance, of equal quality, or at equal stages of development. These are all subjective attributes, which are judged differently in different contexts. This section ends with a policy recommendation outline that is based on computational attributes with objective bases.

3.4.1   Computational Process Definitions

In order to discuss the computational process, consider Fig. 3.1, which expresses some well-known concepts. We use the term **codes** to refer to complete programs with data and say that they are characterized by certain **program structures** and certain **data structures**. Either of these may cause severe performance problems (e.g., program structures with many nested procedures or a lot of branching, or data structures consisting of pointers for sparse arrays). Large programs rely on **libraries** of small programs, which supply standard functionality that users need not write. We refer to a **problem** as the data presented to a program. A problem's size may be large, (e.g., a production run), or small (e.g., a debug run), and we refer to the number of words of problem data as the **data size**, which naturally affects computation time. Numerical problem **types** may be characterized by condition numbers, or stiffness, which indicate how difficult it may be to solve a given problem and also influence computation time. When a program is presented with a problem and run on a machine, a **computation** results. This term refers to all of the dynamics of executing the program on the given problem.

The feasibility of solving a particular problem computationally depends upon how fast the computation proceeds, so performance becomes a critical issue in determining feasibility. Beside being affected by data size and problem type, the performance of a given program on a given architecture is determined by its program structures and data structures. A given code can be transformed into many different, equivalent forms, each leading to a distinct computation that produces the same results. Thus, by using well-designed libraries and compilers and either writing or using good application software, users can obtain much better performance than would be possible with weaker software. The potential performance

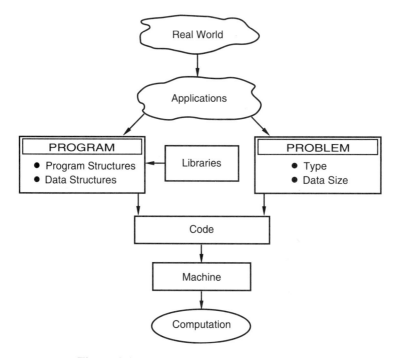

Figure 3.1. Computation Process Definitions

increases may be on the order of a factor of two on a sequential machine, and a factor of $P/2$ on a P-processor parallel machine. Often, programs are initially developed in straightforward, unoptimized styles and then restructured for higher performance on particular machines. Thus, the original code structure together with the power of any restructuring techniques applied are major determinants of performance. We next present some aspects of a code structure taxonomy and discuss corresponding performance levels on high-performance systems.

3.4.2 Computational Types

Many programs run well on supercomputers today. For two decades people have written *vector* programs for the vector processors of CDC, Cray, Japanese super-computers, minisupercomputers, and other systems. In the 1980s, people began to develop successful *parallel* programs for the parallel systems of Alliant, nCUBE, Intel, TMC, and other companies. We can categorize these as *slow-memory* parallel or *fast-memory* parallel computations, depending on the kind of machine on which they run well, a distinction that we clarify below. For the moment, it will suffice to identify slow-memory parallel computations with today's distributed and mas-

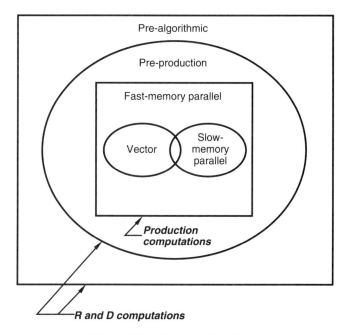

Figure 3.2.   Computation Type

sively parallel processors (MPPs). Beyond these types of computation are several other types that present additional difficulties.

Fig. 3.2 shows a Venn diagram of five computational types (see labels inside regions) and it relates them to the resources they require (cf. Section 3.4.3). The vector and slow-memory parallel programs may both run well on the same machines, but some codes that run well on vector machines will not do well on slow-memory parallel systems, and vice versa. Fig. 3.2 shows increasingly larger classes of computations (discussed below) which enclose these well-understood areas. As more of these are understood, they will be reduced to one of the three types of fast-memory computations shown. If certain problems of parallel processing can be solved, one can expect that all high-performance machines of the 21st century will deliver fast-memory parallel computations.

Fig. 3.2 points out a central problem in HPC today: there is a gap between what we have, computationally, and what we need. On the one hand, using the terminology of Section 3.4.3, production computations are commonly relied upon in many fields, and many designers strive to do new R and D computations. On the other hand, in many cases the equipment available is not suitable for these needs. Vector machines are well developed, but limited in potential for speed enhancement; slow-memory parallel systems are commonly available but limited by performance bottlenecks and high cost at the high-performance end; and fast-memory parallel systems have not been developed in large-scale sizes. Current MPP manufacturers have found it easy to build slow-memory parallel systems and hard to evolve to fast-memory systems, whereas fast-memory parallel systems have mainly been built in smaller sizes and have faced software difficulties in providing general-purpose computing capabilities. The inner rectangle of Fig. 3.2 is missing in the real world, in the form of large, scalable practical systems, although several feasiblity-level implementations have been completed. One goal of the book is to clarify this problem, discuss its importance, and outline steps toward solving it.

3.4.3   Resources Needed for Computational Types

These recommendations are offered in the Practical Parallel Processing Policy (P^4) sense (see Section 2.8) and can be applied at the level of an R & D organization owning multiple systems or the HPCCI program with a national network of diverse systems.

Consider the allocation of resources among the various competing types of applications and program structures. In a broad sense the areas are competing for money and very limited human and machine resources. Hence, it is quite important to identify distinct types of computations, and to discuss which kinds of resources should be applied to each. We will not discuss the merits of various disciplines, only the resources best suited to the various program and data structures that arise in all disciplines.

Production Computations

Easiest to deal with are the vectorized and vectorizable codes, because they can be allocated machine time on a wide range of commercially available systems. Almost as easy to deal with are the slow-memory parallel codes, many of which have been well understood for a long time, which can easily be run on any parallel system and mainly need machine time. For example, with techniques that are well understood using MPPs, certain areas in computational fluid dynamics, computational chemistry, electromagnetics, and seismic signal processing can produce new results and insights that have wide applicability. In the commercial world several organizations are using MPPs for database applications, and Teradata Corp. (now part of ATT/NCR) developed a substantial business around parallel transaction processing systems.

Although there are today very few parallel production codes being run on traditional Cray multiprocessor systems, a notable early example of a fast-memory parallel production code is a parallel weather forecasting code at the European Center for Medium-Range Weather Forecasting in England. A number of examples were also developed on Alliant Computer Systems machines in the 1980s. Certain codes in the areas described in Table 3.2 fall here on various current systems from SGI, Convex, and others. Such established areas can be run on dedicated systems or can be given special allocations of weekend and evening hours on shared systems, because they are guaranteed to produce useful results in predictable ways.

These three classes of computations may all be characterized as **production computations** in that users are willing to pay for major amounts of machine time to help them solve problems in these computational areas. The remaining computations are termed **R & D computations**, in which programs are being developed to become production codes, or are at even earlier stages where people are exploring the possibilities of high-speed computation to augment their theoretical and experimental work. We categorize the R & D computations as pre-production or pre-algorithmic (Table 3.2 also contains a number of these).

R & D Computations

Pre-production computations include those just outside the reach of well-understood computational areas, and those to which not much computing has been applied, but which bear strong similarities to computationally successful areas. Examples here are molecular dynamics in pharmaceutical design and research, coupled fluid and structural dynamics in airplane simulation, or computational combustion in engine design. They consist of established computational fields that are advancing some frontier. In many areas, two-dimensional physical computational models are well established, but three-dimensional problems that better match the real world need development. Other examples require the adaptation of a successful code to a new application or the adaptation of two codes (e.g., the air flow around an airplane and the structure of the airplane itself) to work together (e.g., to simulate an airplane in actual flight conditions). These areas demand the most attention from policymakers because there are many such topics and each has its own scientific and technological merits. Furthermore, each presents its own difficulties.

Finally there are certain **pre-algorithmic computational problems** whose solution would help solve important problems in science and engineering that are overwhelmingly large. These can be relatively easily formulated mathematically, but are well beyond the present horizons for high-speed computers. There are obvious algorithms to try, but their feasibility is questionable and major efforts are required to find the right computational techniques. For example, quantum chromodynamics (QCD) physicists may be able computationally to solve the quark confinement problem and produce fundamental insights about particle physics, but as currently formulated, problems with well over 10^{20} variables must be solved, and even a teraflops machine would require 3 years simply to access each variable once! As another example, the human genome mapping problem has overwhelming complexity when viewed in terms of our present understanding.

These are important problems, and their solution should be set as long-term goals for computational scientists. To solve these problems, we need a broad attack that includes fast hardware and good software, as is required for most scientific computation. However, the QCD problem might benefit even more from a new set of orthogonal functions that would reduce the computational requirements, and the human genome problem might benefit greatly from computer databases of simpler animals, such as crayfish or cat genome mapping efforts, that would simplify the human genome problem. We call these problems pre-algorithmic to denote the fact that with today's machines and algorithms, we do not know how to solve the central problems; only greatly simplified problems can be attempted, and these require huge amounts of machine time to yield partial results relative to the whole problem's solution.

Thus, we should regard the slow-memory parallel problems as straightforward, allocate great amounts of computer time to solving them, and expect new insights in the short run. Other problems should be studied intensively because of their importance and pre-algorithmic nature, and as such be given money for mathematical, algorithmic, and even special-purpose architectural research, as well as limited machine cycles to develop computational insights. But this should be done in a manner where each field prioritizes its problems and then, together with a range of computational experts, establishes a set of sub-problems and a time table. Sub-goals, conditional funding steps, and reevaluation points can then be discussed rationally.

The positive side of this approach is that these areas have common hardware and software needs, so that by sharing certain development work, we can accelerate progress and decrease costs relative to our present approach of putting small amounts of money everywhere.

It is impossible to predict with any accuracy when and where computational insights will provide breakthroughs in applications. Indeed, many computations, with a range of parameters, are required before a user group can infer some new technological or scientific idea from the results. However, there have been many examples of such successes in the past, and the more realistic 3D models provided by massive memories and supercomputer speeds will expand this in the future.

3.5   System Software Design Goals

System software is the glue that binds applications codes to hardware systems, and its design has major performance consequences. At the lowest level, the operating system causes the hardware to start and stop parallel tasks, it decides which tasks can run with others, and it generally manages the hardware and software system resources. One level up, the compiler translates user-language programs into machine-language programs and can restructure the program and data structures in the process. The compiler as well as users depend on a third type of software: algorithm libraries, which provide functionality that is common to many programs, but that no user has the need to write. Each of these system software components can substantially affect performance. Nevertheless, no amount of software can overcome architectural flaws, for example to reach a peak speed that is fundamentally unreachable because of architectural bottlenecks. For a wide range of views on this subject, see [BDKK94].

A fourth system software issue is the programming language or environment through which users express themselves to the computer. Problem-solving environments (PSEs) are evolving rapidly in which users do not write programs but rather specify problems to be solved. Computer-aided design (CAD) systems, which have been in use in various engineering disciplines since the 1970s, or spreadsheet and word processing software, which swept the PC world in the 1980s, can be regarded as the prototypes for future PSEs. A PSE can relieve the user of most programming burdens, and can also ensure high performance if the system itself is well-implemented. Thus, such systems are likely to be used in more and more applications areas in the future.

Today we still must use programming languages for high performance computing and even in the future, PSEs will be written by programmers. Thus, the programming language and compiler issues will continue for certain classes of users. Programming languages themselves are much like natural languages in that many can co-exist, people can be multilingual, and certain ideas are easier to express in one than in another. However, as PSEs become more prevalent, traditional language design will become less important and ultimately one can even imagine very high level languages and PSEs for system software development, so that our traditional image of what programmers do will vanish. Nevertheless, for HPC, language issues currently remain at center stage. Some advocate languages that will enable users to achieve higher performance by expressing detailed ideas about the relationship of a user's code to the system, but this is a step backward, as it lowers the language and thought level and increases the users' time to solve problems. In fact, if we had high-performance hardware, and good system software today, languages would not be an issue in performance discussions.

This eternal struggle between system designers with limited techniques and end users with infinite wish lists can be temporarily broken from time to time by producing breakthrough computer systems. However, ordinary systems and their user interfaces change slowly over time. The following principle seems to combine the breakthrough and slow evolution cases, and govern most successful changes:

Principle of Immediately Usable Change
Unless a new system provides huge cost-performance, functionality,
or usability gains,
evolutionary products are accepted much more easily than revolutionary ones.

The rationale for this principle is that users often behave as follows in assessing new, improved products that perform approximately the same function as existing products. Even though a new product has a few differences or shortcomings to which they must adjust, computer customers generally prefer a new product that resembles the old product they have been using, over another new product whose usability or appearance is different, but is an "improvement" over the old product. Furthermore, users seem less willing to accept a new software system containing new ideas to be *accepted* up-front that are "greater in scope" than those that can be *abandoned* after the adoption of a competing software system. However, when functionality changes at the level of Visicalc or Lotus 1-2-3 appear, or cost-performance and usability changes at the level of the first Apple PC or laptop system occur, whole new markets arise instantly. This **innovator's edge** is often much more dramatic in the marketplace than the attacker's advantage of Section 1.5. It is as if users evaluated a personal criterion of *(effectiveness change)/(cost in effort)* and applied a threshold to proposed changes. In short, when confronted with new software, users are willing to expend effort only in relation to relatively short-term gains.

The principle reflects several historical facts. For example, despite the invention of a series of new and improved programming languages over the past 30 years, engineering and scientific users have never dropped Fortran. Instead they have made changes to it every ten years, mostly by adding new features that allowed continuing use of most old features, so that Fortran 90 of the 1990s contains many innovations over Fortran 2 of the 1960s, although many basic similarities remain. Thus, after adopting a new Fortran, users have slowly been able to drop old language features from their programs, while they had only to accept a few new features up front with each new language version release. In contrast, over the years, higher performance computing has on various occasions been promised to people who would write all of their programs in some new way, for example, in dataflow languages, but such ideas have never attracted large followings, even though they may have had merit.

To apply this principle to present circumstances, consider that sparse array computations are very common in practice, but cause serious inherent performance problems that have not been overcome in the practice of parallel computing. Today most manufacturers ignore the problem, although researchers continue to study its software and hardware aspects. We can evolve toward production parallel systems that deal with sparsity well by providing new hardware support and algorithms, as well as by constraining the users somewhat in how they express themselves. Good parallel programming styles must be developed, as occurred with the structured programming concept of the 1970s, which successfully recommended that programmers using traditional languages should follow certain programming styles to produce more reliable software. Thus, some principles of parallel software engineering will evolve, beyond those of current sequential software engineering. On the other hand, a complete sparse computation software system – PSE or even library – would be an enormous market success.

We should always be on the lookout for new programming languages, because revolutions *are* possible for certain communities of users; for example, LISP, C, and C++, each quickly found substantial followings. However, to succeed, new languages must somehow make the users' work substantially easier through functionality or performance, whether it be to solve problems in production industrial codes or academic research codes. In the short run, because parallel computing promises speed, some users are willing to go to any lengths to exploit the speed of a given system. In the long run, though, parallel computing must be looked upon as a potential replacement for sequential computing and to achieve success, programming tasks must become straightforward and the field must move toward broad adoption of PSEs.

3.6   Benchmarks Representing System Workloads

Given the complexity of parallel computer systems and the great variety of applications in their workload, how can designers cope with the central problem of parallel computer system design, namely that many types of programs lead to serious performance degradation on any particular system. A straightforward and plausible approach is to extract benchmark codes from the real world. Requirements for the success of benchmark code suites can be characterized in two ways: basics that are necessary to be useful, and additional features that are sufficient to gain broad success. This section gives a brief outline of these ideas.

A. Requirements Necessary in Basic Benchmarks:

1. Representation of a large, interesting set of computations.

2. Reduction in volume of the large set.

3. Relatively fast running time.

4. Easily portable to many computer systems.

5. Minimal human time required to run codes and interpret results.

6. Public availability of codes and accurate, replicable results from running them.

B. Requirements Sufficient for Broad Benchmarking Success:

1. Utility in computer system selection.

2. Utility in software selection.

3. Performance improvement insight for architectures, operating systems, compilers, and libraries.

4. Insight about languages and user time expenditure in the programming process.

5. Insight into deliverable performance across applications, data sizes, and types of computations.

Historically, researchers have focussed mostly on List A and have extracted kernels from real applications codes and run them as representatives of whole codes, measuring their elapsed time or computational rate, e.g., megaflops (millions of floating-point operations per second). For example, 20 kernels of 10 to 100 lines of code each, provide a tremendous volume reduction over the tens or hundreds of thousands of lines of code in real applications, and may satisfy most conditions of List A. They also provide some information for List B, but if one designs a machine to run them well, that machine will have little relation to performance on the real applications from which they were selected. Without attempting an explanation here, suffice it to say that complexity is the issue; compilers may become confused and architectures overloaded from running complete codes even though they may do perfectly well on kernels.

It has long been common practice to reduce a given machine's performance to a convenient single number for comparison purposes. Examples include the clock speed, the peak speed, the megaflops of some benchmark, and the arithmetic mean or harmonic mean of the megaflops for a set of benchmarks. The unspoken belief is in the **single number hypothesis**: that one number is sufficient to characterize performance or at least to rank order several machines.

For more realistic tests than kernels provide, people have chosen well-known and widely used library-entry algorithms as benchmarks. For example, the solution of a system of linear equations (the Linpack benchmark), or a fast Fourier transform (FFT) which are widely used in applications provide "name recognition" for a wide audience of users and are popular in advertising computer systems. This approach also eliminates the problem of having to choose a method of combining several benchmark performances (e.g., the means above). However, we shall see that on a given system there can be variations by factors of ten or one hundred in performance from one whole application to the next, so it is absurd to infer anything from this **single benchmark hypothesis**, except the degradation in performance from the peak that that algorithm suffers.

3.6.1 LLNL Loops Example

Some real data will illustrate the difficulties of benchmarking and performance analysis. Consider the LLNL Loops [McMa86] run on two similar and competing vector processors of the early 1980s, the IBM 3090 and the (Hitachi manufactured) NAS XL/60 as shown in Fig. 3.3.

First, suppose that we had wanted to examine the IBM 3090 to determine its speed. Had our test suite consisted of seven particular LLNL Kernels (1, 3, 4, 7, 8, 9, 18), we would have concluded that this machine delivered 20 to 50 megaflops. Unfortunately, if we had bought the machine on that basis and our first users brought in codes represented by nine other kernels (2, 5, 6,10,11,13,15,16, 24), we would have discovered that its performance was only 3 to 7 megaflops, an error of about a factor of 7.

Suppose that being more cautious we were to have compared the two machines before buying one. If we had chosen by chance only the programs that deliver high megaflops on one system or the other (e.g., kernels 1,3,4,7,8,9,18, and 23, with top performance above 20 megaflops), we would have concluded that the IBM 3090 was clearly the better of the two machines (in 7 of 8 cases). Had we chosen the kernels of medium performance on either system (e.g. kernels 2,5,6,10,12,17,19,20,21, and 22, with top performance in the 8 to 20 megaflops range), we would have concluded that in 7 of 10 cases the NAS XL/60 was best. Even if one sees past the flaws in the single number and single benchmark hypotheses, the performance conclusion depends on the choice of kernels or benchmarks in a suite.

Overall, Fig. 3.3 shows that that each of these machines is a clear winner (by more than 50%) in nine different cases. Furthermore, the ratio of highest speed to lowest speed is 14.8 for IBM and 14.5 for NAS, so an equally wide range of performances is under consideration on each machine. The introduction to this chapter mentioned that high performance computers have **unstable** performance characteristics; a small change to the system or workload can produce large performance differences, and these are examples of such instabilities. When the *workload* is varied by examining two codes running on one machine, the ratio of the best to worst LLNL Kernels produces instabilities of nearly 15X on both machines. When we perturb the *system* by running one code on two similar machines, another instability results as IBM wins by 1.5X or greater for nine different codes, while NAS wins by 1.5X or more for nine other codes.

These two systems are not some historical anomaly. Unfortunately, the performance levels of many comparably priced high-performance systems are as difficult to compare as the two systems considered here. In order to help clarify such comparisons, in Chapter 5 we introduce the systematic study of performance with varying systems and codes, and in Section 6.7 we present more details about performance stability.

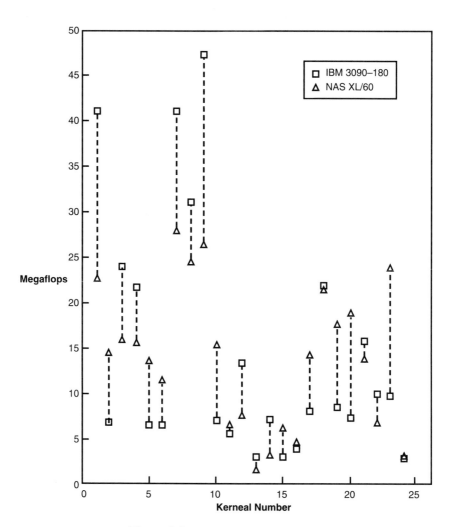

Figure 3.3. LLNL Fortran Kernels

3.6.2 Policy and Conclusions

To satisfy any of List B, a benchmark suite requires much more breadth of coverage than an algorithm or set of kernels can provide; the SPEC and Perfect benchmarks are moving to fill this need. List B also requires measurement of much more than a single number for the codes considered. Some new macroperformance measurements are required, as we shall see in the latter half of this book, and more detailed microperformance measurements (as are now made by computer engineers) are also required. A policy issue of great importance is that performance evaluation hardware must be provided within delivered systems and associated software must be available and easily usable to satisfy List B.

The most common approach to benchmarking is to provide programs with data sets to be timed on various systems. Instead of forcing everyone to run given programs, a set of problems can be specified and then programs can be written by experts for each computer system (parallel systems have evolved to require quite different programs). This approach satisfies many of the criteria, but it violates A.5. because multiple person-years of expert time may be required on each computer before benchmarking can begin. This approach has been used effectively by certain agencies with relatively simple problems to aid in machine selection, e.g., the NAS Parallel suite for computational fluid dynamics, and the NSA suite for intelligence-related computations. It is widely used in the transaction-processing community with the TPC benchmark.

Whereas computer systems get progressively faster, fixed data sizes become dated as the years pass. An ideal suite might allow presentation of the computational work done in real-world problem terms on each system, in a standard amount of time. Over the years, more complex problems in each application area would be reported as solved, computationally, in the standard time allotment. This approach has been discussed over the years, but it presents formidable difficulties, including the fact that algorithms and the scopes of computations change with time. A fixed representation of what computers must do to solve useful problems in each appication area is impossible, although for a given algorithm the idea has been used in the Slalom benchmark. In reality, it is inevitable that benchmarks must change and evolve over time, regardless of how they are initially devised.

There is no single right answer here; the diversity of computer applications also implies that a diversity of computer systems are required. Since the benchmarking and performance analysis questions are extremely complex and difficult, answers are hard to get. It is possible to draw complexity and procedural analogies with clinical trials of medical treatments, which have recently been fraught with claims of misconduct and misrepresentation. Although such problems have not arisen in performance evaluation, their prevention may benefit from the observation of the renowned clinical trialist Richard Peto, that "ignorance is the biggest form of misconduct" in clinical trials [Nowa94]. In HPC performance analysis, greater skills are called for in defining the problems to be solved, selecting benchmarks, designing and conducting experiments, and analyzing the results.

We conclude that the single-number hypothesis and single-benchmark hypothesis, both of which have played useful roles in the past, can now be renamed the **single number fallacy** and the **single benchmark fallacy**, respectively. To move ahead, the HPC world must do some careful planning and hard work to enter a new era of performance understanding and improvement.

3.7   Open Performance and Future Benchmarks

Closed systems were the downfall of many 1970s' computer products and ultimately of many manufacturers, when open systems that allowed easy user migration swept the marketplace. Open hardware (e.g., IEEE arithmetic and bus standards) caused some design problems, but it was easy and often advantageous for most manufacturers to accept. Open software (e.g., Unix) allowed users to have the same programming environment from one manufacturer's machine to the next, and it allowed third-party software vendors easily to port their system and applications software to each platform. Thus, from the user's perspective, with open systems, choices come down more to cost and performance than to what functionality and software may be available on each system, because most good software is ported to all systems. Cost is obvious to users, but performance is not. Open systems allow easy performance comparison of specific computations but do little to promote *broad* performance understanding, leaving the user with no guidance except the customary caution, Caveat emptor. In the 1990s the same openness that came to hardware and software system components in the 1980s will come to overall system performance understanding.

In the late 1980s two performance consortia were formed to take steps in satisfying List B of Section 3.5. The SPEC and Perfect benchmark suites were developed by teams that had industry-wide representation from the workstation and supercomputing domains, respectively. These group efforts were intended to foster open system comparison and understanding, as well as improved future system designs, based on broad sets of user codes. The initial phases of both efforts showed that defining benchmarks in this manner was possible, and that there was great public interest in the effort. Computer manufacturers knew that something was needed, although they supported these efforts with some ambivalence because detailed comparative performance information was to be generated and widely disseminated. After five years of experience, both groups now have substantial data on a number of machines, have produced second versions of their benchmark suites, have merged into one organization to strengthen their efforts, and can be expected to fulfill the goals of Lists A and B. There are still very hard problems to be solved that require industry-wide cooperation and that could benefit from academic as well as government participation (and vice versa). As more information is collected and disseminated, the SPEC-Perfect organization will be more broadly used by producers as well as consumers of computer systems. This work has been much less glamourous than building new systems, for example, but in the future it will become the cornerstone of new system design.

Computer manufacturers *owe* their customers broad performance insight as is planned for the new SPEC-HPSC (High-Performance Steering Committee) results. While human nature and corporate policy may resist revealing weaknesses, participants in such group HPC performance studies as Perfect 1 and SPEC-HPSC share information about performance with other companies and learn a great deal about their own systems in the process. It is interesting to observe that Thinking Machines Corp. resisted joining both efforts and appeared over a long period to favor quoting only proprietary performance results that could not be compared with the competition (recall Section 1.2). While participation in open performance efforts does not, of course, guarantee the success of a company or its HPC efforts, the importance of such participation will grow in the future.

As was true with the original Perfect 1 reports [BCKK89, Poin90], the benchmark codes should be selected and results presented by applications area, attempting broad coverage. The SPEC-HPSC organization plans suites in a number of areas, and eventually joint efforts with various professional societies would lead to results of wide practical use. It is even possible to imagine the benchmarking of proprietary software packages running standard problems. This would provide an obvious user service, but would also provide the ultimate in design information to system designers.

Open performance standards will evolve in the 1990s to provide what users and system designers need. The necessary characteristics include:

1. Codes from many applications, drawn from various emerging discipline-specific benchmark suites, such as graphics, signal processing, and transaction processing, as well as the more broad-based suites, like the traditional SPEC-Perfect. For a survey of benchmarks, including transaction processing examples, see [Gray93].

2. For each benchmark, multiple data sizes that are chosen to represent a range of typical uses of the code.

3. Decomposition of the codes into a suite of enabling, time-consuming algorithms, and a separate algorithmic level of benchmarking that contains this complete algorithm suite. This suite would contain items that have not typically been regarded as algorithms, such as data set-up and post-processing for scientific codes.

4. Hardware designed into each system that monitors performance and collects important performance data on disk files as each benchmark runs.

5. Software that analyzes performance data and provides users with standard reports. It will also allow users to probe existing data more deeply, and to request

new data and its analysis.

When open performance standards become commonplace, users will easily understand what performance level they can expect for their immediate applications, and they will also be able to gain insight into other applications, perhaps areas of future interest. Hardware and software manufacturers will also have a much easier time understanding their systems' performance in each market segment. However, the big benefit should come through *improving* system performance. With broad-based performance information will come insight into how to build better systems, whether they be general purpose or specific to particular types of computations.

The Grand Challenges (Section 3.3) may be thought of as a generalization of the Perfect or SPEC benchmarks. They are large programs that advance the frontiers of computer applications in all directions. Progress on the Grand Challenges should be recorded in a National Performance System and be available to the public on a national network (Section 10.4 develops this idea further).

Sidebar 12: The Rules of Benchmarking

Benchmarking requires rules that are easy to follow and easy to enforce. This is obvious when one observes two page spreads in the *Wall Street Journal* or *TIME* magazine featuring SPEC results. People from more than 20 companies meet frequently for SPEC benchathons to demonstrate their performance to each other, select new benchmarks, and establish new rules. About 20 Fortran and C codes are run, each with the best compiler options known; the time is measured relative to an historical baseline (a DEC VAX of the 1970s, for SPEC89 and 92), and a relative speed improvement is recorded. In addition to selecting compiler option flags, SPEC benchmarkers are not permitted to adjust anything about the codes. Over time, compilers have become so complex, even for sequential systems, that they now provide options for experts that are well beyond the comprehension of ordinary, naive users. It is important to report performance results that are available to ordinary users as well as experts; clearly, most users do not want to become performance experts. Thus it is also important that compiler writers make available as much performance as possible, to users. In 1994, SPEC adopted a baseline run rule for workstations that requires uniform compiler flag setting across all benchmarks.

To illustrate typical SPEC results, Fig. 3.4 shows the report on floating-point results for an IBM POWERstation 370/375 with a RISC processor, measured in 1993. The bar chart shows the SPECratio, that is, the running time on a VAX 11/780 divided by the running time on this system. The horizontal line is a mean of these ratios (see Sidebar 19, Chapter 8, for details), which is referred to as SPECfp92.

These are scientific and engineering codes, and fp denotes floating-point arithmetic which is required by such codes; these are all Fortran codes, except alvinn and ear, which are written in C. Note that the system hardware and software details are specified at the upper right, and at the bottom, various command-line flags are shown under "tuning parameters." For example, at the bottom of the list, fpppp uses only the -O option, which enables the compiler's optimizer. However, other codes use several special optimizations, some via the KAP preprocessor, that challenge naive users.

This information serves users if it presents performance that they can reasonably obtain. However, it serves only the manufacturers if it presents performance levels that ordinary users would not normally obtain, for example because the tuning requires expert information or because the preprocessor is not normally provided with a system. The baseline rule was adopted to improve the usefulness of the SPEC data to system users.

The Perfect 1 benchmarks reported two kinds of results for high-performance computers, that spanned the old SPEC rules in complexity. **Baseline** numbers were intended to measure the architecture and the compiler for the codes as they are, with more constrained compiler rules than SPEC had. Because substantial performance improvement is often possible by hand-adjusting the codes or giving assertions and directives to the compiler, Perfect 1 rules allowed this and reported the results as **manual** numbers. The original Perfect Club kept information about the amount of human effort required to obtain the manual performance level, in an attempt to satisfy criterion B4 of the previous section. It also divided the codes into four applications areas as a step toward B5.

3.8   Testing for Practical Parallelism

To be satisfied, any test for practical parallelism must be passed by a number of codes. Choosing these codes is obviously a matter for each machine's customers to decide, for example, by running a complete set of codes for each potential user. As a compromise, publicly collected and distributed benchmark suites – for example SPEC-Perfect, or Grand Challenge codes – are useful for the purpose of providing general information to the community. After any set of benchmark codes is chosen, there are several possible ways to apply performance thresholds in deciding whether practical parallelism has been demonstrated. These are illustrated in Fig. 3.5:

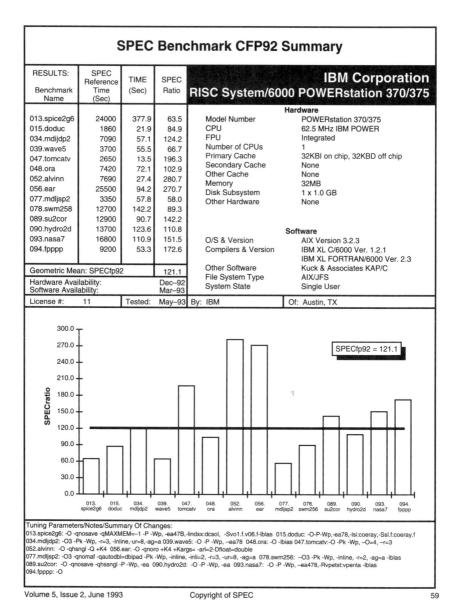

Figure 3.4.   SPEC Report for IBM POWERstation

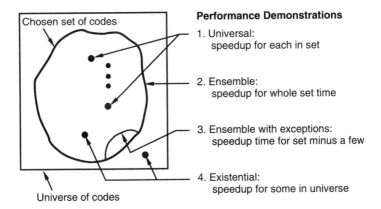

Figure 3.5. Testing for Practical Parallelism

1. **Universal**

   Each desired threshold is exceeded for each code in a generally acceptable set. Thus each user represented by the benchmark suite would be satisfied with the given machine.

   This is an idealized criterion which appears impossible to achieve, partly because there are always new users and new codes, but more importantly because with today's machines and software systems, almost any set of independently selected codes will contain a high percentage of serious performance-degrading difficulties.

2. **Ensemble**

   Each threshold is exceeded by combining the performance numbers for the whole set of codes (e.g. considering the sum of the running times). Thus, the user community as a whole (but not each user, individually) as well as the computing facilities' managers would be satisfied with the given machine.

   An ensemble demonstration is easier to manifest than a universal demonstration, but today's state-of-the-art systems are incapable of even this, for most realistic sets of codes.

3. **Ensemble with Exceptions**

   This is the same as the Ensemble test, except that n of the test-suite codes are excluded from consideration. Thus, some users are excluded a priori from the user community. This test becomes easier and easier to meet as n increases and, of course, the results become less appealing at the same time.

4. **Existential**

For some selected codes in the universe of all codes, good performance is demonstrable. This is the level of performance evaluation that the MPP community engages in today. It is totally unsatisfactory to almost everyone except those individuals whose code has been run. Comparisons to the rest of the community are typically impossible because people often create specialized codes to demonstrate performance, so the codes cannot be ported to other machines.

Passing the Turing test for an artificially intelligent computer system requires that an observer finds it impossible to distinguish the machine from a human via keyboard communication. Similarly, passing tests for practical parallelism must eventually be made a contest between sequential and parallel computer systems. Just as the Turing test depends on who the observer is and who the supposed human is, so do practical parallelism tests depend on which user workload is chosen as "observer," and which sequential machine and system software are chosen for a comparison baseline. (Section 5.6 below specifies five practical parallelism tests, and subsequent chapters discuss them in detail.)

3.9   Policy and Conclusions

This chapter has pointed out various limitations on what computers can and cannot do. The limitations range from fundamental logical and mathematical constraints to practical issues about speed and size. In the past, as computer speeds have increased, so have the sizes and complexities of the problems that computers could solve. Parallelism offers an opportunity to go beyond the speeds obtained from making faster hardware circuits by exploiting physical principles. Instead, by making architectural and software innovations, the potential exists to scale speeds in a new way that is limited only by machine size. This raises design problems that now need urgent attention because of the additional observation that sequential speed increases are flattening out.

Computers are used in many ways and with varying degrees of efficiency. This chapter has outlined the manifold uses of computers, their broad benefits, and the multiple uses of application software. Because code structures influence parallel performance very significantly and data sizes determine which problems can reasonably be attacked by particular systems, the use and structure of today's parallel systems should be very well matched. Important and complex choices must be made based on limited information. Thus it is crucial to have widely available comprehensive performance information from benchmarks representing real applications. The process of thinking through the potential uses of these systems in the light of comprehensive macroperformance information can lead to the most effective uses of existing machines, and to strategies for improving future systems. The notion of Grand Challenge computations arose in the 1980s in this regard, but it has now been reduced to a slogan for funding justification. Without an agenda for understanding that is supported by vigorous experimental activities, this situation will not improve.

The United States has *de facto*, but not *de jure* industrial policies. Agencies have set their own directions depending on their missions (ARPA has pursued military goals, and DOE has pursued military and domestic goals) and others have followed the directions of the research community (e.g., NSF). In the case of HPC, all of these agencies would benefit from a large dose of reality, administered through a public performance database. At the same time, industrial organizations would benefit tremendously from this information. The emergence of parallel processing will be most effective if the process is managed so that the benefits of performance improvement are felt as soon as possible in each new system. While government agencies have dawdled, the industrial and academic sectors have jumped into open performance activities in the late 1980s (SPEC and Perfect), but these activities are mere beginnings that demonstrate the feasibility of a major effort. Politicians will continue to pontificate about whether we should have more formal industrial policies, bureaucrats will continue to make policy by their daily actions, and industry will continue to design the best products they can while making as much profit as possible from selling them. Meanwhile, a relatively small investment in obtaining and disseminating facts must be made. At one extreme, this will help to self-correct Washington policies, and at the other extreme it will help the industrial and academic sectors to move directly toward better HPC systems.

CHAPTER 4

PARALLEL SYSTEM ARCHITECTURE

Dozens of parallel computer architectures have been built and sold in the past fifteen years. We will not focus on the details here, but simply observe that many of the architectural ideas of the past, plus a number of new ideas were implemented and sold in the 1980s, so a wide range of designs have now been tried in the marketplace. Two points are noteworthy about these efforts:

1. No system has emerged as a standard parallel architecture in the manner that past sequential systems have, and companies continue to vary their architectures radically from one system to the next.

2. Very little performance information is available from the earlier parallel systems — the good or the bad — upon which designers can base future efforts.

One objective of this chapter is to characterize all of these parallel architectures in sufficient detail to develop macroperformance models for them and to discuss performance improvement techniques. Our overall objective is to move the world forward to develop practical parallel systems in this decade.

There are two halves to the problem of obtaining good performance for HPC Systems: the system and its load. Chapter 3 outlined key issues about the load and discussed computational Grand Challenges which justify the need for ever faster computer systems. We note that there is in fact one Greatest Grand Challenge (GGC) of HPC that must be solved in this decade. The GGC is to solve the problem of designing practical parallel systems so that we will be able, forevermore, to improve computer performance through parallelism, even if clock speeds increase only modestly.

4.1 HPC Casualties and Survivors

In the U.S. alone, since the mid-1980s, the casuality list among major HPC efforts is startling: CDC-ETA, Denelcor, Supercomputer Systems, Inc.(with IBM),

ELXSI, Thinking Machines, Floating Point Systems, Cray Computer Corp., Alliant Computer Systems, Astronautics, Scientific Computer Systems, Kendall Square Research, Stardent (Stellar plus Ardent), BBN Computer, Celerity, Multiflow, Cydrome, Masscomp, Myrias, and so on. These were all well-funded start-up companies or well-established companies that ventured into the market with parallel products and later collapsed or terminated their HPC activities; countless other efforts ventured into parallel processing and got nowhere. Their machines ranged from supercomputers (over $20M) to high-end workstations (under $100K). They all had intelligent, experienced people; they all developed working systems and some sold hundreds of systems before failing. So why did they fail? Generic answers include: managers with poor business sense, system designs that were inferior to the competition, use of the wrong technology for implementation, a bad world-wide economy, an oversupply of good designs relative to the market size, or an attackers frenzy (recall Chapter 1).

Some insight about the failures can be obtained by examining the survivors. Cray Research and the Japanese supercomputer makers — Fujitsu, NEC, and Hitachi — survive from the 1970s at the supercomputer end of the spectrum, and IBM continues with its high-end 390-line of vector/parallel systems and new MPPs. Thus, an installed base, name recognition, and large cash reserves are helpful. Currently surviving start-ups of the 1980s with parallelism include Convex/HP and Sequent, who each gained initial market share by providing an open systems alternative to the traditional closed systems from Digital Equipment. In addition, they offered improved price/performance, but neither staked their products on innovations in parallel processing, instead they relied mostly on multiuser multiprocessing. Both had severe problems in redefining themselves after their early successes. To summarize: one group of survivors includes large traditional companies who moved ahead with new products, and start-ups who improved features and price/performance of the traditional companies' products.

Next we turn to surviving companies that have succeeded in producing parallel systems with relatively long lifetimes. The special-purpose but large and important transaction and database market was discussed in Chapter 3. Innovative start-ups include Teradata, which was bought by NCR-ATT, and nCUBE, which now has close financial and software ties with database-maker Oracle; these are companies that developed very focussed markets, and exploited them well, providing easy interfaces for users, that require no knowledge of parallel processing. Sequent has also embraced this market for its longer-term survival.

Another category includes leading-edge U.S. high performance MPPs, which until 1994 included machines from Thinking Machines, Intel, MasPar, and Kendall Square Research. MasPar began with strong business ties to DEC and is producing SIMD machines which are very powerful for long-vector processing, an area that is not widely regarded as a general-purpose market. The other three sold supercomputers into the general-purpose marketplace but their products engendered wide

Figure 4.1.   Product Development

debate, and had fragile markets because they were not general-purpose systems. Intel has initiated a new effort in the commercial market segment to attempt to correct this situation. However, TMC and Kendall Square suffered severe financial difficulties in 1993-1994 and in the 3rd quarter of 1994 Thinking Machines entered Chapter 11 to reorganize its finances and concentrate on its existing customers, and KSR effectively terminated manufacturing.

Europeans have struggled with parallel processing throughout the 1980s and several national and EC-wide projects have failed, despite handsome funding. Meiko, a British company with strong U.S. ties is one notable MPP survivor of the European efforts; it stunned the U.S. marketplace by winning an order at the Lawrence Livermore National Laboratory, a bastion of HPC and in the past a buy-American stalwart. Having bought Seymour Cray's machines for decades, the Meiko decision was announced by LLNL after cancelling an order in late 1991 for a Cray 3 from Cray Computer Corp. (which sold no machines and went bankrupt in the first quarter of 1995.).

This simple analysis, yields three categories of high performance computer survivors:

1. Large, ongoing firms with evolving products, and start-ups that offer follow-on products to such firms' products.

2. Innovative start-up companies with very focussed markets.

3. Innovators in the general purpose marketplace.

Fig. 4.1 summarizes these three categories of product developers. A company's history, product traditions, and even system features all strongly influence new product development by ongoing companies and startup imitators, and this push corresponds to category 1. Customers and competitors also pull suppliers and this can stampede companies into imitating the competition with poor products, but it may also move companies into important, expanding markets as in category 2. Generally, those forces lead to evolutionary change, not dramatic revolutionary innovation; however in HPC it has had both effects.

The technology push is what often spurs innovators to truly major steps forward. The construction of MPPs from new, commodity technology including microprocessors, large memories, and open operating systems has led in category 3 to a series of high peak-performance systems that were sometimes easily produced but require further system refinement to become generally practical.

Let us return to the dozen failed companies listed earlier. Some of those failures thought they were in category 1 or 2, but all thought they were also in category 3. Innovators are the force behind the Computer Revolution, the darlings of venture capitalists and large company R & D budgets, and the embodiment of the American Dream. So why did they fail? Mainly, they all failed because the practical parallel processing problem is much more difficult than everyone thought. Secondarily, they failed because there was a tremendous amount of competition among groups that did not really know how to solve the problem. A final factor is that the cost of designing and producing proprietary technology (rather than using sometimes less effective but much less costly open/commodity technology) can be very damaging to relatively small companies. Eventually this will contribute to a convergence on widely-used, common hardware and software technologies.

4.1.1 The Future

As a community of users and designers we have learned a great deal about parallel processing, but what we know about performance at the system level is mostly qualitative and intuitive. There are detailed quantitative analyses of parts of the problem, but the nonlinear complexity of whole systems makes these fractional analyses of little use in designing better systems. The most obvious thing that we have not done is to collect detailed macroperformance data about these systems for analysis and system comparison. After 15 years and billions of dollars, the community of users and designers is still groping intuitively for a solution.

The reason that we have not collected and analyzed data is that it is difficult and time-consuming work, no one knows exactly how to proceed, no one has been willing to pay for it, and it is not nearly so much fun to do or invest in as designing new world-class supersystems based on one's keen intuition. A major theme of this book is that we need a world-wide industrial, academic and government cooperative effort to measure and analyze performance, and to develop rational performance-improvement methods.

This situation could not continue in traditional engineering fields. When an airplane engine design causes crashes, an automobile design has its wheels fall off, or an appliance design tends to burn houses down, engineers *fix* the problems. They do not offer a new design for customers to try, and then "see if it works." Sequential computer systems are less complex than parallel ones, but they do have nonlinearities that defy system analysis by any means short of simulation. However, through extensive simulation, microprocessor designers can now predict (but not globally optimize) delivered performance to within a few percent, and this must be the goal for parallel system designers as well.

Let us return to category 1 briefly with respect to the future. A successful old-line company cannot continue without substantial forward-looking plans. As the sequential speed squeeze (cf. Chapter 1) occurs in the 1990s, only the most astutely managed companies will survive. By clinging to traditional systems and technologies, IBM and DEC both suffered major upheavals in the early 1990s, being victims of the attackers' advantage in sequential computing. For example, IBM offered a textbook example of the dynamics of Fig. 4.1 in its handling of the RISC processor, which was invented by John Cocke at Yorktown Heights, after years of compiler and architecture study. Cocke's *technology push* to the first RISC implementation failed to gain sufficient support, as IBM was determined to preserve *company traditions* in the mainframe business. Finally, the *market pull* created by startup workstation companies brought forth the IBM RS6000 microprocessor, which is now moving into mainframe replacement architectures.

The market of the 1980s belonged to the PC and workstation manufacturers, and the 1990s will likely belong to those companies that can innovate using open systems, open performance, and parallelism. The workstation manufacturers have all begun to move toward open performance, with SPEC, and have now introduced parallel products, so it is likely that these companies will become the next battleground for survival. For example, in the style of IBM and DEC earlier, RISC innovator Sun Microsystems had half the workstation market (but has been losing market share), the widest software offerings, and often the lowest priced models; but it was slow to adopt parallelism, and has had clock speeds among the slowest in workstations. Not only will there be a struggle among workstation manufacturers, but there will be a head-on confrontation with personal computers, which will erase the traditional price and performance distinction between workstations and PCs.

4.2 Fast and Slow Memory Computations

In Chapter 3 we used the terms "fast-memory parallel computation" and "slow-memory parallel computation," which are expanded here. We use the terms "fast" and "slow" to express the operational abilities of a hardware system to meet the memory demands of a compiled code. From the point of view of the code running in each processor, if its memory demands are met on time, then the memory system appears "fast" to that processor. An **acceptable fast-memory parallel computation** is one for which, throughout an entire computation, each processor's memory demands are met on time, in that each processor does not notice significant degradation from its cache's acceptable uniprocessor performance. If a parallel computation is an unacceptable fast-memory parallel computation, but if its performance is still acceptable, we call it an **acceptable slow-memory parallel computation**; such computations arise where great parallelism can overcome the memory delays presented to individual processors and produce acceptable overall performance relative to the number of processors in the system. Any other computation has unacceptable parallel performance. Details about definitions of acceptable performance are given in Section 6.5 and Chapter 7.

4.2.1   Uniprocessor Memory Speed

The speed of a single processor, e.g., workstation, is dependent on the speed of its memory system. To greatly simplify the discussion, assume that the processor (CPU for Central Processing Unit) can perform operations in one time unit by accessing data in its fast (register and cache) memory. If the data is not available in fast memory, we have a cache miss and the instruction execution slows down by a factor of 10 to 50 because access to main memory is required. Historically, caches of the 1970s were useful for *enhancing* system performance, but in the 1980s they became *necessities* as CPU performance increased much more than did main memory speeds. By introducing two levels of cache, installing separate data and instruction caches, etc., computer engineers have done an excellent job of hiding the main memory latency of modern uniprocessors. Thus, a computation that has good addressing locality and therefore generates an acceptably high cache-hit frequency is well regarded and runs as an acceptable **fast-memory sequential computation**.

4.2.2   Parallel Memory Speed

In parallel computers data must be communicated between processors or between processors and remote memories, and the time required to pass this data is a crucial issue. If one processor is to access data in another processor's memory, it clearly must pay at least the time that a sequential machine would require for memory access, but there are additional penalties in a parallel machine, because some kind of interconnection network is required. First are the hardware delays: passing signals along wires causes a delay of more than 1 nanosecond per foot, and there is additional delay through the switching devices used to route the data to its destination. As modern microprocessors are appearing with clock periods of 5 nanoseconds and below, propagating a signal across a printed circuit board requires a significant fraction of a clock. Secondly there are operational delays caused by conflicts between two or more data items that are directed along the same path by a computation. On top of these delays, for actually transmitting the data, there is the address translation time, i.e., the time required for deciding to which memory unit a given memory request should be routed. This latter step can largely be accomplished through hardware (as in most shared-memory systems), or can require software intervention (as has been typical of distributed-memory message-passing systems). Section 4.3 presents block diagrams of basic distributed-memory and shared-memory systems, and item 4 of Section 4.5 discusses the ideas of these two types of memory addressing.

Because they are relatively easy to design and build, distributed-memory message-passing parallel systems became very popular in the 1980s [Seit85], [FJLO88]. Using off-the-shelf components, they appeared to be inexpensive, and by using simple interconnection networks, they appeared to be scalable up to large numbers of processors. But due to the message-passing paradigm, their performance was poor whenever there was much network traffic in a computation. In fact, the generation of MPPs produced in the early 1990s have system-wide memory access delays on the order of 100 μs, so using processors whose clock periods are on the order of ten nanoseconds, the processor experiences a memory-access delay that is a thousand-fold worse than a cache access. Thus, if a computation largely avoids use of the system-wide memory, generating mostly local memory addresses, it may run as an acceptable slow-memory parallel computation; otherwise it will run very poorly and deliver unacceptable performance (see Sections 6.5 and 7.2.5). To make matters worse, in a P-processor system whose total main memory size is M words, such computations effectively have a memory size of only M/P words.

On the other hand, shared-memory systems [GGKM83, GKLS83], have tended to use custom parts which appeared expensive, and because they have tended to use more complex networks, their scalability has been more questionable than distributed-memory systems. Today's shared-memory systems with a few tens of processors have shared-memory access times that are not substantially worse than the factor of ten degradation experienced by uniprocessors for cache misses. Thus they often can run jobs as acceptable fast-memory parallel computations, and each processor has access to the full M words of system main memory.

Overall, shared-memory computers have system memory access times that are one or two orders of magnitude smaller than distributed-memory computers, but the existing shared-memory computers have one or two orders of magnitude fewer processors than distributed-memory MPP computers. Whether or not these shared-memory architectures can be scaled up substantially without degrading shared-memory access time, is one of today's important architecture questions. If parallel processing prevails in the 21st century, it will almost certainly be because system designers have been able to achieve fast-memory parallel computation for most users. This can be expected to happen only through the solution of hardware and software problems at the system level, while fully accounting for the applications demands of users. For more about memory size requirements and technology, see Section 6.6.

Sidebar 13: Clock Speed

Every step inside a computer is driven by an electronic clock whose ticks move the system's state forward. In the time between clock ticks, data bits move between adjacent pairs of registers, much like students move between classrooms when the bell rings, each following a different path, generally with different path lengths.

The clock period can be made as fast as desired (within a broad range), but to be practical, data must move forward a substantial distance in each clock tick. The clock is adjusted when a system is designed, to accommodate the longest logic path between any adjacent pair of registers. The path length is determined by delays in transistor devices (silicon or other semiconductor) plus conductor delays (on-chip metal layers, connectors, and wires). These delays are determined by physical laws; the speed of a signal on a wire is less than the speed of light in free space, about 1 foot per nanosecond. Each machine operation takes one or more clock periods to complete, but no operation can be performed in less than one clock. Thus, speeding up the clock results in speeding up all of the computer's operations, but the laws of physics eventually present insurmountable limits to practical clock speed increases.

Historically, early computers had clock speeds in the millisecond range and we are now approaching the nanosecond level: roughly a factor of a million in 50 years. Together with perhaps a factor of 10 achieved by other architectural advances, uniprocessors have gained about 10X performance per 7 years. However, the Cray 1 had a 12.5 ns clock and the Cray 2 a 4 ns clock 15 years later, so the fastest system clocks are gaining less than 1.7X per 7 years now, because physical limits are being hit. Similarly, the Intel x86 line has moved from 210 ns in the 8086 of 1978 to 15.2 ns in the Pentium of 1993, a factor of about 14 in 15 years, or about 3.7X per 7 years, which demonstrates the same slowing trend as in supercomputers. The fastest commercially available clock speed today is 2 ns in the Hitachi S-3800 vector supercomputer. The Cray 3 (the only one delivered was loaned to NCAR) had a 2 ns clock and the CRI Cray C-95 plans a 2 ns clock.

The fastest microprocessor today is the DEC Alpha processor. DEC's announcement of the Alpha with a 5 ns clock period in 1992 promised a 25 year lifetime for the Alpha line with a 1000X performance growth over the period. The company projected 10X from clock speed (300 MHz was announced in 1994), an additional 10X from uniprocessor architectural gains, and 10X from parallel processing. While maintaining the traditional system speed gain of about 10X per 7 years, the projection fits with this book's claim of about 1 ns maximum clock speeds in the next decade, but it posits about 2X per 7 years for clock speed over the next 25 years (a bit more than

Cray's in the 1980s); the remaining 100X comes from architecture and software. Thus DEC is projecting that the cube root of future performance gains will come from clock speed, whereas almost all of the historical gains came from the clock. Most of the rest of the projection comes from parallelism, because uniprocessor speed gains are now substantially tied to pipelining and superscalar issuance of more than one operation in parallel.

The Intel record of the past 15 years, based on a typical metric (Dhrystone MIPS), shows a total gain of 336X; for an earlier, similar view, see [GGPY89]. Thus, architecture and software have provided 24 times the 13.8X clock speed gain mentioned above. Depending on the exact period chosen, Intel microprocessors have recently been attaining about the square root of their performance gains through clock speed advances. In summary, historical system performance improvements were in direct linear proportion to the clock speed, in the past decade this has dropped to a square root effect, and in the next two decades it appears likely to drop to a cube root effect. In fact, a collection of data in [BuWe94] predicts a mere 800MHz clock rate (1.25 ns cycle time) for microprocessors in 2011, in an upbeat article! Sidebar 19 in Chapter 6 discusses memory and system aspects of chip size and speed.

The crucial point here is that the relatively easy historical computer speed gains from clock speed advances are now being replaced by gains from software and architecture. These latter gains are not, unfortunately, across the board gains; they tend to be much more application/computation dependent and are therefore more difficult to design and deliver for general purpose use. Of course it is always possible to design special purpose hardware that runs very fast (e.g. digital signal processors, graphics processors, or multimedia processors) but to succeed, this approach must be general purpose enough to have a sufficient production volume and lifetime.

It is important to realize that the arguments presented here do not depend on whether the limit is 1 ns or even .1 ns, but rather that there is some physical limit that is being hit. Technology breakthroughs are always possible; to succeed they must provide low-cost engineering solutions to computer circuit speed problems, not merely laboratory possibilities. Gallium arsenide has been a big disappointment in this regard relative to speed (although it has provided power advantages in some settings) over the past 15 years. Superconducting devices have long been proposed as computer building blocks, optical computers that switch light, not electricity, have gained attention recently, and various quantum mechanical effects are proposed as device physics'

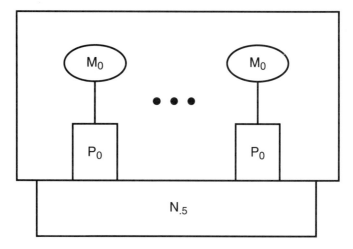

Figure 4.2.   .5-Level Hierarchy

principles from time to time. For any of them to succeed, they must
be competitive with CMOS and BiCMOS devices that have become
the fabric of computers. Since there are no plausible alternatives on
the 5 year horizon, from clock speed considerations alone, one is
led to the inevitable conclusion that architecture and software are the
only escapes in this decade from the speed trap imposed by nature on
general purpose computer hardware.

4.3   General Parallel Machine Model

This section presents a general parallel machine model which is organized recursively using clusters and a hierarchy. As the basis, Fig. 4.2 shows at level 0
independent memory units, M_0, and uniprocessors, P_0, which usually contain registers and caches for fast access to frequently used data. At level .5 these units are
interconnected with a network $N_{.5}$, which may be a bus, mesh, hypercube, shuffle,
etc. This network provides interprocessor communication in some way, perhaps
even to memory, but does not provide shared-memory addressing hardware facilities, so some type of messages must be passed for interprocessor communications.
The first level of shared-address memory space is SM_1 (see Fig. 4.3). Level-0
processors communicate with SM_1 via a shared-memory network, SMN_1.

The distinction we are making here is between direct accesses to memory via
SMN_1, which may fit the fast-memory computation access paradigm of Section
4.2, and indirect accesses to memory via $N_{.5}$, which usually fit the slow-memory

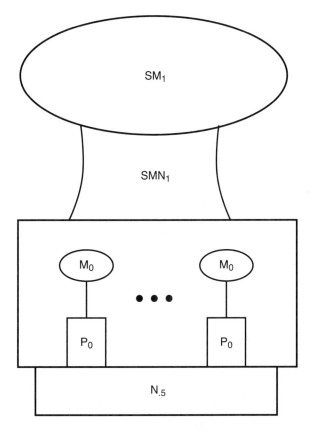

Figure 4.3. One-Level Hierarchy

paradigm. When a code is run on a machine, the *computation* exhibits fast or slow memory, acceptable parallel performance, or has unacceptable performance (see Chapter 7 for a definition of acceptability).

Recursively, we can define a system in half steps by adding network $N_{1.5}$, and shared memory and networks between clusters, SM_2 and SMN_2, etc. Fig. 4.4 shows two levels. $N_{1.5}$, $N_{2.5}$, etc. provide intercluster connections on the processor side of the system. In general, some of these hardware items may be eliminated, e.g., the $N_{.5}$ functions may be merged with SMN_1.

Classes of machines can be defined according to the subscript of the recursion level that defines them. For example:

Class	Real Examples
Class .5	Early Hypercubes, Thinking Machines CM-2

Class 1   Alliant FX-8, Cray, Sequent, SGI
Class 1.5 Alliant Campus-800, SGI Challenge XL,Thinking Machines CM-5,
          Intel Paragon
Class 2   Cedar, KSR

Notice that by definition, machines at any recursion level functionally contain machines at any lower level (however, bandwidths, latencies, etc. could make lower-level machines more effective on some computations).

There are two basic dimensions in which these machines must be exploited: horizontally, via parallel processing, and vertically, via memory-hierarchy management, and we shall expand this in the next section. Notice that particular algorithms may adopt programming models that do not exploit all features of a given architecture. For example, in a Class 2 system, if data is hard to partition, SM_1 may be ignored in favor of data-sharing in SM_2 (see Fig. 4.5), and yet different algorithms may be running on each cluster and intense intracluster communication may be in use via $N_{.5}$.

When sufficiently many computations fail to run efficiently on existing parallel machines, memory bandwidth and interprocessor communication are the prime suspects for improvement. In other words, if by delicate hand-coding it is impossible to use all of the processing power available, the bottleneck is likely to remain in waiting for data from memory or for synchronization signals. Thus, if one has built as good a system as possible with a given technology, to go beyond may require combining these systems as clusters in a larger system. In this way better access to global data and fast intercluster communication may be provided.

As shared-memory machines are designed to contain larger and larger numbers of processors, the clustered-hierarchical model described is likely to become more common for several reasons:

1. Engineering and Marketing

   Engineering considerations dictate physical packaging in units that have intense interconnection among a limited number of processors. Marketing considerations also argue for small as well as larger machines, so a basic building block is attractive. Cost considerations favor few board types used in many system types. Tiny clusters were used in Intel and Thinking Machines systems, and a hierarchy was used in Kendall Square systems. Cedar has a two-level hierarchy that will be discussed later.

2. Communication in Computations

   Computational problems seldom require long-range interaction with the same probability or frequency as short-range interactions. This is intuitively clear from how most of the real world works, although it must be realized that computational algorithms may have communication patterns that are

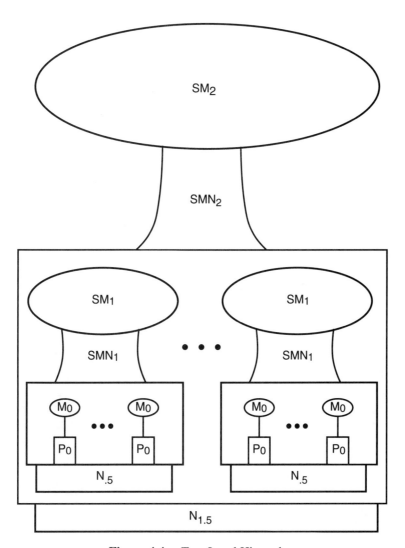

Figure 4.4. Two-Level Hierarchy

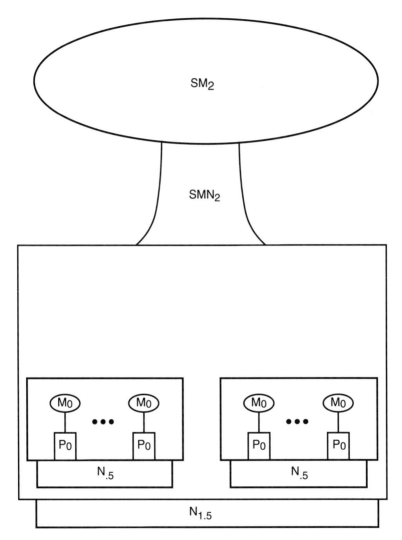

Figure 4.5. 1.5-Level Hierarchy

quite different from their real world problem sources. Thus, widely separated processors should be able to be connected more loosely than nearby processors, in the sense of bandwidth, but not of latency which can ruin performance even if invoked infrequently.

3. System Scheduling

Breaking a large computation into individual algorithms for scheduling leads to individual, tightly-coupled units of work that can be efficiently scheduled onto one or more clusters.

There will always be algorithms and data structures that are inherently global in nature and therefore contradict the use of clusters of processors and a memory hierarchy. However, a machine with this organization also provides both modes of operation, as required.

Sidebar 14: MPP Architectural Swings

To establish a well-pleased customer base, a computer manufacturer must provide systems that allow many users to achieve high performance, and allow most users to carry forward their performance tuning efforts from each system to its successor. While they may not like it, supercomputer users have become accustomed to the necessity of hard work to achieve high performance; but if the work must be redone every few years to exploit a new system, customers will become very unhappy. The Cray line of vector/parallel supercomputers has evolved in various ways over the past two decades, but has kept a solid customer base by maintaining a common instruction set, evolving its architecture, and providing a hardware performance monitor plus software to allow some degree of performance tuning and performance portability between model changes. The massively parallel, distributed memory systems of the past decade have rarely followed this model. The new Cray T3D MPP system is sold as an accelerator to its traditional systems, in an attempt by CRI to deliver systems and share a market in what may be regarded as the best of both worlds.

In 1983 Thinking Machines, Corp. (TMC) began with an aura of artificial intelligence applications, featured LISP as a programming language, and named its system the Connection Machine (some thought, to link with the connectionist models of the mind). Its first system, the CM-1, used up to 64K bit serial processors, had a single-instruction multiple-data (SIMD) architecture, and used hypercube-like interconnections. After market exposure, the CM-1 and successor CM-2 systems provided Fortran programming, and were mostly used in traditional scientific and engineering computations because parallel SIMD systems can be regarded as very long vector machines. One component of TMC's success was that vector machines are much more limited in their speedup potential than parallel SIMD systems are. However, the performance successes users achieved with these SIMD systems had to be seriously reconsidered as TMC produced a successor CM-5 system in 1992 with a different instruction set (Sun Sparc, plus 4 TI accelerator chips per cluster), an MIMD CM-5 architecture, and a fat tree interconnection network. Although the company claimed upward compatibility for CM-2 codes to the CM-5, to achieve high performance required rethinking many aspects of codes for the totally new architecture, and this surely contributed to customer defection and TMC's downfall.

The Intel (now Scalable) Supercomputer Systems Division in Oregon dates from 1984, and has been led technically by Justin Rattner since its founding. The group has produced four generations of MPPs, beginning with the iPSC/1, a hypercube-connected array of Intel 80286 microprocessors. Its current Paragon system is based on clusters of two Intel i860 microprocessors with shared memory for computation, plus one i860 for communication, and a full system may contain up to 1024 clusters. The clusters communicate with each other via message passing over a 2D mesh-connected network. Thus, Intel has changed instruction sets and interconnection architectures, although it has retained MIMD control and a message passing software model over the years.

No standard benchmark suites have been available on either system; performance comparisons are thus very hard to make. No hardware performance monitors are available, and software tools merely tell users what is obvious: the communications networks are usually the bottlenecks. Very little software exists today for automatically laying out data across the systems to prevent communication bottlenecks. There are performance successes on these systems, of course, for codes with much parallelism and little need to communicate, but the same may be said for any LAN (local area network) connected collection of workstations.

It is reasonable to assume that the designers of these computers have solved some interesting and important system problems for practical parallel processing, but it is not clear which problems have been solved. Unless real codes and data sets are extensively measured and made public in comparable forms, many aspects of these efforts are wasted. In particular, the following things should be preserved in such experiments.

1. Reusable system software including compilers and libraries. These efforts have been very weak in MPP companies to date.

2. Reusable, i.e., performance portable, applications programs. These are lost when the instruction set and architecture change radically. Good compilers would help user programs to survive instruction set changes and minor architecture changes.

3. User interface and software development tools including debuggers, performance monitors, some OS features, environments, etc.

4. Intuition within companies and individuals about architectural and software features. This is currently reused only when the same companies or individuals apply their experience.

To date, item 4. is the most important of these mechanisms. It would be much enhanced if detailed performance information were also available in standard form, because the complexity of the systems now prevents people from gathering more than a superficial understanding of what has happened, and human memories of even this are imperfect. Current language design efforts suffer from the fact that they pass to the users a substantial burden that should be borne by well-designed architectures, libraries, and compilers. Passing the burden to end users is the last resort; if the system problems cannot be solved, practical parallelism may have to be defined to include new levels of user participation that far exceed the burdens of programming imposed by the past generation of vector machines.

4.4 Recursive Architectural Performance Model

We now develop a simple, abstract performance model for the hierarchical system model of Section 4.3. It is presented in two parts, one representing the parallelism of a system and the other representing the hierarchical memory structure. The point of developing this model is to enumerate the factors, both good and bad, that affect system performance as one adds to the system's parallelism and memory hierarchy. This is an abstract model whose practical use would be difficult because separating and measuring the factors involved could be very difficult in practice. The model is useful, however, for qualitatively comparing various architectures, factor by factor, and thereby focusing on potential performance hot spots.

Assume that we have two parallel systems with identical .5-level architectures (see Section 4.3), except that one has p vector processors and the other has kp vector processors. The advantages of the larger system are that its peak speed is k times the smaller one, and it has k times the memory capacity and memory bandwidth of the smaller one. Substantial parts of these advantages may be lost in real computations, of course. Each processor may have to communicate and synchronize with k times as many other processors, and for a given problem size each processor sees vectors that are reduced in length by a factor of about $1/k$, which reduces each processor's performance if the vectors thereby become "too short." I/O issues will be ignored here.

We introduce a performance function $perf_i(p)$ which denotes the system's computational rate (e.g. megaflops) delivered using p processors, assuming that the same code is being run to solve a given problem throughout the discussion. The subscript refers to the recursion level (cf. Section 4.3) in the architectural hierarchy under consideration. The following simple relationship describes the overall performance change as the processor count is increased by a factor of k:

$$perf_{i+.5}(kp) = \alpha_1\alpha_2 \ \lambda_1\lambda_2\lambda_3 \ perf_i(p) \qquad (4.1)$$

where
$i = 0$ represents $p = 1$, a uniprocessor,
$i = .5$ represents basic k-processor interconnection, and
$i = 1.5, 2.5, \ldots$ represent combining k clusters of $p = k^{i-.5}$ processors, each combination using another message passing level.

This is a uniform model; more generally, there could be k_i clusters at level i. For completeness, note that $i = -.5$ can be regarded as the bus level of the individual processors.

The performance scaling factors include two potential degradations ($\alpha_1, \alpha_2 \leq 1$):

$$\alpha_1 = vector \ length \ reduction(\tfrac{1}{k}) factor$$
$$\alpha_2 = k-way \ communication - \ and \ synchronization - delay \ factor$$

as well as three potential gains ($1 \leq \lambda_1, 1 \leq \lambda_2 \leq k; 1 \leq \lambda_3$):

$$\lambda_1 = k-way \ processor-count \ increase \ factor$$
$$\lambda_2 = k-way \ memory \ bandwidth \ increase \ factor$$
$$\lambda_3 = k-way \ memory \ capacity \ increase \ factor$$

These factors have complex interactions from computation to computation, with sometimes dramatic effects. However, seemingly anomalous behavior can sometimes be easily explained using these factors. For example, superlinear speedups are often observed for nicely parallel small codes. An oft-reported "insight" is that the whole problem (or much more of it) fits into cache memory when run on a parallel machine, whereas it did not fit on a sequential machine (see Chapter 5). Thus, a substantial speed increase is due to the fact that cache misses are avoided, as reflected in λ_3. On Cedar this benefit of the shared caches has often been measured. Another anomaly for programs with medium-sized vectorizable loops is that the program parallelizes nicely but gets little speedup. The culprit here is often α_1, as the vector speed advantage is sacrificed to parallel speedup. Note that for processors without a vector nature, $\alpha_1 = 1$.

Next, consider the effects of adding another level of shared-memory hierarchy to a parallel system which relies on message-passing communication at its highest level, as described in Section 4.3. As a level of shared memory is added, the system gains additional memory bandwidth, and memory capacity. Furthermore, by communicating through shared memory, the system avoids the overhead time of message passing. On the other hand, for some data, additional latency may be incurred because access to the new global shared memory is required, whereas local memory latency sufficed, previously. Also, for certain data accesses, memory bandwidth may drop because of interference in the global memory network or at the global memory units.

The following simple relationship describes the overall performance change as memory hierarchy levels are added to a parallel system:

$$perf_i(p) = \beta_1 \beta_2 \; \mu_1 \mu_2 \mu_3 \; perf_{i-.5}(p) \tag{4.2}$$

where
$i = .5$ represents processor interconnection only,
and $i = 1, 2, 3, \ldots$ represent shared-memory hierarchy levels.
The memory hierarchy and interconnection network performance scaling factors include two potential degradations ($\beta_1, \beta_2 < 1$):

$$\beta_1 = memory\ hierarchy\ latency\ factor$$
$$\beta_2 = memory\ hierarchy\ interference\ factor$$

as well as three potential gains ($\mu_1, \mu_2, \lambda_3 \geq 1$):

$$\mu_1 = shared\ memory\ advantage\ over\ message–passing\ factor$$
$$\mu_2 = memory\ hierarchy\ bandwidth\ increase\ factor$$
$$\mu_3 = memory\ hierarchy\ capacity\ increase\ factor$$

An illustrative example here is the fact that in some cases [KDLP93], programs can access cluster memory or cache, and global memory simultaneously, thus enjoying a substantial memory bandwidth increase via μ_2. μ_3 represents the advantages of main memory capacity gain which can result in fewer page faults, each of which causes a big time penalty.

As an example of μ_1, note that a RISC processor may execute a simple loop containing a few assignment statements in, say, 100 clocks per iteration. Assuming a 100 MHz clock and a message-passing time of 100 μs, accessing another processor's shared variable in a loop would require the equivalent of 100 loop iterations! A shared-memory access, on the other hand, might take 50 clocks, i.e. half an iteration time, which is a penalty similar to that incurred by a uniprocessor missing on a cache access.

Eq. 4.1 was presented as representing an architectural process that could itself be used repeatedly to construct larger systems. Eq. 4.2 was presented to represent the process of adding a level of memory hierarchy to any system. The architectural processes described by these equations can be used on alternate steps to construct larger and larger systems. Each time Eq. 4.1 is invoked, another level of parallel clusters is connected via message passing; each time Eq. 4.2 is invoked, a new system is defined by another level of shared memory.

The combined performance model for a hierarchical memory, cluster-parallel system is defined by applying Eq. 4.2 for kp at level $i + 1$, to Eq. 4.1 to obtain the following recurrence relation:

$$perf_{i+1}(kp) = \beta_1\beta_2 \ \mu_1\mu_2\mu_3 \ (perf_{i+.5}(kp)) = \alpha_1\alpha_2 \ \beta_1\beta_2 \ \lambda_1\lambda_2\lambda_3 \ \mu_1\mu_2\mu_3 \ perf_i(p)$$
$$(4.3)$$

where the integers $i \geq 0$ represent shared-memory hierarchy levels. This combined form shows the four potential performance degradation factors and six potential performance gain factors discussed above. Hardware and software tradeoffs among these architectural factors must be made in the design of every parallel system, subject to wide workload variations (recall the Central Problem of Parallel System Design at the beginning of Chapter 3).

4.5   Current Parallel Processing Problems

Parallel systems can be characterized in six interrelated dimensions that distinguish them from sequential computers. In these terms, we discuss the solved, well understood, unsolved, and unsolvable problems of parallel computing. The complexity of each dimension and of their interactions define the core of the problem of delivering practical parallelism. The ten architectural factors of the previous section can be seen throughout this section, which addresses design at the system level.

1. Latency

A parallel machine is by definition physically larger than a sequential machine built from the same technology. Making the assumption that arbitrary memory-processor or processor-processor pairs must communicate in general-purpose computations, it follows that in parallel systems larger time latencies must be dealt with than in sequential systems (α_2 and β_1 of Section 4.4). The existence of latency is based on physical laws, so the problem cannot be "solved", it can only be masked. A few examples of dealing with latency follow.

Caches remove latency by keeping local copies of what is in distant memories, but if any processor changes the value of a cached, shared variable, a cache coherence problem develops, as every processor must eventually use this new value. Parallel cache coherence has been solved effectively via hardware for small bus-based shared-memory systems, but the problem is much more difficult for large systems. Larger shared-memory system approaches have included the Kendall Square Research All-Cache system developed by Henry Burkhardt and Steve Frank, and the Stanford DASH [LLGW92], both of which used hardware directories to enforce global cache coherence. Distributed memory MPP's including the Intel Paragon and TMC CM-5, allowed each processor to cache data in its own microprocessor's memory system (which is all that it could address directly), but software message passing with longer latency was required to achieve coherence with other processors. The Cray T3D has global shared memory, but like the above systems only maintains hardware coherence for each processor's local memory. Global software cache coherence proposals [ChVe90] show promise for future MPP systems.

Memory prefetching — accessing data well before it is needed — is another latency masking technique that may be used; for example it has been demonstrated to be effective for some codes on Cedar [KDLP93]. Context switching (or multi-threading) can alleviate latency problems at the instruction level by alternating execution among several instruction streams, so that when one is blocked, another goes ahead. This technique can lead to substantial control overhead in a system. It was used in the I/O peripheral processors of the CDC 6600 and expanded to the CPU in the Denelcor and Tera systems of Burton Smith. When carried to the limit, this is the principle upon which data-flow system ideas are based; each instruction proceeding when its operands are ready.

2. Bandwidth

The rate at which data can be transmitted depends upon the number of parallel paths built for use per transmission (λ_2 and μ_2 of Section 4.4), the clock rate of the system, and conflicts blocking the availability of a path at transmisson time (β_2 of Section 4.4). The number of parallel paths that can be built into a system is a function of system packaging and manufacturing considerations. The clock rate is ultimately limited by manufacturing design rules and physical laws (see Clock Speed sidebar). The availability of a path in the network is strongly related to the quality of network architecture and the severity of the load on the system. Here the Central Problem of Parallel Computer System Design (Chapter 3) dominates; many system networks have been designed without enough detailed analysis and simulation of realistic network loads, with terrible performance consequences for the resulting system. Much experience has been gained with mesh connections (from Illiac IV to the Intel Paragon), interconnected rings (Kendall Square), hypercube networks (from the Cal Tech Cosmic Cube to Thinking Machines), and shuffle networks (Cedar, IBM-RP3, BBN-Butterfly), but the experience is mostly incomparable, and the problem is still unsolved, in a general sense.

Too little bandwidth and too much latency can kill system performance. Systems must be designed with appropriate bandwidth and latency, so that the system can provide most users with acceptable fast-memory parallel computations most of the time.

3. Control

SIMD (single-instruction multiple-data) and MIMD (multiple-instruction multiple-data) system control (see sidebar 14 for examples) approaches have competed over many implementations in the past 30 years. SIMD systems were tried earliest, e.g., Illiac IV, and a few survive, e.g. MasPar. MIMD is theoretically more general than SIMD (i.e. MIMD can easily simulate SIMD but not vice versa), although practical issues have prevented it from universal acceptance and performance domination. As time passes, SIMD may survive in particular applications (e.g. long vectors), but MIMD will be used in the most general purpose architectures.

4. Memory Addressing

The *basic question* is: Can the code executing on a particular processor be written with little need for immediate access to data in various remote parts of the physical system? If the answer is "no," the system design may contain serious restrictions on the code's potential use. Unless the system hardware and software *mechanisms* allow every computation to deliver acceptable performance (recall Section 4.2), a system cannot be regarded as general purpose. The mechanisms by which a code addresses memory are manifold; they may be completely hidden from users by hardware and system software as in most shared-memory systems, or as is common in message passing systems, they may be reflected in the programming language (μ_1, Section 4.4). Many users prefer parallel programming in a style that is similar to sequential programming, but some prefer to think in terms of multiple processes which explicitly pass messages between them. Much heat has been generated by confusing the *basic question* above with the *mechanisms* of memory addressing. The competing memory addressing concepts of message passing and shared memory have come to involve certain hardware and software implementation mechanisms, as well as programming styles and languages. In the end, programming styles and languages are partly application oriented and partly psychological *user issues*, while implementation methods and system architecture are performance oriented *designer issues*. Much experience has been gained with these issues, but there is much hype that confuses the user issues with the designer issues.

5. Programming Model

Many proposals have been advanced concerning how to think about parallel programs and programming. They range from low level synchronization and data movement ideas, to theoretical frameworks embracing parallel programs and architectures, and to the view that most sequential programs should be automatically translated to run in parallel. Programming language modifications have long been proposed as a means of enhancing parallel performance (e.g. dataflow languages).

The problem solving environment (PSE) notion skips programming entirely. In the end, just as a multitude of natural languages and dialects exist and evolve around the world, programming models, languages and styles will never settle down or converge; nor is there any reason that they should.

The software implementation technology for whatever users write in must suit the architecture and deliver good performance. An interesting aspect of parallel programming models/languages is that they may help in defining useful principles of parallel software engineering. In the limit, if all computer use were via PSEs implemented with highly parallel software, everyone would achieve high performance; a reasonable approximation of this ideal appears to be achievable, extrapolating from today's understanding and technology (cf. Chapter 10).

6. Compilers, Libraries, and Operating Systems

Fully exploiting parallel systems will require major compiler and library advances over today's software. This technology will be necessary as the basis for practical parallel system development, although end user paradigms may range far from programming languages and library calls. Even if users exploit parallelism via PSEs, application developers will need tools that are, or are based upon, compilers and libraries. While substantial progress has been made, there are still problems in discovering parallel operations and mapping them to the instructions of real parallel systems, and there are even larger problems in managing parallel data in memory hierarchies. The latter memory-management issues extend to LAN access and optimization, which traditionally have been classified as distributed processing operating system problems. Finally, there are scheduling problems that range from scheduling individual loop iterations to multiple tasks on parallel processors; these generally lie at the compiler/OS interface, but may be handled via hardware in some cases, e.g. loop iterations on Alliant systems. The good news here is that while Amdahl's Law has historically been viewed as retarding progress, as we climb the Amdahl curve, it can provide accelerated performance growth in the future (cf. Chapter 5).

Next we turn to a discussion of techniques for separating these dimensions and cutting through the complexity of macroperformance analysis for parallel systems.

4.6 System Performance Improvement

To understand and improve the performance of a computer system, we must subject the system to a workload, analyze its response, and then if necessary, take steps to improve the performance. This process requires the selection of an application workload, the detection of performance problems, and the attribution of these problems to various system components. In the following, the performance problem scope may be limited to making a single code run better on a given system or may be as broad as producing a new system for which a given suite of codes will perform better than it did on certain previous systems.

We define a code as a collection of **code segments** $(s_1, \cdots, s_m)$ which may be chosen to be subroutines, loops, basic blocks, etc. We define a computer system to be a collection of **system components** $(c_1, \cdots, c_n)$, which may be hardware units such as the adder, divider, memory, etc. or system-software units such as loop startup code, subroutine calling code, etc. The idea is to relate each type of source code construct to those system hardware and software components that contribute to the execution time of the code construct. Now the **macroperformance matrix** of the computation that results from running a code on a system is an m X n array of data, MM, where each element may represent the time consumed (t_{ij}), or computational rate (ρ_{ij}) generated by code segment s_i running on system component c_j over the entire course of the computation. For example, a loop-body code segment s_i would be executed many times, and each execution would contribute additional time to entry t_{ij}, for each system component c_j used. The sum of all t_{ij} elements in a code's MM is the running time T of the whole code.

Fig. 4.6(A) shows a given code running on system A producing macroperformance matrix MM. Using times t_{ij} spent in system components, we can look for code segments that are major time consumers and try to make them run faster by focussing on **row sums** $T(s_i) = \sum_{j=1}^{n} t_{ij}$ of MM (e.g. by use of a profiler).

Alternatively, by focussing on **column sums** $T(c_j) = \sum_{i=1}^{m} t_{ij}$ of MM, we can look for system component saturation points or hot spots, where major fractions $T(c_j)/T$ of running time are spent, and then attempt to improve the performance of weak system components. This type of data would be collected by a hardware performance monitor, or software that instruments the source code. Note that row sums can focus on local performance problems among a group of program segments and lead to performance improvements for a given code. Problems that are global or have a "background" nature can be found through column sums, and these background problems are in fact the system performance bugs that designers seek to remove. For example, a computation profiler could not discover that the divider hardware or loop startup software was causing a problem, but column sums can make this obvious [KiKu93].

Computational rates may be useful in comparing the intrinsic performance of two code segments, often much more effectively than elapsed time can. The fact that a code segment consumes a great deal of time may not indicate a performance problem at all, but may simply indicate the existence of a large data-size computation using an optimal algorithm. Column sums over only those rows with the worst row rates may focus on certain serious system problems. In-depth analysis of code segments with the lowest row rates may also reveal deeper system problems. For more details about performance metrics and how to combine them, see Section 8.1.

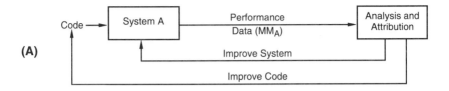

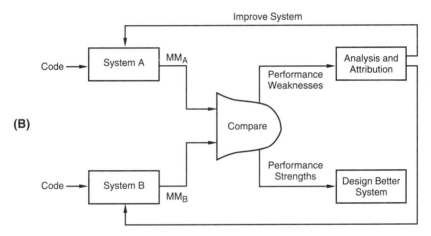

Figure 4.6. Performance Measurement

Fig. 4.6(A) shows two performance improvement loops closing, after the attribution of performance problems, by improvement to the system or to the user code, as discussed above. By using more codes from diverse applications the system improvement process may be enhanced, and m can be regarded as ranging across all of the code segments in an entire application suite.

4.6.1 Comparative Analysis

Next consider the above process being carried out with two similar computer systems, as shown in Fig. 4.6(B), with the sole objective being to build a better system than either of the subject machines.

Whereas absolute column sums $T(c_j)$ were of little interest in the single system case, (instead, $T(c_j)/T$ focussed us on large fractions), by comparing $T(c_j^A)$ for system A with $T(c_j^B)$ for system B, substantial insights may be obtained. For example, one might discover that for the same set of computations on two similar systems with similar overall elapsed times, the adder of system A runs twice as long as the adder of system B, and hence should be redesigned. In general, a better algorithm may be discovered for carrying out a particular hardware or software function by comparing the column sums of several similar machines. As noted earlier, global background problems may be detected and localized by column sum analysis.

By examining fractions of the total computation time spent in each system component, the component balance of two systems may be compared. Intuitively, designers may feel that an ideal system is one in which each component is busy the same fraction of time, or that the fractions of busy-time should be proportional to their component's cost. But in the marketplace the best balance is achieved by the system that executes programs fastest, and the column sum distribution for this case can be observed through comparative performance analysis.

Fig. 4.6(B) shows the two macroperformance matrix (MM) data streams being compared to identify relative weaknesses and strengths. The weaknesses are analyzed, relative performance problems are attributed to the components of one system and may be corrected using ideas from the other system. Alternatively, the strengths of the two systems may be merged into a system that is better than either of the subject systems. This idea can, of course, be extended to more than two systems. This technique is explained in more detail and the results of comparing the Alliant FX/80 with the Convex C240 are given in [KiKu93].

We have discussed macroperformance matrices containing time or rate information. In general, other data may be included as well. For example, one could include detailed information such as average vector length or clocks per instruction for floating-point units, or miss ratios for caches. Thus the macroperformance matrix entries can be regarded as vectors containing, times, rates and other specialized information for certain entries. The definition of rows and columns of MM were left somewhat vague in this section. Columns must obviously be chosen to capture all of the system components that may make significant contributions to overall performance. Similarly, rows must be defined to provide useful resolution of scope in the code stream.

A major issue for the future is that computer manufacturers must provide the hardware and software necessary to make these measurements. Historically, it has been necessary to attach external hardware (e.g. logic analyzers) to systems to glean such data. Cray Research produced its hardware performance monitor (HPM) [Lars85] which was a major step forward in providing runtime counts for various instruction categories. Experimental systems of DEC, IBM, etc. in the 1970s and 1980s have included various hardware and software for performance analysis, and Cedar has extensive performance analysis hardware and software [KDLP93]. Most microprocessor systems now include such facilities, e.g. Intel Pentium and DEC Alpha, but it is seldom made available to users. As open performance becomes common, it will be a requirement, the functions monitored will become standardized, and the results measured will play a major role in system evaluation. This information will also be used in the compilation process. Ultimately, such data will provide a clear, rational vehicle to communicate user needs to system designers. This completely avoids the difficulties of benchmark selection described in Chapter 3, but at the cost of much more data for statistical analysis.

Sidebar 15: The Missing Middle

From two diverse camps, the hard-core supercomputer users and the wide-eyed workstation devotees, a consesus has arisen in many peoples' minds that practical, general purpose massively parallel supercomputers are a straightforward consequence of today's technology. Each group seems to believe that certain missing technology is firmly in the hands of the other group. This middle technology *does not* exist today, however, so the belief that practical, general purpose MPPs are currently within reach is a myth. We shall sketch naive versions of the reasoning that is in popular use today in each of these camps.

Hard-core supercomputer users always want access to the fastest possible systems and will engage in enormous extra efforts to exploit them. Cost has usually been irrelevant for these people, because they can make the case to their research sponsors that a big breakthrough is imminent; however, money is now getting tighter. These people have noticed that ECL clock speed increases are flattening out and that CMOS workstation speeds have continued to explode. They have also tried parallel processing on 8 or 16 processor Crays, etc., with only modest success, but believe that somehow they will be able to effectively exploit thousands of processors with a little more work; MPPs using CMOS microprocessors seem to be a hardware panacea. These supercomputer users assume, along the way, that the workstation community has developed good software for distributed processing, that workstation environments are as easy to learn as PCs, and that CMOS speeds will increase indefinitely. They expect that MPPs will allow their computing costs to drop sharply, machine availability to increase, and peak performance to increase forever.

The workstation devotees' uniprocessor speeds are now approaching (within a factor of 2 to 5) those of supercomputers, and often far exceed supers in delivered computations per dollar. Global data communication networks have enjoyed great gains and HPCCI sponsors as well as private carriers are now serious about providing very high bandwidths and access for the masses. These workstation people know that their systems are easier to use than supers (even if they must serve as system managers for all of the boxes in their offices). All that is really needed, they think, is to combine the best ideas of parallel supercomputer architecture and system software with the best emerging microprocessors, to build really fast, general-purpose MPPs that are easy to use. As an alternative, networks of already installed workstations or small parallel systems, built using emerging high-speed interconnection technology, seem to be a ready made HPC solution that allows them to expand their current environment beyond their office walls.

Because of the enormous complexity of MPP systems and their many potential uses, there are widespread feelings among members of both above-mentioned user groups that they alone are somewhat slow in catching on to the latest technology which so many others talk as if they understand. The hyperbole generated as a result of MPP manufacturers' advertising, supercomputer centers seeking users, MPP system research groups advocating their own ideas, workstation manufacturers competing with raw megaflops per dollar, government HPCCI employees seeking bigger budgets, and so on, is overwhelming. Thus it is easy for these two groups to reach the consensus that by porting all of today's best software to some emerging MPP system built from CMOS RISC processors, all of the HPC problems will be solved. Instead they must come to the realization that at this time, while the HPC Emperor is not naked, neither is he decent.

4.7   Conclusions and Policy Recommendations

Practical parallel processing will require effective memory systems as described in Section 4.2. The MPP systems in use today deliver acceptable, slow-memory computations for certain codes, and today's shared memory machines deliver acceptable fast-memory computations on a wider class of codes. Ideas are emerging now to build architectures that are capable of acceptable fast-memory computations and slow-memory computations, as required on various applications. It seems likely that hardware will not be the ultimate problem standing in the way of practical parallelism; software will be. Nevertheless, there are subtle interactions between hardware and software (see Sections 4.4 and 4.5), so practical parallel systems will have architectural features that require an evaluation jointly with the system software. The techniques described in Section 4.6 will be useful in this evaluation and tuning process.

One major policy issue is that computer manufacturers must provide hardware and software subsystems that promote performance monitoring to provide data whose analysis will lead to the improvement of future systems. Another major policy issue is that general macroperformance data must be collected and made publicly available for comparative analysis. These are not matters for government policy-makers, but rather for industrial consortia, with the help of government and academia.

Government can provide network access to the National Performance System (recall Section 3.7) via national network subsidy, and can finance part of the effort of building the system and collecting and analyzing data, especially through the participation of its many labs who own HPC systems. Academia can help define the metrics, do some measurements, and use the data in research projects focussed on future systems and distant-horizon questions. Industry must lead the effort because it alone understands the need for the effort and can evaluate the usefulness of the information in various time-frames. All three groups must overcome some inhibitions about publicizing performance information concerning systems in which they have major vested interests. The magnitude and complexity of the problem is such that the program must be designed to encourage broad participation; a fruitful cooperation will promote the usefulness and wide dissemination of the results. Accelerated progress toward the Greatest Grand Challenge of practical parallelism will be the consequence of such cooperation.

CHAPTER 5

A PERFORMANCE OVERVIEW OF PARALLEL PROCESSING

Chapters 1–4 have argued that high performance computing is a very important topic, that obtaining stable performance on parallel systems is a difficult problem, and that high performance computing, based on parallelism, is not progressing satisfactorily. They have also suggested that a broad-based quantitative understanding of existing systems is necessary to make progress in parallel system design. The rest of the book outlines a plan for collecting, analyzing and understanding data about parallel system performance with the goal of developing methods for building practical parallel systems.

Chapter 5 is an introduction to parallel system performance. Although these systems are very complex, there are some obvious relations of importance in understanding their performance. As presented in Chapters 3 and 4, delivered performance depends upon the system and its workload. We can represent this with a performance function $perf(system, code)$, where $system$ represents the hardware and system software, and the $codes$ range over some workload. Many questions arise here, including: what performance function should we use and how can the system and the codes be characterized? These subjects are all discussed in Chapter 5 and in addition, we discuss performance limits. The chapter concludes with five tests for practical parallelism that are developed further in subsequent chapters.

Overall it must be realized that high performance computer systems are highly unstable; a small change in some aspect of the system, including the workload or system hardware/software structure, can cause a major performance variation. The consequences of this are:

The HPC Performance Law (see also Murphy's Law)

"If any system component *can* damage parallel performance, it will."

Because of the nonlinear complexity of the entire process of delivering parallel performance, it defies analysis. We currently can hope to analyze well, only small parts of the whole process, or alternatively, to obtain very superficial analyses of the whole process. An overall point of the book is to discuss the difficulties that can create system performance degradation and methods through which system macroperformance can be expressed.

The process of how we design future parallel systems is the concern in Chapter 5, rather than which measures to use or which system details to examine. This chapter synthesizes several ideas that have arisen in the community into practical parallelism tests (PPTs), and these tests seem to provide a reasonable basis for future progress. They are brought together here to form the cornerstone of a proposal for a forward-looking performance evaluation and improvement plan. Subsequent chapters will expand upon these ideas to develop a strategy for performance evaluation and improvement.

5.1   Understanding and Improving Parallel System Performance

We introduce the function

$$perf(system, code) \tag{5.1}$$

by first discussing choices for the *perf* function itself, and then by varying its two arguments independently. The most obvious performance function is the *running time* of a particular code, but since times for dissimilar codes and differing data sizes are difficult to compare, *rates* are often preferable, for example, such measures of operations per time unit as megaflops or instructions per clock.

In general, the *speedup* of one system over another for a given code is useful for comparing any pair of systems, and for parallel computations, the speedup over a single processor achieved by multiple processors is another obvious choice of performance function. There can be difficulty here in defining what we mean by "the same code" on two different systems, but to avoid further discussion let us assume that a given code defines a process that for the same input data produces the same results on either system. This leads to the notion of **relative performance**, which we express for two systems and two codes as:

$$rel\,perf(system\,A, code\,1, system\,B, code\,2) = \frac{perf(system\,A, code\,1)}{perf(system\,B, code\,2)}. \tag{5.2}$$

If we use running time T as the *perf* function, speedup Sp as the *rel perf* function, and restrict ourselves to a single code, we can write

$$Sp(system\,A, system\,B, code\,1) = \frac{T(system\,A, code\,1)}{T(system\,B, code\,1)}. \tag{5.3}$$

Note that in Eq. 5.3, Sp can take on values larger or smaller than 1, unlike the traditional definition of speedup due to parallelism. In most of the book we shall

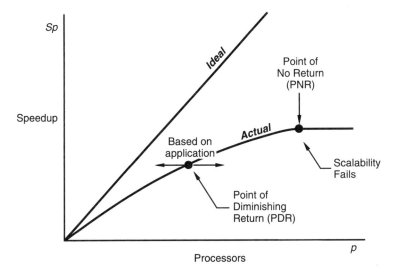

Figure 5.1. Parallel System Performance Sp vs. p

use relative performance measures derived from Eq. 5.2. Speedup is the most familiar of these and we use it, as do both the SPEC and Perfect performance summaries, despite a number of complexities and weaknesses which are outlined in this section. Stability is defined in Section 6.7 and scalability is defined in Chapter 7; both depend on Eq. 5.2 and are used in the PPT's of Section 5.6. Further speedup related definitions appear in Sections 8.1, 9.2 and 9.3.

5.1.1 Sp vs. Parallel System

We simplify the parallel performance modelling problem by discussing only the number of processors used in a parallel machine, ignoring the fact that even for a fixed number of processors, various features of parallel architectures produce performance variations (see Section 5.2). Fig. 5.1 shows what might be expected as more processors are used in any given computation. The speedup cannot exceed p, for a p-processor parallel computation, unless the computation is changed or the architectural resources (e.g. memory per processor) are varied, so this "ideal performance" line is shown in Fig. 5.1. The question is, how close to this line can a computation stay as p increases, and in particular at what value of p does performance drop too far below this ideal line? Rephrasing this as a performance improvement question we have the following. What changes can one make in a new parallel system, to improve the performance vs. processor-count curve of a given system?

The complexity of parallel processing research is revealed by the following range of answers to this question. First, designers can make hardware and architecture changes that remove bottlenecks from an existing system and hence improve performance. Secondly, better system software can be provided, e.g., a compiler that translates each user's programs more effectively to exploit the given hardware system. Finally, the user could write a better program and use better algorithms in order to provide better exploitation of the hardware and software system in solving the original problem, and thus produce better speedup (assuming that, sequentially, the new program runs at the same speed as the old).

These three broad answers embrace almost all aspects of computer science and engineering, and when considered as a whole are *totally overwhelming* to researchers in universities and companies. This breadth of scope in possible approaches to solving a single problem is the cause for the diversity and confusion in parallel processing today.

5.1.2 *Sp* vs. Computation Type

Next, consider varying the applications being solved on a given parallel system with a fixed processor count, and observing the performance levels that result. Whereas, for the previous question we could immediately imagine varying the processor count and easily grasp what effect this would produce, it is not obvious how to formalize or quantify this question. Later in the book we will expand this discussion, but for the moment we will avoid varying the basic application areas of problems being solved, or varying the program and data structures used to solve a given problem, and simply vary the data size, n, for a given choice of program and data structures.

Restricting the question in this way makes it intuitively clear that for a given number of processors P, too small a data size may not produce a speedup that is close to P. But as the data size is increased, performance should increase as shown in Fig. 5.2, approaching some desired level, in the best case. Estimating exactly what levels of performance are desired or can be expected at various data sizes, requires detailed information about the problem being solved and the methods used to solve it, as we shall see later in the book.

We conclude that the question of performance vs. computation type is similar to the question of performance vs. parallel system, but that understanding it requires more detailed knowledge than in the previous case. Just as with the previous topic, a broad spectrum of computer science and engineering expertise comes into play in addressing this topic.

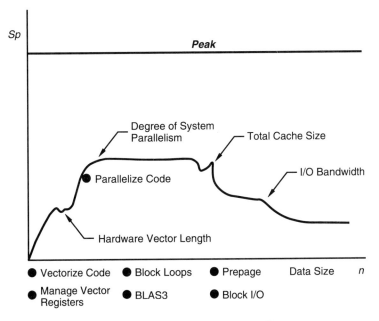

Figure 5.2. Architectural Saturation Sp $vs.$ n

5.2 Technical Introduction to (Sp,p,n)

Using speedup as our performance criterion, we wish to understand how parallel system performance responds to changes in system architecture and the workload of codes being run. As above, to simplify this issue we discuss varying only the processor count for a given system and the data size for a particular code. It is difficult to give a precise definition of what is and is not allowed under the assumption that only the system processor count may be increased. For example, parallel data interconnection and communication facilities must be added to make a parallel system work for most computations and should not be regarded as violating the definition. On the other hand, if each processor chip contains an on-chip data cache memory, then p processors would have p times as much cache memory as one processor — perhaps enough to contain all of the data for the computation — and thus be able to compute with a much faster effective memory access time than a uniprocessor. This can permit superlinear speedups, exceeding a factor of P for P processors, and so would not be allowed under the strict, traditional definition of speedup.

Other resource changes can have similar effects on $T(P)$ and thus give the illusion of superlinear speedups. Processor registers which are *necessary* to program each processor should generally be regarded as acceptable, but as with cache, sufficiently many registers per processor could provide enough extra local memory to modify the effective memory speed. Thus any simple definition of speedup is an idealization and must be applied and interpreted with care in the real world, as microprocessor chips evolve to contain more of the system than was traditionally defined as a "processor."

We use the notation:

$$Sp(system(1), system(P), code\ 1) = \frac{T(system(1), code\ 1)}{T(system(P), code\ 1)} \qquad (5.4)$$

to restrict Eq. 5.3 to express **parallel system speedup,** with the practical assumption that the two systems do have other architectural differences than strictly the number of processors. Since microprocessors now come with registers and cache memory, we obviously want to take advantage of them, and if occasional superlinearities result from this, they should be accepted as a matter of technology advancement.

In what follows, further simplification leads to the traditional speedup definition. We explore the simplified definition to present an idea of the various technologies involved in parallel processing system design, emphasizing the importance of their interactions in determining the resulting system performance.

5.2.1   Sp vs. p

Expressing the time required for a computation using the best-know algorithms on i processors as $T(i)$, we define the traditional standard speedup measure [KMC72] using P processors as

$$Sp(P) = \frac{T(1)}{T(P)} \le P, \qquad (5.5)$$

where it is assumed that no system characteristics are varied besides the number of processors. The notation of Eq. 5.5 is a simplification of Eq. 5.2 that approximates Eq. 5.4, and we use it for theoretical discussions. Requiring the use of best-known algorithms yields conservative, but realistic speedup numbers, although the assumption is implicit in the traditional notation of Eq. 5.5 and, strictly speaking, it violates the "code 1" argument of Eq. 5.4. Later we will discuss experimental data which cuts across these various assumptions (e.g., processors that include cache, and "best-known" algorithms on i processors), and observe that despite all of the above caveats real system speedup usually obeys Eq. 5.5 and has the characteristics of Fig. 5.1. However, one must always be mindful when quoting speedup information that many assumptions are hidden in the measured data. Open performance will standardize certain assumptions, make them explicit and better serve the community.

We denote a variable number of processors as p, in a parallel system consisting of P processors. For any given architectural design, regardless of the cleverness of its designers, inevitably its performance will have the $Sp(p)$ characteristics of Fig. 5.1 as a fixed program and data size are run, using various numbers of processors $p \leq P$, for some engineering choice of P. Even though designers know how to build better systems, there are always physical design constraints that force a fixed size choice for P, and that force designers to make engineering compromises with the ideal architecture in their minds. The α and β parameters of Section 4.4 represent communication with other processors and the memory hierarchy, which introduce these delays in all parallel systems. Thus, plots like Fig. 5.1 will always be true for most computations, with deviations from the ideal Sp being dependent on the particular computations being run. Some computations on a given architecture behave poorly relative to our desires because the problem size is small; others because the computation saturates some part of the system that is underdesigned.

The curve of Fig. 5.1 is constrained by Eq. 5.5 to rise with a slope less than 1 as indicated by the **ideal** line. We show two points of interest on this curve. The **point of diminishing return** (PDR) denotes the number of processors beyond which adding more processors to a computation produces so little performance gain that they are of questionable value. The **point of no return** (PNR) denotes the number of processors beyond which adding more processors to a computation produces no additional performance gain. These intuitive ideas will be expanded in later chapters (cf. Chapter 7 for scalability details).

Just as inevitably as the above, there will always be users with a desire to run larger problems and to use more processors than any fixed engineering design point P, allows. Thus, the necessity of constructing larger parallel systems from smaller parallel systems, seems inevitable. For the doubting mind that seeks the **custom** design of **any** size machine to suit particular problems, consider the following economy of scale argument for interconnecting small systems. Today's microprocessors consume a few million transistors per chip. As single chips (or multichip carriers) grow to 100 million transistors, or beyond, the notion of one processor plus cache on the chip will give way to multiple processors on the chip (carrier). Separate main memory chips are likely to be an economical choice far into the future. In any case, small parallel processor "components" are very likely to become the commodity building blocks used by system architects, and thus the above argument for constructing large systems from smaller ones arises from a purely technology oriented view. We shall refer to such building blocks as **parallel processor clusters** and there are a number of current examples of this trend (Cedar, Dash, KSR, and in a limited way TMC CM-5 and Intel Paragon).

Next consider the problem of using a parallel machine of size P for an arbitrary computation. It is likely that several parallel tasks will arise from a single user's program, e.g. simultaneously executing multiple loops or subroutines; if each user has but a single parallel task of modest size, then a large parallel system resource is likely to serve multiple users at once. Regardless of whether tasks arise from one or more users, it is a natural scheduling strategy to assign each task to one or more clusters for execution. Thus, even if P processors are organized as a "flat" system i.e. in one uniform cluster, some software partitioning of the system would likely be imposed by the operating system in order to simplify its real-time task of assigning hardware resources to newly arrived jobs.

Since hardware clusters might be too small for some tasks, large tasks can be artificially broken into a collection of smaller tasks and handled as above. This would create software overhead and run the task somewhat slower than what could be imagined for a flat machine whose size exactly matches the task. However, trying to avoid this backs one into the impossible corner of having clusters that anticipate the size of each task. The recommended position is to let engineering and technology considerations dictate cluster size, and let system software match the job stream to the hardware.

Our purpose here is to discuss the performance of large computations on large numbers of processors. If each cluster is exploited as fully as possible by the software, there will be some saturation and fall off from the ideal as discussed above. As more clusters are added in response to a larger computational load, it is plausible to expect a *stairstep* performance improvement as shown in Fig. 5.3. If each cluster is performing well the overall performance curve may be quite smooth, although small performance drops can be expected as each new cluster is added. The ideal transition from one cluster to the next is at the point where all existing clusters reach diminishing returns, as shown in Fig. 5.3.

A final aspect of clustered systems is that each cluster can be expected to perform very efficiently when, say, half of the processors are used by all of the other resources of the cluster e.g., memory. Thus, a large parallel machine with P processors and k clusters that is usually time shared by a number of users can provide one user unusually high non-time shared performance by devoting $P/2$ or $P/4$ processors to a single job using all k clusters.

5.2.2 Sp vs. n

We have discussed the fact that as more processors are added to a parallel system a multitude of contributing factors come into play concerning delivered performance. When P is held constant and the data size n is varied for a given program, we have the equation

$$Sp(P, n) = \frac{T(1, n)}{T(P, n)}, \tag{5.6}$$

which is derived from Eq. 5.4 in the form of Eq. 5.5. A number of other factors contributing to system performance reveal themselves in the performance signature

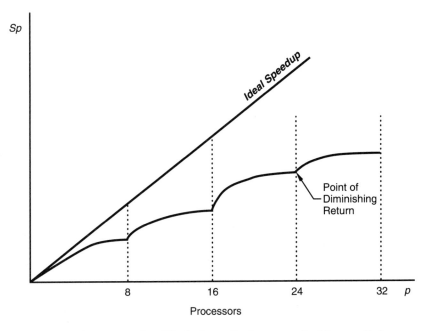

Figure 5.3. How Can We Scale-up Performance Architecturally?

curve of Eq. 5.6 which we plot as Sp $vs.$ n in Fig. 5.2.

Another view of Sp $vs.$ n is that it can help reveal the steps needed to enhance system performance. We may expect to discover hardware and software performance improvement possibilities in a given system when its (Sp, n) curve is compared to those of other systems for some program; when multiple computations are compared on *one* system we may expect to discover software improvements for that system.

Fig. 5.2 shows a typical (Sp, n) curve for one program. We shall use it to enumerate various software performance issues as well as to see how it reveals the system's architectural features. In a sense (Sp, n) shows what the software developer faces when attempting to improve system performance for users. Let us assume the idealization that Fig. 5.2 represents perfectly the workload of a system for some customer; for a realistic understanding of a given system one would have to study a number of such curves for various applications.

For a machine with vector processors, Fig. 5.2 first reveals the vector length by rising (after a vector startup phase, and through some wiggles, not shown) with n until the pipelined units are saturated. Next the parallel processors are exploited, so, after a parallel startup phase, performance continues to rise again (through unshown wiggles) until the system parallelism is saturated. At this point the processors are accessing cache memory for most of their data, but as n increases the cache size is revealed by a performance slump that flattens out as more and more data is accessed from main memory. Finally, the data size exceeds the physical size of main memory, so virtual memory accesses to disk storage begin and the system's I/O bandwidth eventually determines the computation's performance. Note that uniprocessors exhibit all of these characteristics except the parallelism issues.

This system provides "bragging rights" in the range of n that exploits the system parallelism and the cache; advocates of the system dismiss other data sizes as "too small" or "too large." System designers obviously want to make the high performance range as wide and high as possible, and for a given system, software is the answer to improving both width and height. The width of the high performance range can be increased by making smaller or larger data sizes run well. The software that can effect this performance enhancement may be in the compiler and applied to each program to some degree, it may be in system provided libraries which are hand-tuned and used whenever possible, or the users may be asked to provide it somehow, when writing source programs. The following paragraphs provide an overview of these software techniques and Fig. 5.2 locates them with bullets.

To enhance the performance of smaller data sizes for vector processors, more vector code must be found (by any of the three methods above) and the vector registers must be well managed (by the compiler). To exploit the system's parallel processors more parallel code must be found and exploited, and generally the vector and parallel code potential compete in a given source program, i.e., some source code can be compiled either way, until the degree of parallelism is large enough to saturate vector and parallel processing resources.

To enhance system performance for larger data sizes, more locality of data referencing must be found for various levels in the memory hierarchy. The drop off caused by cache size can be avoided by blocking loops so they repeatedly reference the same data in the fast cache memory as do the BLAS3 [AbKL81, GHNP90]. In other words, the flow of the computation can be modified so that rather than accessing the address space of main memory more or less uniformly, the access pattern passes through phases that are clumped on data chunks that can fit into cache.

The dropoff caused by main memory size can be avoided by restructuring the computation to focus on sets of virtual memory data pages that can be simultaneously colocated in main memory. As with cache locality, the program then has phases that consist of working sets of data pages which satisfy all of the addressing requests made for a while, and then move on to a new phase.

These techniques for vector register, cache, and main memory management work because the resulting programs make more references to faster memory and therefore execute faster than other programs which make more references to slower memory. Modern compilers are becoming increasingly able to do effective memory hierarchy management and libraries can be hand-tuned to optimize such matters. Putting responsibility for these issues in the users' hands, even through user-friendly language extensions places enormous burdens on users.

Techniques for enhancing the vector length and degree of parallelism are more natural program extensions than memory management, but ultimately, compiler and library reliance for their exploitation are still very important for several reasons. First, most users do not want to concern themselves with most details of the potential for concurrent operations in their programs. Secondly, they are likely to miss important concurrency potentials, or express them incorrectly for a given system. Finally, even if users get it all right for their system, porting the resulting program to a competing system or the next generation system will very likely require major additional program restructuring. The conclusion is obvious: If users can use vector and parallel language constructs to enhance the programming process, good performance enhancements may be obtained, but if system performance depends on this process, the system designer has made a fatal error.

5.3 Limitations on Performance

Parallel system performance is limited by a number of system architecture and software factors, as well as by the computations being run. The computations involve particular data and code structures as well as a given data size, each of which has performance implications. Together, the data and code structures and the data size help determine γ, the percentage of a program's sequential running time that can be executed in parallel. Exactly how these factors determine parallelism is a difficult subject; for many years the interrelationships affecting delivered parallelism have been core questions in the study of program restructuring, parallel programming languages, parallel algorithms, and parallel architectures.

A very simple relationship between performance and γ was presented in [Amda67] and is often referred to as Amdahl's Law. Using speedup Eq. 5.5 to represent performance, and assuming that a fraction γ of $T(1)$ can fully exploit P processors, while the remainder of $T(1)$ runs on just one processor, we have

$$Sp(P) = \frac{T(1)}{\gamma T(1)/P + (1-\gamma)T(1)} = \frac{P}{\gamma + (1-\gamma)P} \leq \frac{1}{1-\gamma}. \qquad (5.7)$$

We plot the relationship between speedup and γ in Fig. 5.4.

Even though it is an obvious relationship, Eq. 5.7 (and variations of it) has caused much discussion and confusion over the years, probably because of its two idealized assumptions. The assumption that the parallel part of a computation executes fully on P processors is optimistic, while the assumption that the remainder executes on just one processor is pessimistic. A more complete model that can give more optimistic performance estimations was presented in [Bane79]. The model assumed that fractions γ_p of the sequential time executed in parallel on p

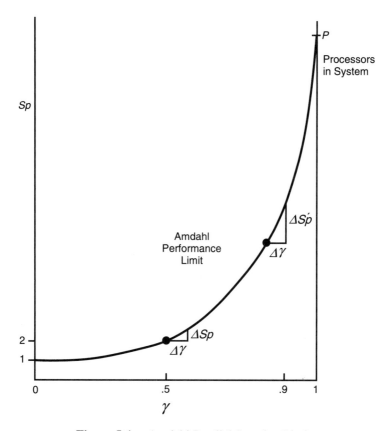

Figure 5.4. Amdahl Parallel Speedup Limit

processors, $1 \le p \le P$. However, experimentally determining γ_p values is very difficult to do before the fact, and after the fact they are of marginal interest since the performance is known; such measurements were made in [LeeR80]. Although one can imagine that the optimistic and pessimistic assumptions of Amdahl's Law approximately balance each other, parallel system performance estimates could be better or worse than the curve of Fig. 5.4 if more parameters were used. Nevertheless, the Amdahl model is inescapably correct, following the assumptions made in its derivation.

Historically, Fig. 5.4 has been used to argue that parallel processing is a difficult, if not impossible alternative to faster sequential systems. In particular, in the 1960s and 1970s, the slope of the curve presented a formidable challenge to parallel processing enthusiasts. As Fig. 5.4 shows, when γ was in the neighborhood of .5 and the inequality of Eq. 5.7 gave $Sp \le 2$, a reasonable change $\Delta\gamma$, made only

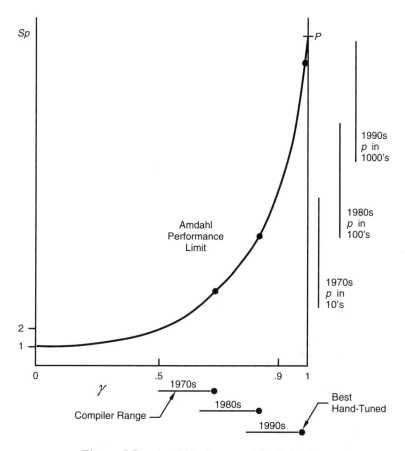

Figure 5.5. Amdahl's Law vs. The Calendar

negligible improvement ΔSp, in speedup. This was the situation when the curve was first presented and it held for many years. However, over the past twenty years, parallel processing has made progress on many fronts, and today computations frequently operate with γ well above .9, as shown in Fig. 5.4. Now, the same (or smaller) $\Delta \gamma$ that made a negligible performance difference twenty years ago, can cause a 16- or 32-processor system to double or quadruple its performance. Still, for any size of P, the $Sp \leq \frac{1}{1-\gamma}$ bound of Eq. 5.7 holds, so for example, even using thousands of processors, if $\gamma = .990$ this model upper bounds speedup at 100.

Fig. 5.5 shows that the magnitude of P has increased substantially over the past three decades, as have γ values for compiled programs and for the best hand-tuned parallel programs. The top delivered parallel speedups have shot ahead in past decades far greater than the averages would indicate. Indeed, as parallelizing compilers have improved and good parallel programming style and know-how have been disseminated, compiled performance has risen dramatically for non-expert users with certain classes of codes. Thus, an outside observer of only the three data points marked on Fig. 5.5, which correspond to the best code running on the largest system available at each time, would correctly conclude that parallel processing has made tremendous progress over the past three decades, but might misunderstand that this is not across-the-board, general purpose progress. These experiences have helped fuel the parallel processing imperative of the 1990s, but they do not imply that practical parallel processing has arrived for ordinary users.

Taken at its face value, Amdahl's Law has served as a cautionary, even threatening guidepost to parallel processing system designers from the 1960s through the 1980s as they have proceeded across the low-γ portion of the curve. For the 1990s and beyond, however, this simple model may serve as a motivating stimulus to the next generation of parallel system designers whose incentive is to climb the steep, high-γ portion of the curve and make practical parallel processing a reality. Overall, this model offers us the optimistic possibility that when sufficiently many design problems have been solved, progress toward practical parallel processing will accelerate.

Sidebar 16: Performance Bounds

Much discussion and confusion arises relative to Amdahl's Law. Like the traditional definition of speedup, Amdahl gave a single formula together with definitions of the terms, so Amdahl's Law cannot be "disproved" as has been claimed by some. For example, people have argued that large parallel machines will, on the average, be used for much larger problems than will small parallel machines; this is certainly a reasonable assumption in most circumstances. But, they have then gone ahead with manipulations of the speedup formula which are falsely claimed to lead to contradictions of Amdahl's formula.

Note that for some computations the fraction γ may be a function of the problem size $\gamma(n)$, since a computation may have a small fixed sequential part, with the rest all perfectly parallel. Thus, if $\gamma(n)$ approaches 1 as n increases, following Eq. 5.7 the efficiency

$$E_p = 1/[\gamma(n) + p(1 - \gamma(n))]$$

gets better as the data size increases, because of increases in the percentage of sequential time that runs in parallel. This can happen even as both data size and processor count increase.

Simple formulas can be misleading and appear overly pessimistic if misapplied, but if understood and applied correctly, they cannot be disproved. It is true that simple formulas are difficult to apply to complex systems and can at best be used only in crude characterizations of system performance.

5.4   *(Sp, p, n)* **Performance Surfaces**

Having explored the relationship between speedup and processor count separately from the relationship between speedup and data size, we now combine them in a three-dimensional surface as illustrated in Fig. 5.6. For most real computations on real machines it is extremely rare to have sufficient data to generate such plots. Nevertheless, the examination of hypothetical plots of (Sp, p, n) reveals the basics of parallel system performance. Later in the book we shall present various hypothetical and measured (Sp, p, n) plots.

Fig. 5.6 shows performance surface projections on the (Sp, n) and (Sp, p) planes which correspond to Fig. 5.2 and Fig. 5.1, respectively. The origin in Fig. 5.6 is fixed at some point where $p \geq 2$ and n is a small problem size. The surface $Sp(p, n)$ may be determined for any (p, n) pair, by computing speedup relative to one processor for data size n.

Our discussion of (Sp, n) pointed out that some range of n gave machine advocates "bragging rights," and we now refer to a performance threshold $\theta(P)$, below which a P-processor system's advocates keep quiet. In the (Sp, p) plane, $\theta(P)$ can be used to determine the minimum processor count (P) machine configuration that advocates would put forward as a "fast system." Concerning Fig. 5.1, we mentioned the fact that as p increases sufficiently, performance flattens (PDR) and then drops off (PNR). Beyond a point of diminishing performance returns, advocates would also keep quiet about large processor counts for a system.

Now for some code imagine sweeping across the (p, n) plane with computations that use various processor counts and data sizes, and observing intervals of good performance by using $\theta(P)$ as well as the point of diminishing returns from additional processors. Fig. 5.6 shows how this process defines some region in the (p, n) plane that, as with a tennis racket, provides a "sweet spot" of performance. The system's advocates will be proud to discuss any computation within the sweet spot. The obvious goal of parallel system design is to maximize the area of this sweet spot and raise the performance within it as high as possible.

The (Sp, p, n) surface provides a basic macroperformance performance image of a computer system which lacks almost all *structural* information about the architecture and software, but does give a broad *behavioral* view of the system. Furthermore, there are some intrinsic qualitative characteristics of this surface that must be understood, and there are also machine specific aspects that are especially revealing and important. For example, there is an intrinsic symmetry because

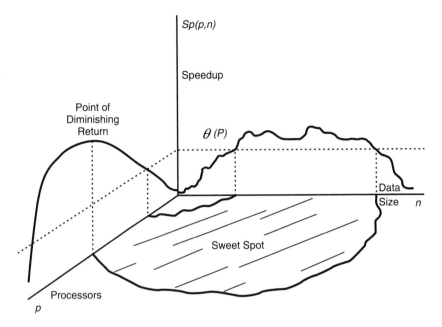

Figure 5.6. Performance Sweet Spot

with increasing processor count (data size fixed), the speedup always starts off
unacceptably and increases, as it does with increasing data-size (processor count
fixed). For sufficiently large data sizes and processor counts, performance always
drops off. However, the points of inflection and the height of the surface reveal
much about specific systems. On the other hand, there is an inherent asymmetry
at the origin when efficiency (= speedup/processors, see Chapter 6), rather than
speedup, is considered, because efficiency falls as more processors are added, and
it is really efficiency loss that determines the PDR. Throughout the book we shall
deal with various aspects of this surface, and we shall define a number of terms
related to it. Thus a subtitle of this chapter (or the book) could be "The Definition
and Understanding of Performance Surfaces for Parallel Computer Systems, and
Their Use In Designing Better Parallel Systems".

Sidebar 17: Benchmark Selection and Compilers

How does one decide whether or not a particular benchmark should
be included or excluded from a given suite? The Perfect suite upgrade
was begun in the early 1990s (Perfect 2) to include a number of larger
data sets as well as codes that were written to run on distributed memory *and* shared memory parallel systems. The goal was to make

Perfect 2 more representative of real programs (large user-defined data sets, LUDS Chapter 6) and make them executable in parallel on distributed memory systems. Because they were ordinary sequential programs, the Perfect 1 codes delivered rather poor performance and were regarded as too difficult or not representative, by distributed memory advocates and MPP manufacturers.

In 1992, the original 1989 SPEC codes for workstations were changed; some codes were added and some deleted from the suite. The most notorious benchmark changed was Matrix 300, a dense matrix multiplication algorithm. It was dropped, largely because its performance had been dramatically improved by the KAP preprocessor; a factor of 10 or more improvement had been achieved on a number of workstations, and this in turn had a noticeable effect on the geometric mean of the whole suite of codes in SPEC 89. Network notes files were abuzz with opinions and gossip about why this happened: who cheated whom by using, or dropping, Matrix 300?

There is an easy explanation for both of the above responses to unusual performance, both good and bad. Manufacturers of sequential and parallel systems are concerned not only about performance, but about the relative performance of various computations on a given machine. Large downward or upward swings are embarrassing because they deviate from the norm. The most desirable systems provide stable performance from one computation to the next, and therefore do not surprise users.

The loop blocking transformation that boosted Matrix 300 was invented in the 1970s [AbKL81], and implemented in the Parafrase 1 system at the University of Illinois. It was implemented in KAP in the mid-1980s for parallelism and memory hierarchy management. When KAP was applied to SPEC 89, loop blocking simply did what it had always done, but applied to a program that did only matrix multiplication, its effect was dramatic. Uninformed people thought – and still think – that Matrix 300 was "cooked" by ad hoc hacking. In fact, loop blocking is powerful in localizing data addressing and therefore can transform nests of two or more loops from slow memory computations into fast memory computations; cache misses are sharply reduced because loop blocking causes repeated use of small blocks from large arrays, once they are in cache.

People were confused because the tremendous improvements obtained with Matrix 300 alone were not seen in whole codes; the confusion can be resolved by consulting the Amdahl curve (which applies to any pair of fast and slow resources). In a whole application code that depends substantially on matrix multiplication, the effects of cache optimization on matrix multiplication will be diluted by other parts of the code whose time is not reduced. An important reason to retain algorithm-level benchmarks like Matrix 300 in a suite is that it allows the community to track the progress of key components of performance, as well as more global effects.

The new SPEC HPSC (High Performance Steering Committee) is planning to collect discipline-specific benchmark suites and to decompose from these the important and enabling algorithms, to form a support-code suite. This will eventually allow algorithm substitution in the support code suite, whose performance can be tested in the discipline-specific benchmarks.

Benchmark suites should be as complete as possible to show overall performance and pinpoint problems. Whole codes are the composition of many small algorithms whose top performance is necessary to achieve top performance on the whole codes. If we were able to decompose all large programs into a set of key algorithms, then we would only have to benchmark these algorithms. Unfortunately, we do not know how to do this today, so collections of real programs from various fields with various data structures and sizes is the best we can do.

5.5   Compilers and Software Effects on Performance

Parallel computer systems have extreme performance sensitivity to the structure of their software. The compiler is the software component that interfaces user codes with the hardware, and thereby doubly exposes this software performance sensitivity. Problems can arise in the users' source code or in the compiler itself. Compilers that restructure user programs for performance have become very complex over the past 25 years of development [Bane88],[Poly88], [Wolf89],[ZiCh91], and we will only outline the subject here.

Modern restructuring compilers can be regarded as three-stage processors of users' source programs. Stage one is a global restructurer which has a broad scope within the source code. It can make transformations that are generally required for a certain class of architectures, and also transformations that are machine specific.

For example, the restructurer can analyze multiple procedures to gather information for transforming one particular procedure, and it can rearrange the procedures as it goes, e.g. substituting one into another to reduce communication overhead. It can rearrange the loop structure of a procedure, deciding which loop should be on the inside and which on the outside in maximizing the parallelism of a loop nest, while minimizing the effective memory latency (i.e. making a fast-memory computation from a slow memory one — recall Chapter 4). Restructurers produce new programs that are similar to the originals, but whose structure may be changed so much as not to be easily understandable by the original authors.

The next stage is one of optimizing the resulting program structure, specifically for a given system. This is the traditional role of compilers, but now the input is a version of the original code that has been restructured specifically for the architecture of a given system. Thus, the restructurer makes it easier for the machine-specific optimizer to work. In all of this discussion, the layman must be aware that compiler people use "to optimize" to mean "to do the best known thing subject to the constraints perceived." Improving compilers amounts to providing them with better perception of the constraints and more powerful transformations for certain code segments on each architecture.

The final stage is to take the optimized program and generate executable machine code. The resulting output code is expected to be well matched to the specific machine for high performance. However it may lead to poor performance when run, because of deficiencies in the original concept of the program, in the program structure that expressed the ideas, or in the compiler itself. The range of these deficiencies may be from absolute (logical or mathematical) in nature and impossible to remove by compiler, to architecture-related and thus potentially removable by compiler enhancement. Absolute deficiencies may be removed by rethinking the program and rewriting it or by deleting parts of it and linking the program to optimized libraries.

5.5.1   Roles of Restructuring Compilers

Compilers play many roles, but in high performance systems their roles are more important and they are more difficult to play well than for lower performance systems. We outline four roles here.

1. Performance

Compilers can play a very important performance role in parallel systems. Once a computer system has been built, including with it various engineering compromises and bottlenecks, the compiler can still help to mask architectural performance bugs by matching a program to the system's strengths and avoiding its weaknesses. If the compiler is strong it can salvage reasonable performance from an otherwise poor code-machine match; if it is weak it can destroy the performance of a good code-machine match. The magnitude of the leverage that compilers have is illustrated by the Amdahl curve (Fig. 5.4).

2. Portability

If the program and data structures have been specified appropriately, a sufficiently strong compiler can provide performance portability between computer systems. This becomes increasingly difficult as the systems become increasingly diverse. Two systems of the same architecture, but with different processor counts, cache memory sizes, etc. are the easiest. Two systems of the same manufacturer with minor "improvements" are next. Two systems with major architectural differences may be impossible, subject to the actual differences, the structure of a given code, and the compiler's power.

3. Match Mind to Machine

Not initially performance oriented is the link to the user's mental programming processes provided by the compiler-language pair. A given language provides for the manifestation of the user's ideas in one of many possible forms in that language, which may be sequential or may contain a model of parallelism that best suits the user's outlook and the type of real-world problem being solved. In the end, the compiler tries to restructure whatever program the user produces into a high performance form, subject to the issues discussed above.

4. Problem Solving Environment Development

Finally, all of this fades if the user can find a PSE or even a good library that suits the application. Then, programming work can be replaced by application-oriented work and the user's time to solution drops sharply, new users are enabled, etc. However the PSE developer now depends on the compiler and library writer to provide high performance within the PSE.

Restructuring compilers are repositories for all of the best programming tricks for a particular architecture as well as for knowing how to apply them based on users' naive presentations of what they want to compute. In the 1980s, restructuring compilers moved from a research phase to production use. Because they are often caught between horrible user programs and serious machine bottlenecks and are thus unable to perform well, they appear to be weak in many cases. In the short term it is extremely important to strengthen them, but at the same time programming style must improve (language evolution and parallel software engineering principles can help this), and architectures must improve as well. In the longer term there is little doubt that PSEs will emerge that are most cost-effective for most users of parallel systems, but before this happens it will be necessary to have major advances in restructuring compilers.

Sidebar 18: Parallelism Applied

How do the abstractions about parallelism and ideas of this book apply to the real world? The complexities of the problem have been referred to repeatedly, and we will illustrate them with a real world example. Mainframe computers have been the workhorses of the computer world for decades; about one-third of IBM's current revenue comes from mainframe hardware and software. While this $20 billion per year is a substantial sum, it has been estimated that the worldwide software investment in the 35,000 installed IBM mainframes is $1 trillion [Lohr93]. This enormous estimate – the U.S. Federal budget is about $1.5 trillion and the U.S. Gross Domestic Product is over $5 trillion – if amortized over 10 years, amounts to a plausible $3 million per year for each system. Even if the error in this estimate is a factor of 10, it is clear that the IBM mainframe business has a major economic influence. But the cost of mainframes in $/MIPS [Million Instructions Per Second] has become very high relative to microprocessor-based systems, so as micros are incorporated into mainframes (NCR, Amdahl, IBM, etc.) the IBM hardware revenues from mainframes drops quickly.

Consider some of the technology ambiance in which mainframes exist. Elsewhere in the book we note that transaction and database processing, a major business and mainframe workload, are well-suited for parallel processing. A central vs. local system debate has continued for years (cf. Chapter 10) and is familiar ground for data processing and mainframe managers looking for more cost-effective solutions. If there is a performance weakness in the Amdahl's Law sense, parallel processing can still survive if a fast, special purpose processor is available (as the Cray had a fast scalar processor to backstop its vector units), and we shall see roles for specialized computers shortly. With this background the combination of new microprocessor technology, networking technology, and parallel software technology have set the stage for a major change.

By combining these technologies in the last decade, computers have literally been placed in the hands of people with all job descriptions. Now, *clients*, including nurses with PCs connected to a hospital-wide LAN, truck drivers with dashboard-mounted PCs connected to cellular phones, and airline reservations agents with international satellite communications, can access file-server systems containing large databases, and compute-servers providing specialized processing power. These *servers* are often microprocessor-based systems at the upscale end of workstation product lines, with price tags in the $100,000 range. The file servers have parallel (RAID) disk drives attached for fast, reliable access to massive data banks. This model of a computer system, has become known as the **client-server model**.

As a threat to the $5 million per system mainframe business, the client-server model offers a tremendous economic incentive to customers, with $5,000 PCs providing many functions at the clients' fingertips, and $100,000 servers offering specialized functions that can be added incrementally, as needed, to a shared network. This "right sized" computing facility approach may seem too good to be true, and often it is. The mainframes have tremendous resiliance in absorbing peak loads that smaller systems cannot handle, and established software services do not appear overnight on new distributed systems. In fact, the mainframes, or their successors can often be configured as one of several "right-sized" servers in a client-server model. However, the bottom line is that traditional mainframes *are* losing market share to the client-server approach of applying functional parallelism. Parallel tasks are assigned by function to different systems (client and server computers), finer grain parallelism is exploited within tasks to process databases in parallel or access disks in parallel on RAID disk farms, and clients will soon use low level parallelism within 2 to 4 processor personal computers. The enterprise-wide computation is now being executed using functional parallelism on a network of computers, each of which has internal parallelism.

The computer companies that survive in this marketplace will be those that can provide the right hardware and software for each class of business, and this will require a wide range of technology integrated into complex parallel, multicomputer systems. Although this business climate promotes the rapid growth of new companies that provide PCs and servers, networking services (3Com, Novell, etc.), and specialized application software, there will not be an easy or quick transition for many customers nor for the established mainframe vendors. In fact, the New York Times referred to Nick Donofrio's job as President of IBM's high-end Enterprise System division as "perhaps the toughest management job in America" [Lohr93], even though he is not the president of IBM.

5.6   Parallel Processing Needs, the Practical Parallelism Tests, and the GGC

Throughout our discussions the term "practical parallelism" has been used to refer to the eventual goal for parallel processing technology. This section defines five practical parallelism tests that allow us to discuss the subject's parts throughout the remainder of the book. The first three tests follow the discussion of this chapter, although formal definitions come in later chapters; before listing the tests we present background material explaining tests 4 and 5.

The parallel systems that everyone seeks must have a certain performance robustness to qualify as practical. In particular one must be able to run codes on a certain range of processor counts, not just on the whole machine or some fixed segment of it. This is the case because a user may want to pay for different performance levels at different times, the O.S. may face scheduling constraints when the system is heavily loaded, etc. We will refer to this as **processor-count**

scalability on a given parallel system (as noted in Fig. 5.1). Similarly, for a given processor count (i.e. a whole system, or some part of it), it must be possible to run any given program with a variety of data sizes. We refer to this as **data-size scalability**. These two concepts combine to form PPT4 (see Chapter 7 and Section 9.1 for details).

Finally, it is necessary that any practical parallel system should pass reimplementability tests. **Architectural scalability** or **architecture reimplementability** requires that systems with a sufficiently broad range of processor counts must be implementable using the same basic architecture, without varying the underlying hardware technology. This allows a range of system performance levels to be implementable with a given technology. The last test that practical parallel systems face, is that of **technology reimplementability**. The issue here is that a successful architecture cannot depend uniquely upon a given technology for its implementation. When a new technology mix becomes current, a successful system must be reimplementable. One way of failing this test is by using very fast, unusual hardware in one part of the system, relative to the remainder of the system, so that if the remainder of the system is reimplemented in a faster, new low-cost technology, the one part, having no new faster technology base, becomes a bottleneck. The two ideas of this paragraph form the basis of PPT5 (see Section 9.6 for details).

Practical parallelism has not yet been demonstrated; in fact, no standard definition of it is in use. It seems clear that there should be "laboratory level" and "commercial level" criteria for judging practical parallelism, and we will now propose five Practical Parallelism Tests. When all of these tests can be passed in the course of ordinary computer engineering, we will have solved the Greatest Grand Challenge (GGC). The discussion is informal here, and later in the book each test is expanded in detail.

At the laboratory level, we will use as our criterion for the success of parallelism,

The Fundamental Principle of Parallel Processing (FPPP):
Clock speed is interchangeable with parallelism while
A.   maintaining delivered performance, that is
B.   stable over a certain class of computations.

There are really three statements in the FPPP: first, the well-established point that high peak speeds are possible through parallelism, and then two important constraints, A and B, that we shall use as Practical Parallelism Tests (PPT's) 1 and 2, respectively:

Practical Parallelism Test 1: Delivered Performance
The parallel system delivers sufficient and efficient performance, as measured in speedup or computational rate, for a useful set of codes.

Practical Parallelism Test 2: Stable Performance
The performance level demonstrated in PPT1 is within a specified stability

range (ratio of performance levels) across useful sets of similar codes, as the computations vary with respect to program structures, data structures, and data sizes.

Next we discuss two additional tests that must be met if one has demonstrated the FPPP and wants to use it in a commercially viable product:

Practical Parallelism Test 3: Portability and Programmability
The computer system is easy to program and to port codes to, for a general class of applications.

Practical Parallelism Test 4: System Scalability
For computations ranging widely over useful programs, the P-processor system is scalable if it is both

a) Data-size scalable:

a sufficient range of data sizes can be effectively run on each chosen $p \leq P$, and

b) Processor-count scalable:

a sufficient range of processor counts, $p \leq P$, can effectively run each code.

Finally, if the first system is a success and the company producing it is to survive over time, the system must demonstrate:

Practical Parallelism Test 5:
Architecture and Technology Reimplementability
The system architecture must be capable of being reimplemented with:

a) a sufficiently broad range of processor counts using current technology, and

b) new, faster or less expensive technologies as they emerge, using much larger processor counts than current technology allows.

It is important to realize that, despite the great enthusiasm for parallel processing today, not even the Fundamental Principle of Parallel Processing has been demonstrated beyond rather narrow classes of computations. Substantial amounts of work will be required before the remaining three PPT's are passed. In the following chapters, we will expand these ideas and illustrate methods by which the community can observe the PPT's and track progress toward satisfying the GGC over time.

5.7 Conclusions

The first five chapters have outlined the importance, technicalities, and difficulties of solving the problems of practical parallelism. Chapter 5 has presented a number of difficulties in achieving good practical parallel performance, and an overview of the many approaches to improving parallel performance.

We have seen that parallelism can be built into systems in many forms. Each approach to parallelism requires basic changes from the traditional architecture and software of sequential computers. In the past, fundamental changes have been made in other aspects of sequential computing, but parallelism causes the most sweeping changes in thinking and system structure. For example, since the mid-1960s, cache memories have been developed to bridge the gap caused because memory speeds have not kept pace with processor speeds. Today, complex caches are used in almost all processors and they provide important performance boosts to most computations. As processor speed increases have diminished and parallelism has become the major hope for future system speed increases, parallelism is now assuming the same level of importance that cache memory hierarchies have had in past computer designs. However, the difficulties of assimilating parallelism far exceed those surmounted in assimilating caches.

Chapter 5 has presented some simple formulas that are widely used in discussing parallel performance. To move the field forward, the problem of parallel processing performance must be broken into several parts that can be analyzed separately at the system-wide macroperformance level. Major efforts must be made to quantify the important issues and collect data broadly. Then these separate parts must be combined to obtain an overview of each system's performance, and to pinpoint opportunities for substantial performance gains. Currently the field is proceeding as a number of individual technologies, each of which is being improved, but without an overall roadmap, without much measurement of the system-level effects, and most damagingly, with too little an understanding of how each technology affects the others. Focussed groups rally around issues — software is the problem, interconnection networks are the problem, or scalability is the problem — but even if they make important progress, it is only on one facet of the overall field.

The complexity of the interactions among the key parts of parallel systems (cf. Section 4.5), makes it difficult to improve system performance by improving isolated pieces of technology. Based on our observations of key technologies over a number of years, the Practical Parallelism Tests were proposed as an attempt to effect a global combining of performance information. The macroperformance analysis of each parallel system will lead to specific performance improvements that are required in architecture, compilers, and other software. All of these should combine to produce future systems that move the field toward practical parallelism and eventually solve the Greatest Grand Challenge.

CHAPTER 6

PERFORMANCE SPEEDUP AND STABILITY

6.1   Performance Definitions and Bounds

User satisfaction ultimately determines computer system acceptance, and many factors determine satisfaction for various types of users. Computer system performance is one such factor. It cuts across user types, because higher performance allows users to perform a given computation in less time, and it allows them to perform more complex computations in a given amount of time. Many ideas and facts are currently available about parallel computing, but they must be better integrated in order to accelerate parallel system performance progress. Our approach is to define a few parameters and show how measurements based on them can be used to compare parallel systems. We believe that performance improvement can best be accomplished based on comparative system analysis. This follows from the fact that comparison pinpoints differences, and performance differences help pinpoint system bottlenecks, which may be removed in subsequent system designs.

The performance parameters used must be intuitively understandable, as well as easy to measure and work with. In the following, we define several input parameters to the system modelling process, which in turn define several model output values of interest in evaluating performance. We also define several basic ways of expressing measured performance, and present threshold values for each metric that allow us to make distinctions between performance levels. The threshold values that we use represent the state of the art in the field, or in some cases may challenge the field to move ahead. These ideas will be used in Chapter 8 to express real system results that quantify the practical parallelism tests for recent systems.

The performance metrics we use have enough desirable properties to have been useful over time, even though they do have certain weaknesses. As time passes new metrics may be added and the threshold levels may be moved upward to promote progress in the field.

6.2   Performance Metrics Introduction

For over twenty years speedup and efficiency have been used as abstract measures of performance [KuMC72]. Although there are some difficulties in using these definitions in the real world (e.g., how to use the speedup definition if the data is too large for a single processor's memory in a distributed memory system, or whether to be concerned about the definition when more processors increase cache size sufficiently to produce superlinear speedups), they do work reasonably well in many practical situations. A more serious difficulty with speedup and efficiency is that they are usually treated as *single-point values*: for a specific computation on a given machine.

When dealing with real computing systems it is important to consider performance *regions* that have certain properties. For example, it seems desirable to be able to describe simple regions where the delivered performance, e.g., speedup, is above some absolute level, regions where the performance is not too far below the best performance achieved for a given set of computations, or more complex regions defined as logical functions of other regions. It is also important to be able to compare two systems with respect to performance regions.

For at least ten years, the term "scalable system" has been used to characterize systems for which larger numbers of processors than one's current focus, could somehow be used effectively [Lax82, GKLS83]. Currently, every parallel machine is scrutinized for scalability and one hears about scalable software as well. Because of this popularity, it seems unfortunate that there is no clear definition of what scalability means.

For the past 5 years the term "stability" has been used to refer to ratios of performance extremes in a given set of computations [Kuck89, Corc91]. The intuition behind this idea is that users expect some level of performance stability (invariance) as they go from computation to computation on one system or among similar systems.

Because of the current importance of parallel computing, we believe that it is necessary to expand the methodology of parallel performance analysis, so we will present and discuss definitions of the above terms and then use them in subsequent performance evaluation chapters. Throughout the book there are references to the need for macroperformance analysis of systems. Basic **macroperformance data** must satisfy two informal requirements:

A. The data must have sufficient breadth to allow computation of speedup, stability, and scalability information about the system for a reasonable set of codes, and

B. The data must have sufficient depth to allow the generation of a detailed macroperformance matrix (MM, cf. Section 4.6) relating system components to running times, for the codes.

Many variable factors including the architecture, system software, data structures, and program structures affect parallel system performance. All of these variables take on many different vaues in real-world computations and hence can lead to confusion in discussions of performance. However, two overriding factors limit the performance of a parallel system: the number of processors used (processor count) and the size of the data in the problem being solved (data size). Machine size is fixed for a given system, and so we regard it as an independent variable that a user can choose. Data size is independently chosen by the user depending on the type of computation being done, and it could be used to determine the processor resources required for the computation. Compared to the other factors mentioned above, these two can easily be varied explicitly, thus allowing us to perform controlled experiments involving processor count and data size tradeoffs. Finally, we shall discuss a duality between the two which should be borne in mind when considering parallel system performance limitations.

6.3   Speedup and Efficiency

We use P to denote the number of processors in a system or in the part of the system being considered at any moment, and if we are varying the number of processors, we use $1 \leq p \leq P$. While the number of processors being used is clear, the size of a problem can be a complex matter to discuss. The terms "problem size" and "data size" can be used interchangeably in referring to the amount of data used by a computation, but we shall use "data size" for consistency. We shall use N to denote the data size of a problem being solved, where each use of N will require some explanation relative to the program under consideration. Bounds on N are also complex and will be discussed later.

Now, using the parallel system speedup definition of Eq. 5.4, for a system with processor counts of 1 and P and specifying the code by data size N, we obtain the standard idealized definition of **speedup**:

$$Sp(P, N) = \frac{T(1, N)}{T(P, N)}, \tag{6.1}$$

where $T(1, N)$ is the best sequential processor time known for solving a problem of size N, and $T(P, N)$ is the P-parallel processor time required to solve the same problem. Assuming as we did in Eq. 5.5 that all system architectural characteristics except the processor count are invariant,

$$1 \leq Sp(P, N) \leq P. \tag{6.2}$$

This leads to the standard idealized definition of **efficiency**:

$$E(P, N) = \frac{Sp(P, N)}{P}, \tag{6.3}$$

where

$$\frac{1}{P} \le E(P, N) \le 1. \tag{6.4}$$

Computer time can be expressed in seconds or in clock cycle periods and since speedup is a dimensionless ratio, we can compute it using either seconds or clocks. Using clocks, as we will throughout this section, and observing that $T(P, N) \ge 1$ clock,

$$Sp(P, N) = \frac{T(1, N)}{T(P, N)} \le T(1, N). \tag{6.5}$$

Next, we explore the relationship between speedup, processor count and data size in an idealized sense. Fig. 6.1 shows the (Sp, p) plane for a fixed data size N. Initially, Sp is limited by the number of processors; Eq. 6.2 states that the bound has a slope of 1, as the above equations all hold for $1 \le p \le P$. In this region we say that the **processors** are **saturated** by the problem. Eventually, however, the fixed data size limits $Sp(p, N)$. For very tiny $T(p, N)$, speedup can approach $T(1, N)$, as in Eq. 6.5, which provides a horizontal cap on speedup. In this region we say that the **data** is **saturated** with processors, or that the processors are unsaturated by the data. Thus, in Fig. 6.1, the solid line is the speedup upper bound for data size N, and we refer to the knee of this curve as the **saturation break point**.

Fig. 6.2 shows the (Sp, n) plane using a fixed number of processors P. The above equations are now applied to a range of N values denoted by n. Initially the data size limits speedup because of Eq. 6.5, so we say that the **data** is **saturated** with processors, but the processors are unsaturated because the data size does not provide enough work for P processors. Eventually $Sp(P, n)$ is bounded by the number of processors P (Eq. 6.2), which provides the horizontal cap on performance. In this region we say that the **processors** are **saturated** with data. As above, we refer to the knee in Fig. 6.2 as the **saturation break point**.

6.4   Practical Speedup Bounds

In practical situations the above-mentioned bounds are only partially felt; a number of architectural, algorithmic, and software issues intrude before the bounds of Eqs. 6.2 and 6.5 are reached. We now impose some of these on the previous figures. Fig. 6.3 shows (Sp, p) with two curves below those shown in Fig. 6.1 (recall Fig. 5.1). An estimate of actual speedup can be obtained for some computations by using abstract algorithmic time complexity upper bounds; for a program consisting of several time consuming algorithms, this analysis might be carried out in a piecewise fashion. If $f(n)$ is the sequential time complexity and $g(P, N)$ is the parallel time complexity for a given computation, we can express an **abstract time complexity speedup** as

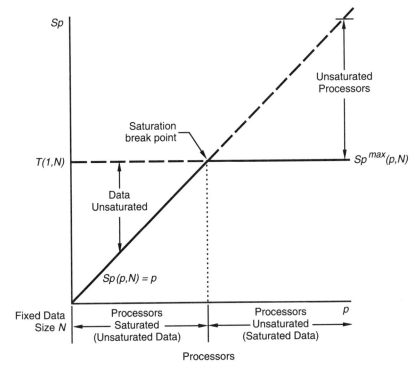

Figure 6.1. Speedup vs. Processors for Fixed Data Size N

$$Sp^{atc}(P, N) = \frac{f(N)}{g(P, N)}, \qquad (6.6)$$

which will generally be much lower than either the bounds of Eq. 6.2 or Eq. 6.5, as shown in Fig. 6.3.

Furthermore, in any real parallel system, as more processors are used in a computation, the overhead of more system-level architectural constraints will be noticed. These include limitations of various memory capacities which lead to additional data latency and bandwidth constraints (recall Section 4.4). We limit this discussion to communication overhead, which varies from one computation to another. Thus, the **system communication constraint function** $\sigma(p)$ (a combination of the α's and β's of Section 4.4) limits the speedup potential of any computation and diverges farther from the ideal as the number of processors used in a computation grows. For codes with little communication overhead, $\sigma(p)$ may be a straight line with a slope close to one for small p. For most codes, as the whole system is loaded with a computation, $\sigma(p)$ has a convex shape with the

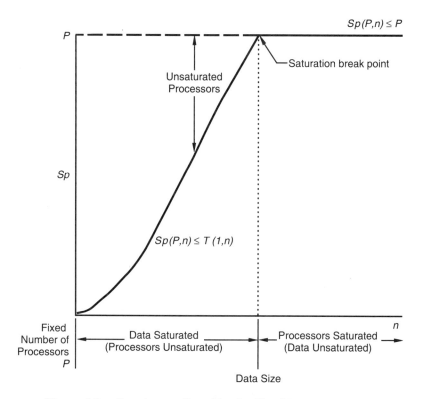

Figure 6.2. Speedup vs. Data Size for Fixed Processor Count

performance eventually dropping due to bandwidth or latency limitations, which is shown as the $\sigma(p)$ curve in Fig. 6.3. By extending Fig. 6.1, we label three processor-count regions in Fig. 6.3. Here we refer to **saturation** of the **system** (in contrast to processor saturation) with data up to the point of diminishing return where we transition to **saturation** of the **data** with processors. Finally, we say that the **system** is **underloaded** beyond the point of no return as speedup falls with the addition of processors. In Chapter 7 we give more formal definitions of these terms.

A similar discussion follows for (Sp, n) with fixed P, as shown in Fig. 6.4 (recall Fig. 5.2). In this case there is a **startup** phase where little speedup can be expected. By any definition of data size, for a sufficiently small n it will be impossible to use more than one processor effectively in a real machine. At some point the data size reaches a critical threshold and, using the crude estimate of Eq. 6.6, good performance increases occur with increasing n, as in the ideal case of Fig. 6.2; this is the **system unsaturated** region of Fig. 6.4. Eventually $\sigma(P)$

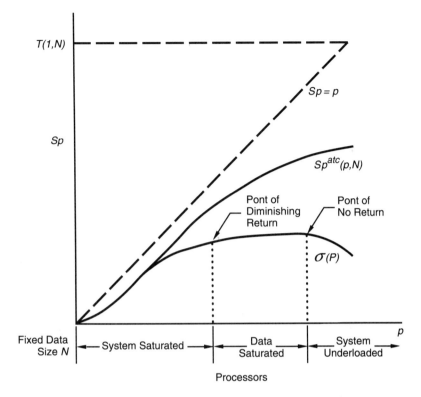

Figure 6.3. Practical Speedup vs. Processors for Fixed Data Size

provides an upper limit on Sp due to various system communication limitations in the **system saturated** region. Finally, as the data size becomes sufficiently large, performance falls as we reach a **system overloaded** state. The data size regions of Fig. 6.4 are labelled accordingly, as is the **saturation break point**. In practice, this curve is more complex than shown, but the notion of a saturation level speedup, Sp^{sat}, at which users feel that the system has reached "good" performance for a given computation is one that we will adopt.

6.5 Acceptable Speedup Relative to Processor Count

Defining performance measures is much easier than using them. In practice it is clear that there are qualitatively acceptable and unacceptable performance levels, whose definitions depend on the user. And then, there are various levels of accept-

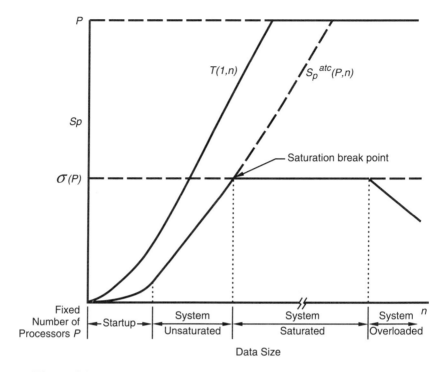

Figure 6.4. Practical Speedup vs. Data Size for Fixed Processor Count

ability. Thus, we are confronted with the question: "How good is good?" We first answer this by expressing speedup as a function of the total number of processors P, for a fixed data size N. Just as users are not concerned about instantaneously inactive gates or circuits in a 64-bit processor, they should not be concerned with in- active processors in a 64-processor parallel system, as long as overall performance is acceptable. However, as peak speed is scaled up by increasing P, delivered performance must also increase. Most people who are experienced with running a variety of real codes and data sizes on parallel machines would be pleased if they could achieve at least a fraction of P or even of $P/log\ P$ (we use the no- tation $log\ P = log_2\ P$) across all their runs, especially as P grows to hundreds or thousands of processors. Note that on a 16-processor machine $P/log\ P$ is 4, on a 1024-processor machine it is over 100, and on 1 million processors it is about 50,000.

The previous sections pointed out that performance saturation of a computation depends on a number of factors and thus is subject to various possible definitions. Chapter 7 will define various minimum performance levels for classifying saturated computations as n varies, but for the interim, following Eq. 5.6, we define a

minimum high-performance speedup level

$$Sp^{Hmin}(P, n) = P/2 \tag{6.7}$$

and expect that this is achievable for a parallel system running well-suited computations with relatively large data sizes. For smaller data sizes or less well-suited computations, we define the **threshold performance speedup** level (recall $\theta(P)$ in Section 5.4) as

$$Sp^{Th}(P, n) = P/2log\ P,\ P \geq 8. \tag{6.8}$$

We refer to performance in the three ranges defined by these two levels as shown in Table 6.1, as **high**, **intermediate** and **unacceptable performance**, respectively. Any performance above unacceptable is termed **acceptable**.

In terms of the 10X/7 years performance improvement that has been achieved over the history of computing, mainly due to hardware speed increases, a 2000 processor machine that delivered acceptable speedup would provide nearly 15 equivalent years of electronics-advancement speed improvement, and a system with about 100 times that many processors would provide about twice that many years of advancement. Thus, if we knew how to build machines that met all five of the PPT's, the threshold level $P/2log\ P$ would provide users with acceptable performance in any future number of years, t, by setting $10^{t/7} = P/2log\ P$. Architecture and compiler technology would be able to replace or augment traditional electronics-driven system performance gains over the years.

Suppose, however, that as we pass 1998, the 50th anniversary of the invention of the transistor, clock speeds stopped improving beyond an asymptote in the range of 1 nanosecond to .1 ns. Further performance improvement would depend on parallelism. Furthermore, suppose that by that time we will have solved the software problems that allow us to pass the PPT's, and suppose that we continue to discover how to make smaller, denser circuits so that ever-larger parallel systems could deliver acceptable performance into the 21st century. Then the issue of data size increase over time becomes a central question, because after the software problems have been solved and most computations achieve acceptable or at least good performance, larger parallel systems will depend on larger data sizes and hence larger memories, to deliver higher performance over time. This leads us to the following subject.

6.6   Acceptable Speedup Relative to Data Size

A user's classification of a particular data size as small, medium, or large depends on who the user is and in which year the classification is made. For example, manageable problem sizes for an undergraduate student's personal computing equipment have increased from slide rule size in the 1950s, to increasingly powerful

Name	Speedup
High Performance Range	$\dfrac{P}{2} \leq S_P \leq P$
Minimum High-Performance Level	$S_P = \dfrac{P}{2}$
Intermediate Performance Range	$\dfrac{P}{2\,log\,P} \leq S_P < \dfrac{P}{2}$
Threshold Performance Level	$S_P = \dfrac{P}{2\,log\,P}$
Unacceptable Performance Range	$1 \leq S_P < \dfrac{P}{2\,log\,P}$

Table 6.1. Performance Levels and Ranges

hand-held calculator sizes in the 1960s and 1970s, to PC's in the 1980s, and will move through sequential workstations to parallel workstations by 2000. As another example, weapons designers and weather forecasters at the national labs have used the fastest available supercomputers from the beginning, but had almost no random access memory in the 1950s and have about a billion words today. Thus, each stratum of computer-user society attacks larger problems over time, and individual members of this society at each stratum tend to be upwardly mobile, as when graduate students go to work in industrial or government labs.

6.6.1   User-Defined vs. Architecture-Defined Data Sizes

At each stratum, for a given code, each user makes various types of runs. We define three sizes of problems, related to these runs. A **small user-defined data size** (SUDS) is typical of a debugging run during code development, with a problem chosen just large enough to exercise important aspects of the code. The results may or may not be physically meaningful, but the user will be able to decide whether the program seems correct. A **large user-defined data size** (LUDS) corresponds to a production run, which may take one hour or more on whatever machine is used. For the experiments we discuss, such a data size would be chosen at a balance point that would not consume too much machine time, would represent as complete a set of real-world data as possible, and would fit reasonably well into the memory system (perhaps exceeding main memory size). Finally, a **medium user-defined data size** (MUDS) lies somewhere between small and large data sizes. Perhaps it would be chosen to be physically meaningful, although quickly runnable even in a time-shared system.

Next we consider data size as defined by parallel machine performance on a given code. We have discussed two system performance levels, a threshold level Eq. 6.8 and a minimum high-performance level Eq. 6.7, which are predefined parameters, as well as the system-overloaded state of Fig. 6.4, which is determined by a computation running on a system (recall the fast- and slow-memory discussion of Section 4.2). We now will identify these three points with small, medium, and large architecture-defined problems, respectively, as shown in Fig. 6.5. It seems intuitively reasonable that a **small architecture-defined data size** (SADS) should be defined by the threshold level of parallel speedup, as defined in Eq. 6.8. Similarly, a **medium architecture-defined data size** (MADS) should be one for which a machine is nearly reaching its top deliverable speed as in Eq. 6.7. Finally, a **large architecture-defined data size** (LADS) should be one that causes a system to lose substantial performance, so, assuming that a computation has reached high performance, we can quantify LADS as the point where speedup drops below $P/2$. Under the high performance assumption, Fig. 6.5 distinguishes three data sizes: too small, acceptable, and too large, where acceptable data sizes are those that lead to acceptable performance, and the other two cases have obvious meanings. In

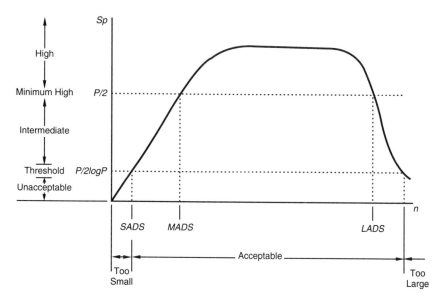

Figure 6.5.   Architecture-defined Data Size Definitions

Chapter 7 we shall expand this discussion to cover all performance cases.

Notice that the small and medium architecture-defined data sizes are functions of the processor count, while the large data size might be determined by something other than the processor count (e.g., I/O latency). Similarly, large and medium user-defined data sizes also depend on the machine size, i.e., the number of processors, and memory size determine what a user attempts to run. A small user-defined data size would usually not depend on the machine size because its running time is very small, but rather on intrinsic details of the program and application, because the user is checking the program's validity.

With this in mind, we can list some desirable and undesirable inequalities. First, a desirable situation would be when

$$LUDS < LADS \qquad (6.9)$$

and

$$MADS < MUDS, \qquad (6.10)$$

so the user would be operating in a high performance state for all runs – medium to large. We show this in Fig. 6.6 as Case A. If

$$LUDS < LADS \qquad (6.11)$$

and

$$MADS < SUDS, \qquad (6.12)$$

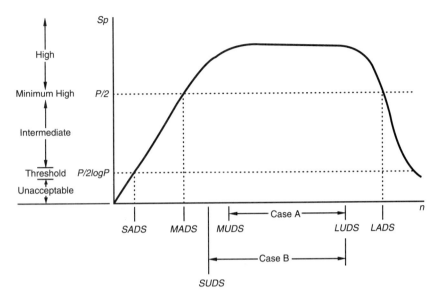

Figure 6.6. User-defined vs. Architecture-defined Data Sizes

then even debug runs would run in saturation, as shown in Fig. 6.6 as Case B, whereas if

$$LUDS < MADS, \tag{6.13}$$

the user would never reach saturation, so most of the machine's resources would be wasted.

6.6.2 Future Data Sizes

Returning to the scenario discussed in Section 4.2, of a future breakdown in clock speed increases, but with large potential increases in processor count and memory size, how much problem size increase would be necessary in the next 50 years to match the effective computer speed increases of the past 50 years? At 10X per 7 years, how could we achieve a 10^7 performance increase by the mid-21st century?

First, we must assume that the parallel software problems of providing excellent compilers and libraries will be solved. Arbitrarily, we will assign two orders of magnitude of performance enhancement to software, although in reality this enhancement would be a function of P and N. This leaves us with the need to explain a natural growth of five orders of magnitude increase in data size over fifty years, or 10X per decade.

Assume that a serious workstation user today has two-dimensional physical problems that fill a 100 MB memory, for example, a 1000 x 1000 mesh with 10 variables using 8 byte words. Over the next fifty years it is easy to expect this to become a 3D computation, which increases the data size by three orders of magnitude (1000 mesh planes), and then to expect at least a quadrupling of the mesh resolution, which requires 64 times more data, for five orders of magnitude, total growth. Alternatively, a 3D problem today with dimension 100 x 100 x 100 using 10 variables would only have to increase its resolution by about 40X in each dimension to provide five orders of magnitude growth in data size. In most cases, as computational data size increases, so does the model complexity, e.g. a physical simulation would include more physics and hence more variables per mesh point.

  Thus we reach the conclusion that future computer speed could continue to accelerate as it has in the past even if clock speeds were frozen. The requirements for this to happen are:

1. solving the software problems and architecture problems that would allow parallel systems to pass the practical parallelism tests,

2. increasing future packaging densities at the rate of 10X/7 years (see Sidebar 19), and

3. increasing problem sizes at the rate of 10X/10 years.

Based on history, the latter two seem likely to continue to happen, but as discussed throughout the book, the first requires new approaches.

Sidebar 19: Chip Size and Speed

  Sidebar 13 in Chapter 4 discussed hardware clock speeds over time. The other basic hardware measure of interest is the feature size in semiconductor chips; how small can wires and transistors become? In the past decade, this has passed through the 1 micron (millionth of a meter) level and will approach .1 micron before 2010. **Moore's Law** (named after a 1964 observation by Gordon E. Moore of Intel [Noyc77], holds that

The number of elements in advanced integrated circuits doubles every year.

This law is widely and loosely quoted, with the doubling period being stretched to two or three years as time passes, but reflects the tremendous progress made since the first production of the planar transistor in 1959.

  There are two obvious contributors to this growth: the reduction of feature sizes within the chip and the growth of chip sizes. Chip (and package) sizes have grown to about 1 in. square, and standard wafers to 12 inches in diameter, but even with the squaring effect, a 10 times larger package side holds only about 7 years worth of transistor-count growth (by the original Moore's Law), so most of the progress has come from smaller feature sizes. The fundamental limitations on feature size are determined by the wavelength of light used in the lithography process of semiconductor chip manufacturing. Continued progress seems assured for beyond the next decade and is relatively straightforward, as long as the fabrication process can be based on light. X-ray lithography and other techniques currently seem too expensive and difficult, but over time practical new approaches may appear. With a drop-off in Moore's Law to doubling in 2 years, memory size increases by 10X per 7 years. A collection of data in [BuWe94], for example, predicts an increase to 64 gigabit DRAM memory chips by 2011, from today's 64 megabit chips — a factor of 1000 which matches the above well. However, a doubling in 3 years would decrease this factor by an order of magnitude.

Memory *speeds* have not kept pace with processor speeds, however. In the past few decades they have gone from speeds that were comparable to processor speeds, to being extremely mismatched. Traditional computers performed typical operations in about one memory cycle period. Current RISC processors can perform one operation per clock period, but memory accesses require about 50 clocks. This has made cache memory systems with 1 or 2 levels very important components of modern microprocessors.

Increasing memory speeds is a problem because it tends to require higher operating voltages and greater power dissipation. However, the trend is to lower voltages to reduce system power dissipation and hot electron effects, and improve reliability. Cooling a system with water or ultimately refrigerating it to superconducting temperatures changes this, but non-air cooling appears very unlikely to become practical for ordinary computers in the next few decades.

The prognosis of much larger memories at about constant speeds, matches well with parallel systems. Each processor added to a system adds a memory unit as well, and if the processor/memory speed ratio is constant, cache systems will evolve to yield well-balanced, high performance microprocessor-memory components. This leads to the assumption that memory size grows linearly with processor count and hence with peak system performance.

Computational time requirements usually grow faster than linearly with data size; for example, n^2 data elements may require n^3 operations or $n^{3/2}$ operations/datum. If the software and system allowed perfect speedup, performance would grow linearly in p, and the architecture would allow memory size to grow linearly in p (as discussed above), but the data required per operation would only grow as $p^{2/3}$ in this example. This would allow space in the system for more cache memory. Of course, it would also be desirable to increase main memory size relatively, as this decreases reliance on disk storage, so $LADS$ grows, ideally allowing $LUDS < LADS$, in most cases.

Any hint that there may be excess memory capacity in the future, however, can be immediately dismissed by realizing another fundamental limitation of computing, **The Law of Large Memory:**

Software abhors vacant memory and immediately fills free space.

6.7 Stability

The relative performance definition of Eq. 5.2 compared two systems, each running a different code. The speedup definition of Eq. 5.3, and all of its further restrictions, restricted this to two systems and a single code. Now we discuss restrictions of Eq. 5.2 to a single system with P processors running two or more codes from an ensemble. In the manner of the speedup definition in Eq. 6.1, and as presented in PPT2 (cf. Section 5.6), we define the **stability** on a given system, of an ensemble of similar computations which may range over K codes and/or various data sizes N_i for the codes, as follows:

$$St(P, N_i, K, e) = \frac{min\; perf(P, N_i, K\; codes, e\; exceptions)}{max\; perf(P, N_i, K\; codes, e\; exceptions)}, \tag{6.14}$$

$$1 \leq i \leq f(K),$$

where i ranges over the total number of data sets used, f represents the fact that each code may have a different number of data sets, and where e computations are excluded from the ensemble because their results are outliers from the ensemble (recall the discussion of Section 3.8, case 3). Thus, assuming that the *perf* function measures performance or relative performance such that larger numbers are better than smaller ones,

$$0 < St(P, N_i, K, e) \leq 1.$$

We write $St(P, N_i, K)$ if $e = 0$. To emphasize large magnitudes, we sometimes use the reciprocal of stability and refer to it as **instability**.

If we are varying the data size for a single program we write $St(P, n, 1, e)$, and if in addition $e = 0$, we simply write $St(P, n)$. **Data size stability**

$$St(P, n) = \frac{min\ perf(P, n)}{max\ perf(P, n)}, \tag{6.15}$$

can be rewritten as

$$St(P, N_{min}, N_{max}) = \frac{perf(P, N_{min})}{perf(P, N_{max})}, \tag{6.16}$$

where N_{min} and N_{max} are the data sizes of min and max observed performance, respectively, and could be written more pedantically as $St(P, (N_{min}, N_{max}))$. Using St as *rel perf*, this is a restriction of Eq. 5.2 to data size variation. Recall that Eq. 5.4 was a restriction of Eq. 5.2 to system variation, and this led to the speedup definition of Eq. 6.1. Thus, a symmetry of speedup and stability arises from the definition of relative performance.

In contrast to Eq. 6.15, if code variation corresponds to varying only programs (with one data set each), we define **program stability**. We write $St(P, K, e)$, since $f(K) = K$, and if $e = 0$ we write

$$St(P, K) = \frac{min\ perf(P, K)}{max\ perf(P, K)} \tag{6.17}$$

or

$$St(P, K_{min}, K_{max}) = \frac{perf(P, K_{min})}{perf(P, K_{max})}, \tag{6.18}$$

restricting Eq. 5.2 to program variation.

Whereas *perf* can represent time or a computational rate in the definition of speedup, for stability it can represent speedup or a rate, which ideally remains constantly high across similar computations. However, *perf* cannot represent time, because running time performance *obviously* varies with running time so stability would generally be a nonsensical measure of times. Stability must be defined for a set of *similar* codes and *similarity* is subjective. As examples, a transaction processing suite, a graphics suite, or an engineering and scientific suite like the Perfect codes can be regarded as *similar* in the application of $St(P, K_{min}, K_{max})$. As discussed earlier, speedup varies with data size; this suggests that $St(P, n)$ must be applied to an ensemble of comparable codes, e.g. the various codes must have *similar* data sizes. Various notions of data size definition were discussed in Section 6.6. In Chapter 7 we will expand this idea, defining scalability using $St(P, n)$ in conjunction with speedup and efficiency performance levels.

A number of different rate measures may be used as the *perf* function; for example, the Perfect codes are scientific and engineering computations, and use the traditional megaflops (millions of floating-point operations per second) as a rate measure [BCKK89]. To avoid debating how to define floating-point operation counts, Perfect codes simply use the floating-point counts obtained from the Cray

Hardware Performance Monitor [Lars85], when measurements are presented. The Perfect 1 codes each have a single data size that is best described as SUDS, and the codes all have comparable running times.

Applying $St(P, K, e)$ to real computational rates (megaflops), Table 6.2 shows that for the past 20 years, from the VAX 11/780 through various modern workstations, a code instability of about 5 has been common for the Perfect baseline codes (cf. [Poin90]). Table 6.3 shows code instability data for the SPEC 92 floating-point benchmark suite using the SPECratio metric. The SPECratio metric is a relative performance speedup metric (Eq. 5.3), which compares running times for each code on each system, to a VAX 780. This table was derived for 1993 workstations from various issues of [SPEC93] (see Sidebar 12, Chapter 3 for an example). Each system shown has a SPECratio swing (i.e. ratio), from the best code to the worst, in the range of 3.7 to 7.8. The particular pairs of codes that cause the maximum swings, vary substantially from system to system. Therefore, regardless of whether the VAX 780 might have had unusually spotty performance (which few users of that popular system would probably have felt, and Table 6.2 shows to have a 5(1) Perfect instability), these current workstations all exhibit the performance instabilities shown, across the SPEC codes. The workstations have clock speeds in the range of 50 to 200 MHz, and there is little correlation between instability and clock speed except that the DEC Alpha with a 200 MHz clock has the highest instability. The DEC Alpha has long hardware pipelines and has been likened to the Cray 1 architecture; in fact it has similar instability to the Cray 1 (cf. Table 8.3).

Sidebar 20: Practical Performance Stability

A number of philosophical questions arise about benchmark selection, and in fact about what ordinary users attempt to use computers for, as we outlined in Section 3.4. For users, the time to problem solution is the main concern. In the benchmarking process, manufacturers want to present representative and realistic numbers, win in comparison to other current systems, and improve their products in the long run.

Recalling the discussion of Matrix 300 (Sidebar 17), it could be argued that benchmark selectors maintain an instability of no more than 6 by rejecting codes that violate that instability level. On the one hand, that is what happened with Matrix 300. On the other hand, Matrix 300 was a singularity in that it caused much discussion in SPEC. Furthermore, nothing similar has happened with the Perfect codes. Notoriously difficult-to-optimize codes are included in the suites; for example, SPICE fits this description and yet appears in both suites.

The direct explanation of why Matrix 300 deviated so far from
the other benchmarks, is that unlike other SPEC and Perfect codes,
it is a low-level algorithm which could be automatically optimized to
a high degree. Amdahl's Law (Section 5.3) shows that whole application performance can depend on the worst-performing component
algorithm, rather than the best. Whole application performance will
indeed improve substantially when we have very high-perfromance
libraries that can be used to construct whole applications.

The most plausible explanation of an instability bound of 6 follows
a complex, natural process. The programs that people write become
widely used only if they effectively solve real problems in reasonable
times. Benchmarkers choose from the universe of effective user codes,
and do it with a combination of altruism for the user and competition
with other manufacturers. Thus, the observed instability of 6 simply
arises from the natural selection of effective user codes across many
applications, and reflects a natural range of performance mismatches
between useful codes and useful systems.

We shall assume that codes running worse than this range are not
generally regarded as effective by the user community. However, we
use the notation of stability with *e* exceptions, to hold the historical instability level of 6, but allow flexibility in claiming stable performance
for any suite of codes on a given system.

Users are evidently not concerned with these levels of performance variation
among programs on workstations, and we will judge practical parallel systems on
similar scales via PPT2.

When data size is varied for a single program on a workstation, lesser variations
are typical, and show up mostly as the data becomes large enough to overload the
system. We have little experimental data in this area, but arbitrarily forcing the
data size to vary on two Perfect codes yielded instabilities up to about a factor
of two. We know of no systematic experimental study of $St(P, n)$. It is reasonable to assume that users do not attempt to vary n over a range that would force
$St(P, n) < St(P, K)$ for the range of programs K, with which they normally
deal.

We define an **instability parameter** π^{in} where

$$\pi^{in} \geq 1, \tag{6.19}$$

and its inverse the **stability parameter** $\pi^{st} = \frac{1}{\pi^{in}}$. Over a range of programs, we

Decade	System	Perfect Baseline Instability
1970s	VAX 780	5 (1)
	DEC 6000-410	4.7
1980s	STARDENT 3010	5.1
	SUN SPARC 2	5.37
1990s	IBM RS6000	5 model average

Table 6.2. Perfect Workstation Instability

Workstation (1993)	SPECratio Instability
DEC 3000 Model 500X	7.77
HP 9000 Model G/H/160	3.70
IBM RS6000-POWERstation 370/375	4.84
Motorola Series 900	5.19
SGI INDIGO 2	4.56
SUN SPARCstation 10 Model 40	4.16

Table 6.3. SPEC Workstation Instability

will define a system as **stable** if

$$\frac{1}{6} = \pi^{st} \leq St(P, K, e), \qquad (6.20)$$

for small e, and as **unstable**, otherwise, capturing the notion of Tables 6.2 and 6.3. If on some architecture, the interprogram performance were to vary by substantially more, the net effect could be noticed by many users.

The Perfect code performance of a number of recent supercomputers [Corc91] shows that there are about two orders of magnitude (100X) in performance variation across the Perfect suite on all of these machines. Thus, the program instability of supercomputers has been an order of magnitude (10X) worse than that of workstations. This has been a prime factor contributing to the confusion in the supercomputing marketplace, and the widening price difference between supers and workstations has been another major factor. As more parallelism is used in supercomputers, this instability will continue to grow, unless we can develop machines that pass PPT's 1, 2 and 3. For further discussion of stability and real systems, see Section 8.2.2.

6.8 Summary

In this chapter we have discussed several examples of the functions *perf(system, code)* (Eq. 5.1) and *rel perf*(2 *systems*, 2 *codes*) (Eq. 5.2). Several kinds of *perf* and *rel perf* functions have been introduced. In fact "speedup" has been used in several different senses, to refer to: the *observed* performance ratio of two systems running a computation; certain *specified levels* of performance, whether or not they are achieved by particular computations; and *theoretical abstractions* about the speedup of particular computations. Speedup and stability have been shown to arise symmetrically from *rel perf* by varying the processor count and codes, respectively. Parameters linking these abstractions to reality have also been discussed.

Chapters 6 and 7 introduce a great deal of symbolic performance notation. As a summary and quick reference, a glossary is introduced in Tables 6.4 (A) and 6.4 (B). This glossary will be continued at the end of Chapters 7, 8, and 9 to aid the reader in relating and referring back to these definitions.

The row labels of Table 6.4 (A) indicate the above-mentioned uses and the columns are self-explanatory. The *system* argument of Eq. 5.2 and its derivatives, is represented simply by P and p and needs no further explanation. Table 6.4 (B) shows the types of data sizes used to represent the *code* argument, and has labels similar to Table 6.4 (A). Finally several parameters have been introduced which will be used throughout the book, and are summarized in Table 6.4 (C).

The relationship between speedup, stability, efficiency, processor count, and data size are summarized in Fig. 6.7, which is an elaboration of Fig. 5.6. Efficiency,

Performance Functions			
Type	Symbol	Name	Definition
Observed	$Sp(P,N)$	Speedup	Eq. 6.1
	$E(P,N)$	Efficiency	Eq. 6.3
	$St(P,N_i,K,e)$	Stability	Eq. 6.14
Specified	$S^X(P,n)$	X-Performance Speedup	Eq. 6.7, 6.8
Theoretical Abstraction	$Sp^{atc}(P,N)$	Abstract Time Complexity Speedup	Eq. 6.6

Performance Function Glossary (A)

Data Size			
Type	Symbol	Name	Definition
Observed	$XADS$	Data-size X Architecture-Defined Data Size	Section 6.6
Specified	N	Fixed Data Size	General Use
	$XUDS$	Data-size X User-Defined Data Size	Section 6.6

Data-Size Glossary (B)

Performance Parameters			
Type	Symbol	Name	Definition
Speedup	π^{Hmin}	High Performance Minimum	Eq. 7.8
	π^{Th}	Threshold	Eq. 7.9
Stability	π^{in}	Instability	Eq. 6.19
	π^{st}	Stability	Eq. 6.19

Parameter Glossary (C)

Table 6.4.   Glossary of Performance Terms

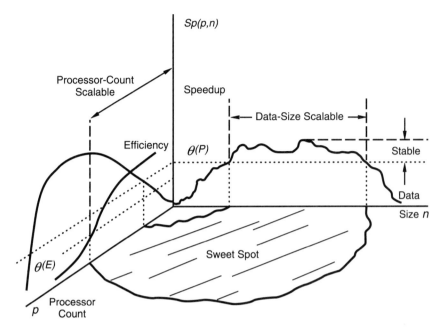

Figure 6.7. Refined Performance Sweet Spot

$E(p, n)$, has been added on the (Sp, p) plane, and as p increases, it falls from 1 for a uniprocessor to some threshold value $\theta(E)$, beyond which performance is unacceptable. Poor efficiency and the point of diminishing returns (PDR), which we used as a cutoff in Fig. 5.6 are closely related; we will formalize these ideas in Chapter 7 in discussing the details of scalability.

Stability is seen in Fig. 6.7 as a representation of the performance surface ripples. A stable region is one in which the performance variation is not too great. The sweet spot of Fig. 6.7 can now be seen to be a region in which speedup, efficiency, and stability are all sufficiently high, and processor count has not increased beyond the point of diminishing speedup returns. These intuitive notions will be formalized in Chapter 7.

A major goal of this book is to promote macroperformance analysis of parallel computer systems. Currently, performance is too frequently discussed only qualitatively, especially in a global sense, e.g. people simply claim that a particular system is "scalable to more than 2000 processors," with little further explanation. Quantitative statements are made about single performance points, e.g. peak speed or 1K Linpack results are quoted for a system, although this would be inadequate, even for special-purpose systems. Even data that is more meaningful, e.g. Perfect code megaflops, represents each program with only a few numbers for a single data size. Performance regions for each program must come to be understood and used in performance analysis and the resulting general-purpose system improvement process. Furthermore, sweet spots for the individual programs in a whole workload must be considered collectively in assessing general-purpose system performance. The workload varies, of course, from one system to the next, further complicating the subject. This chapter and the next provide a framework upon which we can build toward these macroperformance goals. Chapters 8 and 9 will present some real data to demonstrate the application of this theory to general-purpose system analysis and design.

CHAPTER 7

PERFORMANCE SCALABILITY

Performance scalability is a central issue in parallel computing. While spectacular isolated performance demonstrations may excite people in the short run, performance that holds up across machine sizes and problem sizes for a wide class of users, sells computers in the long run. Indeed, performance scalability is a necessary condition for parallel computing to replace sequential computing in any market segment. While scalability is a widely discussed and much desired property of MPP's, there has been no clear definition of the term. By defining scalability and discussing its technical components, one can expect a better understanding of how to achieve it. By measuring and analyzing these technical components, the community can better understand what progress is being made and what the key unsolved problems are.

We shall define several input parameters to the system modelling process, which in turn define several model output values of interest in evaluating performance scalability. The three-dimensional space in which we work is (speedup, processor count, data size) space, which we denote by $(Sp(p, n), p, n)$. This is a generalization of the (Sp, p) and (Sp, n) models presented in Chapters 5 and 6 (recall Section 5.4).

Designers and users of parallel computer systems want efficient and stable performance, as discussed in Chapter 6. In the context of this section, they also want machines that perform well over a wide range of data sizes using any number of processors available in the system. In what follows we will use efficiency, speedup and stability to define processor-count scalability and data-size scalability, and in terms of these we will define scalable computations, program scalability and system scalability. In the end, demonstrating system scalability over a satisfactory range of p and n, for a satisfactory range of programs, implies satisfying PPT4 (recall Section 5.6).

We define regions of scalable performance using the following logic, which is summarized in Fig. 7.1, where upper case letters represent constants, lower case letters represent variables, and X, Y, and Z are parameters. As the processor count is varied for a given program and data size, we say that a system is **processor-count scalable** $PSc(p, N)$ at all points (p) for which the system performance exceeds

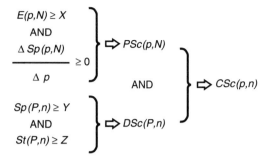

Figure 7.1. Scalable Performance Overview

a given efficiency level and the speedup increases as processor count increases. As the data size for a program is varied for a given processor count, we say that the system is **data-size scalable** $DSc(P, n)$ at all points (n) for which the system performance exceeds given speedup and stability levels. **Scalable computation** points $CSc(p, n)$ for a program are particular processor counts and data sizes for which the system is both processor-count scalable and data-size scalable. A **scalable program** is one with a sufficiently broad range of scalable computation points. A **scalable system** is one on which a broad range of scalable programs have been demonstrated.

The reason for defining scalability theory is to apply it in practical performance analysis and system performance improvement. The (Sp, p) model reveals for a given system and code, the maximum processor count that can reasonably be used for a computation and hence defines the processor-count scalability region. It also gives the maximum reasonable speedup possible. "Reasonability" is related to efficiency and the performance gained by using incremental processors, as shown in Fig. 7.1.

The (Sp, n) model yields for a given system and code, the minimum and maximum data sizes that provide performance above a specified speedup level, and hence defines data-size scalable regions. Globally, the (Sp, n) model defines saturated speedup points $(Sp^{sat} = Sp^{max}/\pi^{in})$ that are within the distance of the instability criterion (π^{in}) from the maximum speedup (Sp^{max}) measured for a given computation, and hence defines data-size scalable regions of highest performance. The stability definition of Eq. 6.15 is used in this process with $perf$ represented by Sp, to provide speedup range conditions as shown in Fig. 7.1.

This ties together two intuitive ideas discussed in Chapter 6. The saturation point (Sp^{sat}) for a computation is where, starting from low performance and increasing the data size, a user feels that the system has reached a "good" performance level $(\theta(P)$ in Fig. 6.7). The tolerable instability (π^{in}) for a computation is the performance degradation factor, starting at the maximum performance and varying the data size, that the user feels is "acceptable." What we are doing in $DSc(P, n)$ is equating these two notions of "good" and "acceptable" performance. In the future, more refined analyses may lead to sharper definitions, but for the present this simplification seems reasonable.

The following discussion is quite general and contains several parameters. In order to use the ideas, these parameters must be given values, and to help advance the field, the values should be adjusted over time. It is important to realize that the parameters must be assigned a consistent set of values for each machine size, P. We will not always state all of the conditions necessary for applying each definition in what follows, because the conditions are easy to construct, when needed. In Section 7.3 we give an overview of the limits on the conditions developed and used in Section 7.2. As we use the model later in the book, we will state values for the parameters, as required.

7.1   Processor-Count Scalability Definitions

Throughout this chapter we will refer to the performance levels and ranges defined in Table 6.1 as well as the architecture-defined data sizes and ranges presented in Fig. 6.5. It is also useful to have a set of processor-count points and ranges, as discussed in Section 5.2, and we define these now.

As the processor count, $p \leq P$ in a P processor system, increases for a given program and data size N, speedup usually increases initially, but eventually flattens or drops off. When the incremental performance gain obtained by using additional processors is too low, we have a reached a point of diminishing performance return, and when speedup becomes flat we have reached a point of no performance return, as presented in Fig. 6.3. To simplify matters in what follows, we assume that $Sp(p, N)$ has been smoothed so that it rises monotonically to a single **maximum speedup**, Sp^{max}, and that the maximum number of processors used, $max\{p\} = p^{max}$, is a uniquely defined processor count. Using the speedup differential with respect to p, we define the **processor-count point of no performance return** p^{nr} as

$$p^{nr} = p \ni \frac{Sp(p, N)}{p} = 0. \tag{7.1}$$

For a given **diminishing performance return parameter** π^{dr}, we define the **processor-count point of diminishing performance return** p^{dr} as

$$p^{dr} = max\{p\} \ni \frac{Sp(p, N)}{p} \geq \pi^{dr}, \tag{7.2}$$

which can be identical to p^{nr} in certain cases. We define the range of processors for which a system is **processor-count scalable**, $Sc(p, N)$ (which we also write for emphasis as $PSc(p, N)$) as

$$PSc(p, N) = Sc(p, N) = \{p\} \ni 1 \le p \le min\{p^{dr}, P\}, \qquad (7.3)$$

and we define the **maximum scalable processor count** PSc^{max} as:

$$PSc^{max} = min\{p^{dr}, P\}. \qquad (7.4)$$

For Eqs. 7.1 and 7.2 to be of practical use, it is necessary to specify magnitudes for p and π^{dr} (or their product) and define Sp, perhaps as $[Sp(p, N) - Sp(p - k, N)]$ or $[Sp(p, N) - Sp(p/k, N)]$, for some k.

We shall distinguish performance levels as a function of p, just as we did with $\theta(E)$ in Fig. 6.7. Because we wish to present constant contour lines that distinguish performance levels, we use efficiency to determine straight lines in the (Sp, p) plane. Using **efficiency parameters** π^{E^X} and $\pi^{E^{X+1}}$ to denote performance levels X and $X + 1$, respectively, in a hierarchy that will be specified in the following section, we define **efficiency range** X, $E^X(p, N)$ as:

$$\pi^{E^X} \le E^X (p, N) < \pi^{E^{X+1}}. \qquad (7.5)$$

We define the **maximum useful processor count at efficiency** X, $p^{max}(E^X)$ as

$$p^{max}(E^X) = min \begin{cases} p^{dr} \\ max\{p\} \ni \pi^{E^X} \le E(p, N) < \pi^{E^{X+1}}. \\ P \end{cases} \qquad (7.6)$$

Finally, we define the range of processors for which the system is **processor-count scalable at efficiency** X, $PSc^X(p, N)$ or $Sc^X(p, N)$ as

$$PSc^X(p, N) = Sc^X (p, N) = \{p\} \ni 1 \le p \le p^{max} (E^X). \qquad (7.7)$$

7.2   Performance Level Scalability Definitions

We shall define four ranges of acceptable performance in the following, each of which begins at a minimum performance level. Within each of these ranges, we define data-size and processor-count scalability ranges. The first and last ranges are determined by the high performance and threshold performance levels, respectively, and these are prescribed levels (recall Eqs. 6.7 and 6.8). The other two are useful ranges of performance that fall between high and threshold performance; their saturation levels are determined by the actual performance characteristics of a computation, rather than predefined levels. Each of the following subsections deals with processor-count scalability and data-size scalability. In subsequent sections we discuss combining them to define program and system scalability.

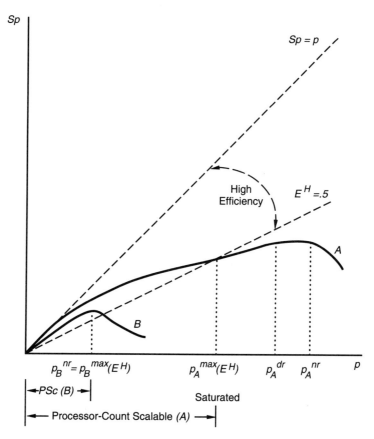

Figure 7.2. High Efficiency Processor-Count Scalability (Sp, p)

7.2.1 High Performance Scalability Definitions

Processor-Count Scalability Definitions

Choosing an efficiency parameter π^{E^X} for a given system defines a range of processors with efficiency level X performance. Using $\pi^{E^H} = .5$ as the high efficiency parameter (recall Eq. 6.7), curve A in Fig. 7.2 shows that following Eq. 7.6 the $E^H = .5$ line defines $p_A^{max}(E^H)$, the upper limit of **high efficiency processor-count scalability** PSc^H for the computation shown. Note that p_A^{dr} and p_A^{nr} occur to the right of $p_A^{max}(E^H)$. Illustrating the other option in Eq. 7.6, curve B in Fig. 7.2 shows $p_B^{max}(E^H)$ defined by the speedup differential at the point of no performance return (Eq. 7.1), before the high efficiency parameter line is intersected. In each case, the processor-count scalability range is shown on the p axis. We

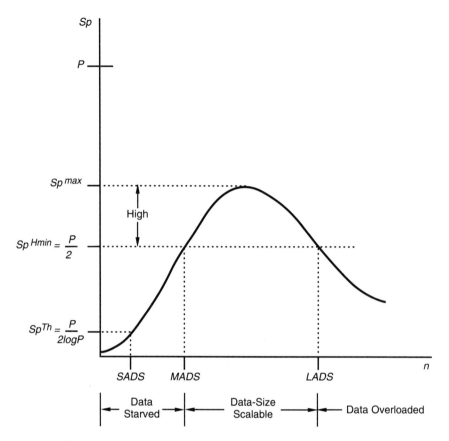

Figure 7.3.   High Performance Data-Size Scalability (Sp, n)

will make the same parameter choices in subsequent models to keep the discussion simple.

Data-Size Scalability

By choosing two speedup parameters, we shall determine three data sizes and three data-size ranges. Following Eqs. 6.7 and 6.8, we denote the **minimum high speedup parameter** as π^{Hmin} and the **threshold speedup parameter** as π^{Th}. By assigning values to these parameters, we define the **high-performance minimum speedup level**

$$Sp^{Hmin}(P, n) = \pi^{Hmin} = P/2 \qquad (7.8)$$

as in Eq. 6.7, and the **threshold speedup level**

$$Sp^{Th}(P, n) = \pi^{Th} = P/2 \, log \, P \qquad (7.9)$$

as in Eq. 6.8. Fig. 7.3 shows these and also shows that the threshold level defines data size $SADS(Sp^{Th})$, while the minimum high-performance level defines data sizes $MADS(Sp^{Hmin})$ and $LADS(Sp^{Hmin})$, as in Fig. 6.5. We say that to the left of $MADS$ the system is **data starved**, between $MADS$ and $LADS$ it is **data-size scalable**, and beyond $LADS$ it is **data overloaded**. When running a given computation, we arbitrarily say that it saturates the system at a speedup no lower than $P/2$, so the **high-performance saturated speedup** level, $Sp^{Hsat}(P, n)$, is defined as

$$Sp^{Hmin} \leq Sp^{Hsat}(P, n) = \frac{Sp^{max}(P, n)}{\pi^{in}}, \quad \pi^{in} \leq 2, \qquad (7.10)$$

invoking the instability parameter π^{in} of Chapter 6.

This leads to a definition of the range of data sizes for which a computation on the system is **high saturated speedup data-size scalable** $Sc^{Hsat}(P, n)$ (which we also write for emphasis as $DSc^{Hsat}(P, n)$) as

$$
\begin{aligned}
DSc^{Hsat}(P, n) &= Sc^{Hsat}(P, n) \qquad (7.11)\\
&= \{n\} \ni MADS(Sp^{Hsat}) \leq n \leq LADS(Sp^{Hsat}).
\end{aligned}
$$

Generally, we shall write $Sc^{X}(P, n)$, or $DSc^{X}(P, n)$, to denote data size scalability at speedup level X.

Speedups in the **high performance range**, $Sp^{H}(P, n)$, are defined by

$$P/2 = Sp^{Hmin} \leq Sp^{H}(P, n) \leq P. \qquad (7.12)$$

When the maximum measured speedup for a computation, $Sp^{max}(P, n)$, is in the high performance range, $St(P, n) \geq 1/2$. In the following sections, π^{in} is not constrained as it is here ($\pi^{in} \leq 2$), and this allows Sp^{Xsat} a wider range. We take the position that to be rated as high speedup, a fixed performance level should be required of a computation, instead of using the floating levels of later sections. Furthermore, even if π^{in} has been set to less than 2, achieving a high level of performance justifies bounding Sp^{Hsat} by a fixed parameter, π^{Hmin}.

7.2.2 Intermediate-High Performance Scalability Definitions

A system may be quite acceptable to users even though it performs below $Sp^{Hmin} = P/2$, in which case we invoke the stability parameter π^{st} to define data-size scalable

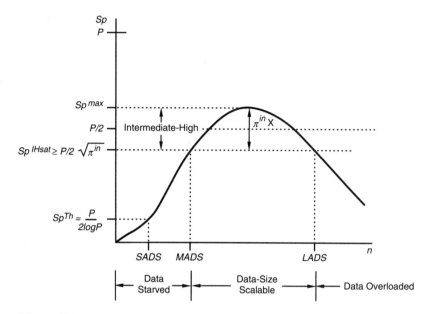

Figure 7.4.   Intermediate-High Performance Data-Size Scalability (Sp, n)

performance. Section 6.7 showed experimental evidence for $St(P, K, e) \geq \pi^{st} = 1/6$, and mentioned that in practice, one might expect $St(P, n) > St(P, K)$; in the following discussion of $St(P, n)$ we assume that $\pi^{st} \geq 1/4$, and in Section 7.3 we discuss issues concerning the range of π^{st}.

Speedup in the **intermediate-high performance range**, $Sp^{IH}(P, n)$, is defined by

$$Sp^{IHmin} \leq Sp^{IH}(P, n) < Sp^{Hmin}, \tag{7.13}$$

where (using $\pi^{in} = 1/\pi^{st}$),

$$Sp^{IHmin} = \frac{\pi^{Hmin}}{\sqrt{\pi^{in}}} = \frac{P}{2\sqrt{\pi^{in}}}. \tag{7.14}$$

Note that $Sp^{IH}(P, n)$ is undefined when $\pi^{in} = 1$, because $Sp^{Hmin}(P, n) = P/2$.

Given an empirically determined $Sp^{max}(P, n)$, by invoking π^{in}, we define the **intermediate-high performance saturated speedup level** $Sp^{IHsat}(P, n)$ by

$$Sp^{IHmin} \leq Sp^{IHsat}(P, n) = \frac{Sp^{max}(P, n)}{\pi^{in}} < Sp^{Hmin}. \tag{7.15}$$

If, for a given computation, $\pi^{st} Sp^{max}(P, n) < Sp^{IHmin}$, then the computation's saturation point is below the intermediate-high performance range, which leads to the next section. Otherwise, Sp^{IHsat} defines two problem sizes, $MADS(Sp^{IHsat})$ and $LADS(Sp^{IHsat})$, and the threshold speedup level determines $SADS(Sp^{Th})$ as before, as shown in Fig. 7.4. The region of **intermediate-high data-size scalability** DSc^{IH}, as well as the **data starved** and **data overloaded** regions, are also defined as before. For $\pi^{st}Sp^{max} < Sp^{IHmin}$, we can determine a reduced intermediate-high data-size scalability range for a given computation between Sp^{max} and Sp^{IHmin}, using $MADS(Sp^{IHmin})$ and $LADS(Sp^{IHmin})$.

We formalize the definition of the range of data sizes for which the system is **intermediate-high saturated speedup data-size scalable** $DSc^{IHsat}(P,n)$ as

$$DSc^{IHsat}(P,n) = \{n\} \ni MADS(Sp^{IHsat}) \leq n \leq LADS(Sp^{IHsat}).$$

$$(7.16)$$

Using $Sp^{IHsat}(P,n)$ we can determine the **intermediate-high efficiency parameter**

$$\pi^{E^{IH}} = \frac{Sp^{IHsat}(P,n)}{P} \geq \frac{1}{2\sqrt{\pi^{in}}},$$

$$(7.17)$$

which is the slope of the line labelled E^{IH} that lower bounds the region in Fig. 7.5. This in turn defines $p_A^{max}(E^{IH})$ and $p_B^{max}(E^{IH})$ for the two examples shown in the figure. These points determine **intermediate-high efficiency processor-count scalability** PSc^{IH} according to Eq.7.7.

7.2.3   Intermediate Performance Scalability Definitions

When performance falls below the intermediate-high range, the next range of acceptable performance is defined while the condition $Sp^{Hsat}/Sp^{Th} = \frac{P/2}{P/2 \log P} = \log P > \pi^{in}$ holds (when $\log P = \pi^{in}$, the minimum intermediate-high performance level meets the maximum threshold performance level).

Speedup in the **intermediate performance range**, $Sp^{I}(P,n)$, is defined by

$$Sp^{Imin} \leq Sp^{I}(P,n) < Sp^{IHmin},$$

$$(7.18)$$

where

$$Sp^{Imin} = \pi^{Th}\sqrt{\pi^{in}} = \frac{P\sqrt{\pi^{in}}}{2\log P}.$$

$$(7.19)$$

Given an empirically determined $Sp^{max}(P,n)$, by invoking the instability parameter π^{in}, we define the **intermediate performance saturated speedup level** $Sp^{Isat}(P,n)$ by

$$Sp^{Imin} \leq Sp^{Isat}(P,n) = \frac{Sp^{max}(P,n)}{\pi^{in}} < Sp^{IHmin}.$$

$$(7.20)$$

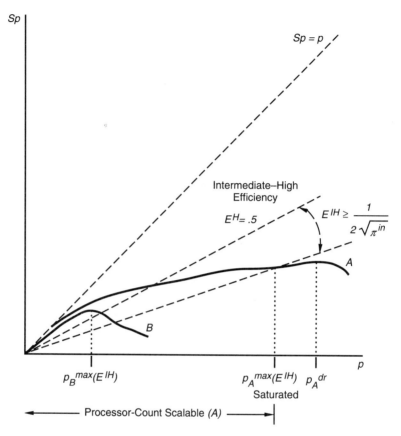

Figure 7.5. Intermediate-High Efficiency Processor-Count Scalability (Sp, p)

If, for a given computation, $\pi^{st} Sp^{max}(P, n) < Sp^{Imin}$, then the computation's saturation point is below the intermediate performance range, which leads to the next section. Otherwise, Sp^{Isat} defines two problem sizes, $MADS(Sp^{Isat})$ and $LADS(Sp^{Isat})$, and the threshold speedup level determines $SADS(Sp^{Th})$ as before. This is shown in Fig. 7.6 together with the three data-size ranges, including **intermediate saturated speedup data-size scalability** DSc^{Isat}. For $\pi^{st} Sp^{max} < Sp^{Imin}$, we can determine a reduced intermediate data-size scalability range for a given computation between Sp^{max} and Sp^{Imin} using $MADS(Sp^{Imin})$ and $LADS(Sp^{Imin})$.

Note that $Sp^{Isat}(P, n)$ can be used to define the intermediate performance saturated processor count p^{dr} in the Sp vs. p plane, as before. Using Eq. 7.7, this determines the **intermediate efficiency processor-count scalability** PSc^I range.

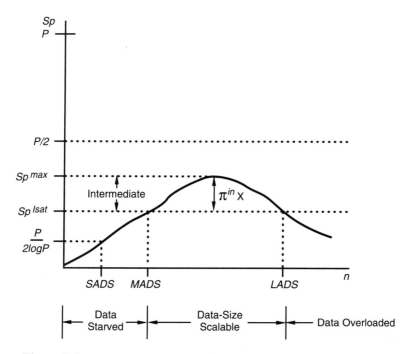

Figure 7.6. Intermediate Performance Data-Size Scalability (Sp, n)

7.2.4 Threshold Performance Scalability Definitions

We regard the lowest level of acceptable performance to be just above the speedup threshold level. Speedup in the **threshold performance range**, $Sp^{Th}(P, n)$, is defined by

$$Sp^{Thmin} \leq Sp^{Th}(P, n) < Sp^{Imin} = \frac{\sqrt{\pi^{in}} P}{2 \log P}, \tag{7.21}$$

where

$$Sp^{Thmin} = \pi^{Th} = \frac{P}{2 \log P}. \tag{7.22}$$

Note that $Sp^{Th}(P, n)$ is undefined when $\pi^{in} = 1$.

Consider two cases of $Sp^{max}(P, n)$. Given an empirically determined $Sp^{max}(P, n) > \sqrt{\pi^{in}} P / 2 \log P$, by invoking the instability parameter π^{in}, we define the **threshold performance saturated speedup level** $Sp^{Thsat}(P, n)$ by

$$Sp^{Thmin} \leq Sp^{Thsat}(P, n) = \frac{Sp^{max}(P, n)}{\pi^{in}} < Sp^{Imin}. \tag{7.23}$$

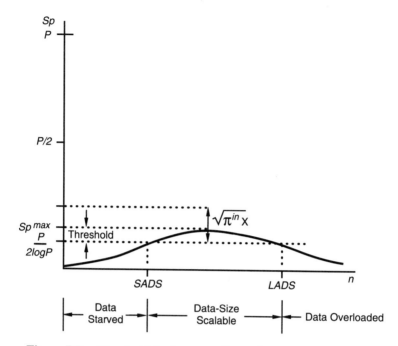

Figure 7.7.   Threshold Performance Data-Size Scalability (Sp, p)

Given an empirically determined $Sp^{max}(P, n)$ in the threshold performance range (Eq. 7.21), we define the **threshold performance saturated speedup level** $Sp^{Thsat}(P, n)$ by

$$Sp^{Thsat}(P, n) = Sp^{Thmin}. \tag{7.24}$$

In the threshold performance case, two parameters, the **threshold performance minimum speedup level** $Sp^{Thmin} = \pi^{Th}$ and the instability parameter π^{in}, determine two problem sizes and three data-size ranges as shown in Fig. 7.7, which also shows how the performance curve determines $SADS$ and $LADS$ as before. These, in turn, define **threshold saturated speedup data-size scalability**. The threshold performance efficiency level of $E^{Th} = 1/2 \log P$ also defines, via Eq.7.7, the **threshold efficiency processor-count scalability range**.

We have defined the threshold performance range to be cut off at π^{Th}. The two ranges above have a width of π^{in}, and the high performance range had a maximum width of 2. In practice, this leaves the door open to expand the acceptable threshold performance range by a factor of $\sqrt{\pi^{in}}$ below the threshold level.

7.2.5 Unacceptable Performance Definitions

If $Sp^{max}(P, n) < Sp^{Th} = P/2\ log\ P$ for a given application, regardless of the problem size, we regard the system as unacceptable for that application. Of course, by selecting some fraction of a whole system as P, the above definitions can be reapplied to define a subsystem of acceptable performance.

7.3   Model Summary and Application

In the above scalability performance models, five input parameters were used to determine all of the output characteristics of the modelling process for a P-processor system. For data-size scalability we used three parameters: speedup parameters $\pi^{Hmin} = P/2$ and $\pi^{Th} = P/2logP$, and instability parameter π^{in}. For processor-count scalability we used two parameters: speedup differential was conservatively set to zero, representing p^{nr} (Eq. 7.1), and the point of diminishing return was established by π^{dr}. We unified the p and n model dimensions by allowing data-size scalability to determine $E(p, n)$ for processor-count scalability (in the high performance model we made independent, but identical choices). Table 7.1 summarizes the data-size scalability performance models and clarifies the parameters chosen.

In practice, people want to talk about the highest speedup level as well as the broadest data-size scalability range achieved by a given program (or set of programs, say, in some application area), even though these are competing concepts. The definitions provide a way of expressing the data-size scalability achieved for each speedup range by a given program. Given a set of programs, at each saturated speedup level discussed above, the minimum range of scalable data sizes can be stated for the whole set of programs. Similar information can be provided for processor-count scalability.

To illustrate the concept for a single program, consider the hypothetical (Sp, n) curve shown in Fig. 7.8. The performance curve intersects the $Sp^{Hmin} = Sp^{Hsat}$, $Sp^{IHmin} = Sp^{IHsat}$, Sp^{Isat} lines, each at two points that define a data-size scalability range, and the size of the range varies inversely with the magnitude of the performance level. Intermediate performance saturated speedup is achieved at $Sp^{Isat} = 9$, leading to a data-size scalability range that spans about three orders of magnitude ($MADS < 10^3$ to $LADS < 10^6$). However, for speedups down to 11.3, intermediate-high data-size scalability is achieved over data sizes that span about two orders of magnitude, and for a range of two units of speedup ($16 \leq Sp \leq 18$), high speedup data-size scalability is achieved over data sizes that span about one order of magnitude. In principle, we could also speak of intermediate performance with a broader range of data size scalability, if we chose some Sp^* such that

Levels	Ranges	
$Sp^{Hmin} \equiv Sp^{Hsat} = \frac{P}{2} = \pi^{Hmin}$	$Sp^{Hmin} \leq Sp^H \leq P$	High
$Sp^{IHmin} = \frac{P}{2\sqrt{\pi^{in}}} = \frac{\pi^{Hmin}}{\sqrt{\pi^{in}}}$	$Sp^{IHmin} \leq Sp^{IH} < Sp^{Hmin}$	Intermediate High
$Sp^{Imin} = \frac{P\sqrt{\pi^{in}}}{2logP} = \pi^{Th}\sqrt{\pi^{in}}$	$Sp^{Imin} \leq Sp^I < Sp^{IHmin}$	Intermediate
$Sp^{Thmin} = \frac{P}{2logP} = \pi^{Th}$	$Sp^{Thmin} \leq Sp^{Th} < Sp^{Imin}$	Threshold
	$1 \leq Sp^U < Sp^{Thmin}$	Unacceptable

Table 7.1. Scalable Performance Levels and Ranges

$$Sp^{Imin} \leq Sp^* < \frac{Sp^{max}}{\pi^{in}}, \qquad (7.25)$$

if we claimed speedups only in the range of Sp^* to $\pi^{in} Sp^*$, and a data-size scalability range defined by Sp^*. Any performance curve can be characterized in a manner similar to the above discussion, spanning the lowest to the highest performance levels achieved.

The various parameters in the model of Section 7.2 must be chosen in a consistent manner for each system processor count under study. The inequalities shown in Table 7.1,

$$P/2logP < \frac{P\sqrt{\pi^{in}}}{2logP} < \frac{P}{2\sqrt{\pi^{in}}} < P/2, \qquad (7.26)$$

are pairwise consistent as long as $\pi^{in} > 1$ and $Sp^{Imin} < Sp^{IHmin}$, because the latter implies that $\pi^{in} < logP$. In addition to this internal consistency, the inequalities must be consistent with $1 \leq Sp(P,n) \leq P$. To avoid degeneracy of the threshold concept, requiring $1 < Sp^{Thmin}$ implies that $P \geq 8$. The instability definition requires that $\pi^{in} Sp^{IHmin} \leq P$ and using Eq. 7.15, this implies that $\pi^{in} < 4$, or more generally that $\pi^{in} < (\frac{P}{\pi^{Hmin}})^2$. Note that if $\pi^{in} Sp^{IHmin} = P$,

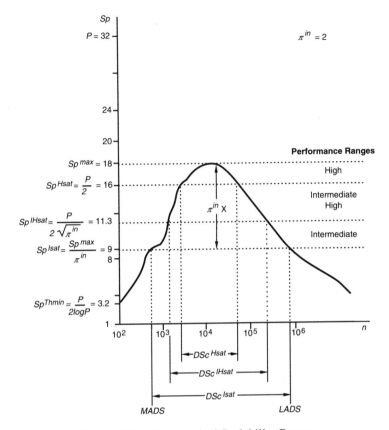

Figure 7.8. Hypothetical Scalability Ranges

the intermediate-high performance range totally overlaps the high performance range. The intermediate-high performance level requires that both $\pi^{in} < 4$ and $\pi^{in} < logP$, and the latter can be ignored if $P \geq 16$.

If $\pi^{in} \geq 4$, intermediate-high performance is undefined, but for intermediate and high performance to remain defined, we must have $Sp^{Imin} < P/2 = Sp^{Hmin}$, and using Eq. 7.22, this implies that $\pi^{in} < log^2 P$, or more generally $\pi^{in} < (\pi^{Hmin}/\pi^{Th})^2$. If $\pi^{in} > log^2 P$, threshold performance reaches up to Sp^{Hmin}.

Note that if $\pi^{in} = 1$, the threshold performance range shrinks to zero at the threshold performance level, and the intermediate-high performance range shrinks to zero at the high performance level. This leaves intermediate performance as the only separation between the threshold speedup level and high saturated speedup level. We summarize the ranges of the model's applicability in Table 7.2, where *undef* means that the performance range is undefined for the values of π^{in} shown,

Instability Range	Performance Ranges Defined			
	Th	I	IH	H
$\pi^{in} = 1$	undef	OK	undef	OK
$1 < \pi^{in} < 4$	OK	OK	OK	OK
$4 \le \pi^{in} < log^2 P$	OK	OK	undef	OK
$log^2 P \le \pi^{in}$	OK	undef	undef	OK

Table 7.2. Model Performance Ranges vs. Instability Ranges

and *OK* means that the performance range is defined.

In general, linking the data-size and processor-count scalability models as we have done here to make a uniform model is unnecessary, and it may sometimes be desirable to choose their parameters independently. This becomes an issue when we wish to combine the two into one three-dimensional model, as follows.

7.4 Scalable Computations, Programs and Systems

Viewing the three-dimensional surface of speedup vs. processor count and data size for a program allows overall performance insight, as in Fig. 6.7. In these terms we can define a computation as scalable at all points on the surface exceeding some threshold. In particular, we can apply the thresholds of previous sections and define a program as scalable at all computation points on the surface that are both processor-count scalable and data-size scalable. These definitions are consistent for uniform models, and for non-uniform models we simply require that both conditions be met independently. Thus, any computation point on the surface is **computation scalable**, $CSc(p, n)$, if it is both processor-count scalable, $PSc(p, N)$, and data-size scalable, $DSc(P, n)$, as indicated in Fig. 7.1. On a given system, a **scalable program** is one that has a sufficiently large computation scalable area, i.e. the computation scalable points cover a sufficiently large area of the (Sp, p, n) surface. A **scalable system** is one that has a sufficiently broad class of scalable programs.

7.5 Designing Scalable Regions

Fig. 7.9 shows an efficiency contour of a scalable computation region in the processor count vs. data size plane. The shape of a scalable region is determined by a number of system characteristics; one objective of system design is to maximize its area for a given scalability definition, and other objectives would be to give it particular shapes. To understand this plot, first recall that a horizontal line within the contour indicates data-size scalability (acceptable stability) and a vertical line

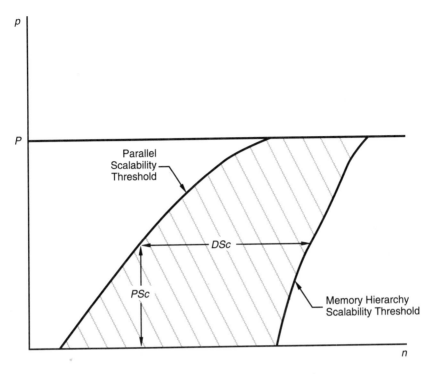

Figure 7.9. Scalable Computation Region

indicates processor-count scalability (acceptable efficiency). Thus, to expand the contour in the processor direction we must make the computation more efficient for large processor counts. This can be achieved by architecture, compiler or algorithm changes. To expand the contour horizontally to the left, we must improve performance for small data sizes, which can also be done by improving the architecture, compiler or algorithm. However, in this regard, assume that we have a perfect architecture with zero overhead for communication, and a compiler that exploits the architecture fully for a given program. The ultimate issue here is the parallel algorithm used, as was indicated in Fig. 6.3.

To expand the contour to the right requires better performance for large data sizes, which is mainly related to improved memory hierarchy performance and is beyond the scope of our present discussion. There is a vertical cutoff here, if the memory hierarchy offers uniform performance across all processor counts, but assuming that more processors (clusters) provide more I/O capability, the contour slopes up as shown.

Because it is constrained by the parallel architecture, compiler, and algorithms

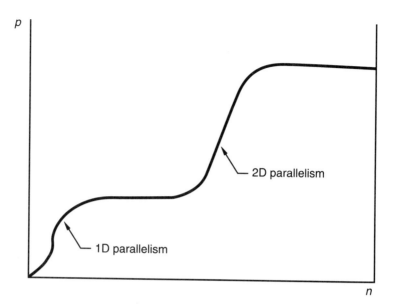

Figure 7.10. Two Dimensional Parallel Scalability Region

used, we shall refer to the curved contour constraining scalability to the left and upward as the **parallel scalability threshold**, whereas the vertical line to the right is a **memory hierarchy scalability threshold**.

The parallel scalability threshold reflects algorithmic approaches to exploiting the parallelism in a given computation. Consider a three-dimensional problem which we parallelize in two dimensions, first in one dimension, and then as the problem size grows sufficiently large, we exploit the second dimension. The parallel scalability threshold would reveal this process as shown in Fig. 7.10, where the two types of parallelism are obvious.

7.6   Generalization

The previous definitions generalize to families of performance levels and ranges that may be useful as processor counts reach $\frac{P}{2} \gg \frac{P}{2 \log P}$. To illustrate the idea we assign letter grades to performance levels as follows. In the (Sp, n) model, high speedup becomes A-level speedup, with **A-level saturated speedup** and the **minimum A-level speedup parameter** defined by

$$Sp^{ASat}(P, n) \geq \pi^{Amin} = \frac{P}{2} \qquad (7.27)$$

following Eq. 7.10, **B-level saturated speedup** defined by

Speedup Level Letter Grade	Level X Speedup Saturation Parameter π^{XSat}	π^{XSat} for $P = 1024$	π^{XSat} for $P = 10^6$
A = High	$P/2$	512	512K
B	$P/4$	256	256K
C	$P/8$	128	128K
D	$P/16$	64	64K
E = Th	$P/2 \log p$	51	25K

Table 7.3. Speedup Hierarchy Summary

$$Sp^{BSat}(P,n) \geq \pi^{Bmin} = \frac{P}{4}, \qquad (7.28)$$

and so on. Table 7.3 shows that for processor counts up to 1024, grades A, B, C and threshold are sufficient, while for processor counts up to 10^6, adding grade D suffices, assuming that $P/2 \log p$ is still acceptable as the **threshold level**. Other families could be defined by dividing P by functions other than 2^i, which provides rather narrow stability classes.

Just as we defined intermediate-high performance using the instability parameter π^{in}, we can define intermediate letter grade performances. Thus A=High and A^- = Intermediate High, B^- is defined relative to B using π^{in}, C^- is defined relative to C using π^{in}, etc. Fig. 7.11 shows the idea of this speedup hierarchy.

In a similar manner we can define efficiency families for (Sp, p). Thus the efficiency parameter π^{E^A} corresponds to π^{E^H}, so π^{E^A} = .5, π^{E^B} = .25, π^{E^C} = .125, π^{E^D} = .0675 , while $\pi^{E^{Th}}$ = $1/2 \log p$, as before, and following Eq. 7.5, $.5 \leq E^A \leq 1$, $.25 \leq E^B < .5$, $.125 \leq E^C < .25$, and $\frac{1}{2 \log p} \leq E^D < .125$, as shown in Fig. 7.12 for four efficiency levels.

7.7 Glossary of Notation

This is an extension of Section 6.8 which presents further examples of *perf(system, code)*. Table 7.4(A) presents scalability and speedup examples of *perf*. As in Section 6.8 there are functions with observed values, but here, some observations depend on specified parameters. Table 7.4(B) lists several examples of the *system* arguments that are introduced in this chapter, and the parameters introduced in this chapter are summarized in Table 7.4(C).

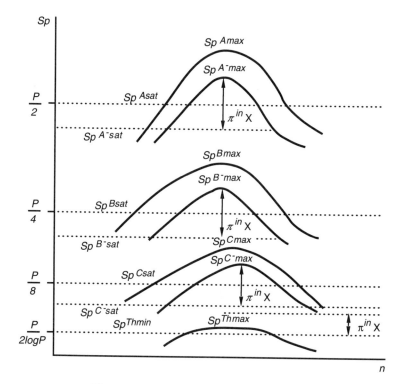

Figure 7.11.   Speedup Hierarchy (Sp, n)

7.8   Conclusion

In Section 6.7, we showed how the definition of relative performance in Eq. 5.2,

$$rel\ perf(system\ A, code\ 1, system\ B, code\ 2) = \frac{perf(system\ A, code\ 1)}{perf(system\ B, code\ 2)},$$

(7.29)

leads to speedup by restriction to system variation (i.e. p variation), and to stability by restriction to code variation (i.e. n variation). To define scalability in this chapter, using the logic of Fig. 7.1 we have used speedup, with time as the *perf* function in Eq. 5.2, and we have used stability, with speedup as the *perf* function in Eq. 6.18 (derived from Eq. 5.2). Thus, we may think of speedup as a first-order *rel perf* function, and stability as a second-order *rel perf* function that employs the speedup function.

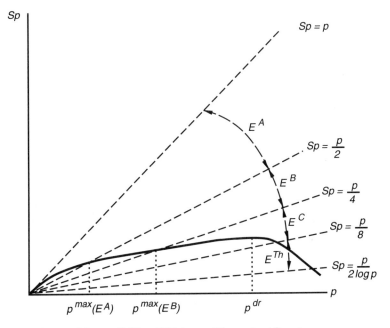

Figure 7.12. Efficiency Hierarchy (Sp, p)

A few parameters with specified values were used for the definitions of this chapter, and perhaps more parameters will be needed as more comprehensive and more useful models evolve. In the following chapters, the values of this chapter are assigned to the parameters. These values were chosen because they seem reasonable from a system design point of view and from the users' point of view. Since the parameter values lead to qualitative statements about performance, it will be desirable to change them as systems evolve over time. In this way, performance models can challenge the field to keep moving ahead.

Chapter 6 gave detailed theoretical discussions of speedup and stability. It opened the discussion of performance regions as a more useful concept than single performance points. This chapter used those results in defining stability. Chapter 7 concludes the theoretical aspects of the book, and we next turn to empirical issues in Chapters 8 and 9. Chapter 9 applies the results of this chapter to PPT4, and in the process, adds a few more definitions that may be considered as extensions of this chapter.

Performance Functions			
Type	Symbol	Name	Definition
Scalability			
Observed	$PSc(p,N)$	Processor-count Scalable	Eq. 7.3
	$PSc^X(p,N)$	Processor-count Scalable at X Efficiency	Eq. 7.7
	$DSc^X(P,n)$	Data-size Scalable at X Speedup	Eqs. 7.11, 7.16
Speedup			
Specified	Sp^X	X-Performance Speedup	Ch. 6 Eqs. 7.8, 7.9
Observed	$Sp^{max}(P,n)$	Maximum Speedup	Section 7.1
Observation Depends on Parameter	$Sp^X(P,n)$	X-Performance Saturated Speedup	Eqs. 7.10, 7.15, 7.20, 7.23

Performance Function Glossary (A)

System Characterization			
Type	Symbol	Name	Definition
Observed	p^{nr}	Point of No Return Processor-Count	Eq. 7.1
	p^{dr}	Point of Diminishing Return Processor-Count	Eq. 7.2
	$p^{max}(E^X)$	Maximum Useful Processor-Count at Efficiency X	Eq. 7.6
Specified	P	System Processor-Count	General Use

Processor-Count Glossary (B)

Performance Parameters			
Speedup	π^{Hmin}	High Performance Minimum	Eq. 7.8
	π^{Th}	Threshold	Eq. 7.9
Efficiency	$\pi_E^{IH)}$	Intermediate-High	Eq. 7.17
	π^{Amin}	A-Level	Eq. 7.27
	π^{Bmin}	B-Level	Eq. 7.28

Parameter Glossary (C)

Table 7.4. Performance Functions Glossary

CHAPTER 8

DEMONSTRATING PPT'S 1, 2, AND 3

Chapters 8 and 9 serve as a report card on both the state of HPC and this book. As a report card on this book, the comprehensibility and potential usefulness of these chapters reflect the value of the definitions and methodology proposed. On this point, each reader will form a personal opinion about how well the kind of data presented here, if expanded and kept current, would help move the field ahead. As a report card on the state of HPC – Table 9.4 in Section 9.7 provides an example – it is important to realize that the data presented reflects the 1992-1993 time frame and is only a tiny sample of what would be available in a National Performance System (cf. Sections 3.7 and 10.4). Finally, in addition to being two report cards, Chapters 8 and 9 are a demonstration that HPC system performance *can* be broken into independent components, quantified, and analyzed at the macroperformance level.

8.1 Performance Metrics

Parallel computer system performance is so complex a subject that it must be broken into a number of pieces to be comprehensible. We have presented speedup, stability and scalability as three constituents into which system performance analysis can be broken. In this chapter, we will use the first two of these three performance constituents to explain the details of Practical Parallelism Tests (PPT's) 1, 2, and 3 which were outlined in Section 5.6. Our objective in defining and discussing the PPT's is to focus on those key system components whose individual performance improvement will lead to overall system performance improvement. The difficulty, of course, is that there are a number of performance benefits and bottlenecks in any given system. One must choose the right bottlenecks to eliminate, and since removing one bottleneck usually exposes others, this process must not do too much relative damage to the other already established benefits/costs of a given system. We must also use the proper metrics to understand various issues, as discussed next.

8.1.1   Relative and Absolute Performance and Cost Metrics

The study of computer system effectiveness is of little real-world value unless the costs of various systems are considered. However, costs are difficult to pin down and compare because of differing customer discounts (e.g., academic vs. industrial sales), because some interesting systems are not commercially available (e.g. academic and industrial research systems), and because of rapid changes in cost over time. Costs are usually of the same real-world importance as delivered peformance levels, and this is indicated by such common measures as megaflops/dollar or dollars/solution for real problems. Because of these variabilities in cost measurement, we shall not attempt to bring them into our discussion; nevertheless, the results of our analysis must be adjusted by costs to be practically applied.

A number of metrics will be used to analyze and explain parallel system performance. We designate as **absolute**, metrics that are expressed for a single system and computation, as functions of running time, data size, costs, etc. Examples of absolute metrics are system cost, dollars per result, and megaflops. We designate as **relative**, those metrics which compare two systems or two computations; they are often dimensionless, and can be expressed at a single point (e.g., P and N), or as a range or region (e.g., of p or n). Examples of **relative point metrics** are speedup and efficiency. The stability and scalability metrics are expressed as a range or region in terms of relative metrics, and are thus **relative region metrics**. Both absolute and relative metrics may have either simple dimensions (e.g. operations executed and speedup, respectively), or normalized dimensions (e.g. megaflops and efficiency, respectively). The distinction is that the dimension of a **normalized** metric has an absolute metric as its denominator; all other metrics are **simple**. Normalized metrics and relative metrics are often useful in making comparisons.

Much of the discussion of Chapters 5, 6, and 7 has ignored the absolute performance level and cost metrics. Speedup, stability and scalability are relative metrics that allow us to compare system performances with respect to architecture and software quality, independently of absolute performance and cost. Thus, even though System A soundly beats System B using the relative metrics, one still must examine absolute performance and cost levels before choosing one system over the other. One way to do this is simply to rank machines on several scales, including (typical examples are listed):

- Absolute simple performance: Total running time for a set of computations

- Absolute normalized performance: Steady state throughput or megaflops

- Absolute cost: Total system and operating costs

- Cost-normalized performance: Absolute performance/Absolute cost

- Relative performance: Speedup, stability, scalability

Such scales would be applied in various ways to different situations. For the purposes of this book, we focus mainly on relative performance metrics, invoking absolute metrics as occasional "sanity checks". The point of this is that we regard certain relative metrics as more universal than most absolute ones, holding across time and technologies, while the absolute metrics invoke important practical realities of the moment. The goal is to develop an understanding of system needs in order to satisfy the PPT's in the long run. Improving system design in terms of relative performance metrics is a necessary precondition, and once this can be regularly accomplished, practical parallel systems can be constructed based on then-current technology to meet the desired absolute conditions.

8.1.2 Program Suite Performance Estimations

The complexities of parallel computer systems lead to large variations in performance from one computation to the next. The speedup discussions of Chapters 5, 6, and 7 have centered on the relative performance of a single system running a single program. Section 6.7 introduced the notion of stability for a collection fo programs (Eq. 6.17) and the following further develops the practical issue of a single system running a suite of programs, generalizing Eq. 5.3 from a single code to

rel perf(system 1, system 2, code suite 1) = perf(system 1, code suite 1)/
perf(system 2, code suite 1).

If a suite of programs or codes (including one program with varying n) is to be discussed as a whole, one is torn between the complexities of looking at a diverse set of numbers, and of combining them into a few characteristic numbers for easy comprehension. It becomes especially difficult when comparing two or more computer systems to grasp the details of a large set of numbers, and yet important details are found among individual numbers. For gross performance comparisons, we will sometimes use mean values to combine the performance rates of a set of computations as follows.

The harmonic mean of a set of computational rates $\rho_i, 1 \leq i \leq K$, for K codes, is defined as

$$Hm(\rho_K) = \frac{K}{\sum_{i=1}^{K} 1/\rho_i}. \tag{8.1}$$

Since the dimension of ρ is [operations/second], the denominator has the dimension of its inverse [seconds/operation]. Furthermore, since each program can have various data sizes (n), the total number of operations to be performed in a set of computations can be regarded as an input parameter to that set of computations. Thus ρ_i for each code i can be regarded as having the dimension [1/time], so the denominator has the dimension [time] for the set of computations. In this sense we can regard the harmonic mean of a set of rates as an indicator of the overall reciprocal running time (rate) of a set of computations on a given system.

Continuing in this manner, the harmonic means of the rates for a suite of codes on one processor $Hm(1, \rho_K)$, and on P processors $Hm(P, \rho_K)$, can serve to estimate sequential and parallel reciprocal running times for the suite, respectively. Harmonic mean analogs of speedup and efficiency are

$$Sp^{Hm}(P, \rho_K) = \frac{Hm(P, \rho_K)}{Hm(1, \rho_K)}, \tag{8.2}$$

and

$$E^{Hm}(P, \rho_K) = \frac{Sp^{Hm}(P, \rho_K)}{P}, \tag{8.3}$$

which we refer to as the **harmonic mean rate speedup** and **harmonic mean rate efficiency**, respectively. The data size parameters are not shown as arguments here, as they are implicitly contained in the rates for each code in the suite. Furthermore, total operation counts approximately cancel out in Eq. 8.2, assuming that the sequential and parallel computations do about the same number of operations.

Another estimator of the performance of a suite of codes, which generally yields a more optimistic result than Hm, is the arithmetic mean of the individual speedups achieved for each code in the suite. We denote the arithmetic mean of a set of numbers $x_i, 1 \leq i \leq K$, as

$$Am(x_K) = \frac{1}{K} \sum_{i=1}^{K} x_i, \tag{8.4}$$

so the arithmetic mean of a set of K speedups is

$$Am(Sp_K) = \frac{1}{K} \sum_{i=1}^{K} \frac{T_i(1, N_i)}{T_i(P, N_i)}. \tag{8.5}$$

Arithmetic means of speedups can easily be raised by a few high values, and are thus poor indicators of weaker codes (see sidebar).

However, for a given set of computations, the ratio of the arithmetic mean of the single processor times, $Am(1, T_K)$, and the arithmetic mean of the parallel processor times, $Am(P, T_K)$, reduces to the ratio of the total running times of the set of computations on one and P processors, and thus can be meaningful, assuming that the data sizes have been chosen in a "comparable" way. We refer to this as the **arithmetic mean time speedup**, and express it as

$$Sp^{Am}(P, T_K) = \frac{Am(1, T_K)}{Am(P, T_K)} = \frac{\sum_{i=1}^{K} T_i(1, N_i)}{\sum_{i=1}^{K} T_i(P, N_i)}. \tag{8.6}$$

The **arithmetic mean time efficiency** is defined as

$$E^{Am}(P, T_K) = \frac{Sp^{Am}(P, T_K)}{P}. \tag{8.7}$$

Sidebar 21: Combining Numbers

Whenever people make measurements and keep statistics, they inevitably combine the numbers to get summaries and dimensionless indices that are simple to understand. Snowfall per season ranks ski areas, earned run averages rank baseball pitchers, and Dow-Jones Industrial Averages rank bull markets. And the fact that a wild river of two feet average depth has a ten-foot deep trench at its center does not deter some people from wading in.

The hidden depths and complexities of analyzing computer system performance data are manifold. Consider the fact that some benchmark suites are reduced to an arithmetic mean (Livermore Loops), and others to a harmonic mean (Perfect), as discussed in the text. To complicate matters, the SPEC benchmarks for workstations are indexed by computing the ratio of the running time for each benchmark on a test system and a baseline system. Then, these ratios are combined using the geometric mean, which for n numbers x_i is defined as:

$$Gm = \sqrt[n]{\prod_{i=1}^{n} x_i},$$

i.e. it is the nth root of the product of the numbers.

Assume that we have measured the megaflops (or some other rate) for four benchmarks. Table 8.1 shows how each mean would combine each of four sets of measurements. We arbitrarily assume that $rate * time = 100$ for each code, so in Case A the rates of 1 lead to times of 100 and the rate of 10 leads to a time of 10, for a total time of 310. The last column is the ratio of Case A to each of the total times. The other columns show the various means of rates and the ratios of each mean to the corresponding value for Case A. Note that in each case the arithmetic mean is the largest, and the harmonic mean the smallest. In particular, Case D shows that when one code performs poorly (measure 1), while three do well (measure 10), the arithmetic and geometric means tend to appear more optimistic than the harmonic mean. In fact, if one is interested in the total running time for the suite,

Case	Rates	*Am*	Ratio	*Gm*	Ratio	*Hm*	Ratio	Time	Ratio
A	1,1,1,10	3.25	1	1.78	1	1.29	1	310	1
B	1,2,3,4	2.5	.77	2.21	1.24	1.92	1.49	208.3	1.49
C	1,3,6,10	5.0	1.54	3.66	2.06	2.5	1.94	160	1.94
D	1,10,10,10	7.75	2.38	5.62	3.16	3.08	2.38	130	2.38

Rate * Time = 100

Table 8.1.   Time and Rate Mean Value Examples

the harmonic mean gives the most accurate indication of the combined numbers (compare the ratios of Hm and time).

8.2   Practical Parallelism Tests 1, 2 and 3

In Section 5.6, the PPT's were introduced, and in Chapters 6 and 7 the details of three relative performance metrics were presented; these included several parameters π. Chapter 6 presented speedup and scalability, with parameter values that reflect current and historical real-world practice. Chapter 7 included a hierarchy of performance levels concerning scalability, for which there is not much historical or even current real-world data. In what follows such data will be presented for the Cedar and Cray YMP systems, and for other systems as we have found it available. As such data becomes more commonly measured, relative performance discussions can become more focused in the future. In Chapters 8 and 9, PPT's 1 through 4 will be discussed in detail, using historical, sequential system parameters in some cases, and using emerging parallel parameters and performance levels in other cases.

In Chapter 7 we discussed the relationship of π^{in} to the performance scalability definitions. When varying n, setting $\pi^{in} = 1$ leads to three performance ranges: high, intermediate and unacceptable, which were introduced in Section 6.5. They will be used here for the discussion of PPT's 1, 2 and 3, with various performance metrics. Since only one data set is provided for each Perfect 1 program, stability as a function of n, $St(P, n)$, cannot be discussed. We will present stability $St(P, K)$, across the Perfect codes, which all have relatively small (debugging-run sized) data sizes, in the discussion of PPT2. In Chapter 9, we discuss PPT4 and scalability, and will force n to vary for a few codes to observe $St(P, n)$ results.

8.2.1   Practical Parallelism Test 1

Practical Parallelism Test 1: Delivered Performance
The parallel system delivers sufficient and efficient performance, as measured in speedup or computational rate, for a useful set of codes.

Practical Parallelism Test 1 (PPT1) is the easiest of the PPT's to meet and has been demonstrated many times by showing that one code and then another runs well on some parallel machine. PPT1 refers to a "useful set of codes," which may be a few codes if a machine is used for nothing else, but to be of general use, should reflect a wide range of computations. As discussed earlier, any benchmark suite, by definition, has deficiencies. On the other hand, sample codes must be chosen to make measurements for improving system performance, and we will present data here about the Perfect 1 codes (see sidebar).

Another use of the relative performance function of Eq. 5.2 is to quantify the performance improvement obtained in hand tuning a code for a given system. There are three basic approaches to tuning, beyond any initial software engineering principles followed to get a code that, among other desired properties, delivers good performance. People make modifications to the program source statements, i.e. manual program restructuring; they give assertions and directives to the compiler about the program, e.g. to ignore certain dependence arcs; and they set compiler command line flags or switches (recall Sidebar 12, Chapter 3), telling the compiler which of its many techniques to apply in what degree for a given program, e.g. to unroll all loops four times. We will call the performance improvement resulting from this tuning, the **tuneup** factor. Letting tuneup Tu be the *rel perf* function in Eq. 5.2, we have

$$Tu(system\ A,\ code\ 1\ tuned,\ code\ 1\ untuned)$$
$$= \frac{perf(system\ A,\ code\ 1\ tuned)}{perf(system\ A,\ code\ 1\ untuned)}, \qquad (8.8)$$

restricting attention to a single system as was done in Section 6.7 for the stability definitions.

In passing PPT1, most systems benefit greatly from the tuneup factor, which is a major distinction between passing PPT1 and PPT3. While tuneup and stability have similar derivations from Eq. 5.2, one wants the tuneup factor to be high because one is working to improve performance, and one wants the stability factor to be high because one expects to avoid performance variations between ordinary runs. Another view of these two functions will be presented in Section 8.2.3.

Fig. 8.1 shows the speedup of Cedar and the Cray YMP-8 when running the manually optimized Perfect 1 codes (recall Section 3.7); the nonuniform axes emphasize the Cray numbers. Note that seven of the thirteen codes (denoted by

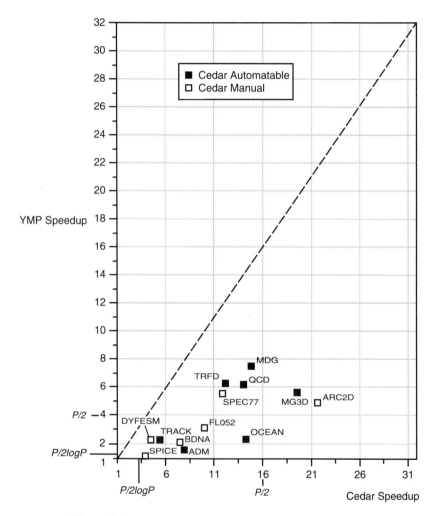

Figure 8.1.   Perfect Manual Speedup — Cray vs. Cedar

Performance Level	Cedar	Cray YMP-8
High $\left(E_P \geq .5\right)$	3 codes	6 codes
Intermediate $\left(E_P \geq 1/2 \log P\right)$	10 codes	6 codes
Unacceptable $\left(E_P < 1/2 \log P\right)$	0	1 code
$E^{Hm}(P, Mf)$	.5 ≥ .22 ≥ .1 Intermediate	.5 ≥ .25 ≥ .17 Intermediate
$E^{Am}(P, T_K)$	.5 ≥ .34 ≥ .1 Intermediate	.5 ≥ .48 ≥ .17 Intermediate

Table 8.2. Perfect PPT1 Summary

solid points) were hand-tuned for Cedar using only methods regarded as compiler automatable. It is clear that there are both good and bad speedups on each machine, although the correlation between good speedups on the two systems is not perfect. In absolute speedup terms the Cray is, of course, limited to a maximum of 8 while Cedar can reach 32, so a comparison that normalizes out processor count can be obtained by observing efficiencies. Normalized measures like efficiency can be very useful in comparative studies aimed at improving system performance.

Fig. 8.2 shows a scatter plot of Cray YMP-8 vs. Cedar efficiencies for the manually optimized Perfect codes. Using the performance categories discussed at the beginning of this section, Table 8.2 summarizes the data by counting the number of codes in each category and also by computing the harmonic mean rate

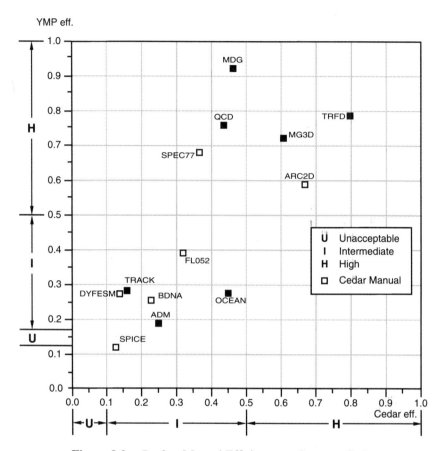

Figure 8.2.   Perfect Manual Efficiency — Cray vs. Cedar

efficiency — using megaflops (Mf) as the rate metric — as well as the arithmetic mean time efficiency as defined in Eqs. 8.3 and 8.7, respectively. The bounds on the latter follow from the definitions, e.g. for Cedar $E^{Th} = 1/2 \, log \, P = .1$.

The 8-processor YMP has about one-half high and one-half intermediate levels of performance, while the 32-processor Cedar has about one-quarter high and three-quarters intermediate levels. Note that the YMP has one unacceptable performance, while Cedar has none. This distribution of data is reflected in the intermediate performance categories derived from evaluating the harmonic mean rate efficiency and the arithmetic mean time efficiency, as marked at the bottom of Table 8.2.

We conclude from this that on the average both the Cray YMP and Cedar perform acceptably, delivering intermediate parallel performance, and thus pass PPT1 for the Perfect 1 codes.

8.2.2   Practical Parallelism Test 2

Practical Parallelism Test 2: Stable Performance
The performance level demonstrated in PPT1 is within a specified stability range (ratio of performance levels) across useful sets of similar codes, as the computations vary with respect to program structures, data structures, and data sizes.

PPT2 is a reflection of the general purpose nature of a system. If there is sufficiently small variation in computational rate from run to run and from application to application, the system delivers stable performance. This, together with possessing the physical resources (e.g., memory size, absolute performance level) required to run all of the jobs presented by some group of users, makes the system a general purpose one for that user group.

Stability is a relative metric; Section 6.7 related its definition back to Eq. 5.2:

$$rel\ perf(2\ systems,\ 2\ codes) = \frac{perf(system\ A,\ code\ 1)}{perf(system\ B,\ code\ 2)}. \tag{8.9}$$

Throughout most of the book, we have reduced the notion of two systems to 1 and P processors on a given parallel system, and the notion of two codes to varying n between two data sets for a given program. However, in Section 3.6 we showed performance variations among the Livermore Loop benchmark programs. Those systems were not parallel, so adapting the notation of Section 6.7, Section 3.6 concerned $St(system, K)$ for the K Livermore Loops. It also compared two similar vector systems for each code in the sense of Eq. 8.9 as $rel\ perf(system\ A1,\ system\ A2,\ code\ 1)$, for each loop.

In this chapter and the next, we discuss parallel performance variations across the Perfect 1 program suite. For PPT2, stability should be considered across a range of n (i.e. $St(P, n)$) and K (i.e. $St(P, K)$), but since each Perfect code has just one data set (as has been true for all broad benchmark suites), we consider only $St(P, K)$ here. This subjects a system to the stresses of a wide variety of program structures and data structures (recall the introduction to Chapter 3), as well as some data size variations between codes. For example, the large data size in MG3D causes I/O performance problems on some systems, and the addressing mechanisms of SPICE defy parallel analysis by all current compilers (although with run-time support, speculative methods offer promise for the future [BEHP94]. These $St(P, K)$ results are wider uses of the stability metric than $St(P, n)$, which represents mere variations of n, but of course, they are narrower than most real-world variations in the loads applied to high-performance computer systems.

As we saw in Section 6.7, sequential machines have traditionally satisfied a remarkably constant stability parameter approximated by $St(P, K, e) = \pi^{st} \geq 1/6$, for suites as broad as the Perfect and SPEC benchmark codes, and it seems obvious that parallel systems should not differ much from this if they are to achieve the same general purpose stature as sequential systems have had. However, Section

6.7 pointed out that supercomputers often have instabilities in the neighborhood of 100 for the Perfect 1 codes.

Table 8.3 shows that both Cedar and the Cray YMP-8 have terrible instabilities for their baseline-automatable Perfect computations; see the next section for a description of the Cedar automatable codes. This is generally caused by several very poor performers (e.g., SPICE) and several very high performers. So we are led to examining the number of exceptions required (i.e., $St(P, K, e)$) to achieve workstation-level stability, and Table 8.3 shows that two exceptions are sufficient on the Cray 1 and Cedar, whereas the YMP needs six — about half of the Perfect codes. Based on this, the YMP cannot be judged to pass PPT2 for the Perfect codes, i.e., it is unstable, while the other two systems do pass with two exceptions, i.e., they are stable. Overall, we conclude that PPT2 is in the process of being passed at this time by real parallel systems.

It may be regarded as absurd to invoke a test that can be passed by ignoring codes that give top performance. On the other hand, consider two points. First, it can be argued that if a few codes produce very high performance, then the user should expect that within the stability parameter range, all codes — or at least most applications areas — *will eventually* perform well, as has been the case with workstations and sequential machines (note that even the 10.9 instability of Cray 1 came close to the workstation level). Secondly, most of the Perfect 1 codes have relatively small data sizes which may magnify certain performance differences, and stability is a measure that is useful for focussing on the *class of codes* that is well matched to the system. Both of these points indicate that the general purpose abilities of a system are indeed related to its stability.

The Matrix 300 benchmarking controversy discussed in Sidebar 17 arises here again. Does the above paragraph mean that if some benchmark runs with a performance ten times greater than all the rest, that the rest are anomalies, or is the one an anomaly? The answer depends on the nature of the codes. The Matrix 300 question is resolved by noting that the code is a single algorithm rather than an application level code. Whole applications typically use a number of library algorithms such as Matrix 300. Thus by Amdahl's Law (see Section 5.3), we realize that the worst segments of code — not the best — usually dictate overall performance.

As a measure of a system's general purpose performance level for any suite of codes, we propose using the harmonic mean of the computational rates of all the codes that satisfy the stability parameter. Thus, given a set of K codes, the stability parameter π^{st} determines the number e of exceptions that must be made (cf. Section 3.8). The outliers included in e have both high and low performances, and denoting these overachievers and underachievers by e_H and e_L respectively, where $e = e_H + e_L$, we denote the harmonic mean of the rates of the remaining codes by $Hm(P, \rho_K, K, e_H, e_L)$, and we refer to this as the **general purpose performance** level of the system.

Cedar	Instability	= 90
	Instability (2)	= 5.8
Cray 1 **(with modern compiler)**	Instability	= 10.9
	Instability (2)	= 4.6
YMP-8	Instability	= 75.3
	Instability (2)	= 29
	Instability (6)	= 5.3

Table 8.3. Perfect Baseline (Automatable) Instability – Cray vs. Cedar

Sidebar 22: Perfect and SPEC

Typical Perfect 1 data is shown in Fig. 8.3, and SPEC performance results were shown in Fig. 3.4. They are similar in that each lists the individual performance information for a number of different codes, and both show aggregated performance information that reduces the complete set of data to a few index numbers.

The SPEC 92 codes include 12 Fortran programs and 8 C programs, each with a single data set. The geometric mean is computed for the 6 integer C codes and also for the 14 floating-point codes, to attempt a distinction between general workstation use and heavily scientific and engineering use. Originally, the SPEC 89 codes

Perfect Benchmarks™

CRAY Y–MP 8 CPUs

Hardware	
Theoretical Peak (MFLOPS):	2664
Clock Period (ns):	6.0
Number of Processors:	8
Memory Size (Mbytes):	1024
Precision for **real** (bits):	64

Testing Environment	
Location:	Cray Research
Submitted By:	Charles M. Grassl
Date Submitted:	October, 1991

Software	
Operating System:	UNICOS 6.1
Fortran Compiler:	CF77 5.0

Derived Statistics	base	opt.
Instability:	75.38	68.14
Harmonic Mean:	25.66	123.95
Geometric Mean:	51.99	286.03
Arithmetic Mean:	107.07	457.33
Benchmark Megaflops:	60.42	559.38

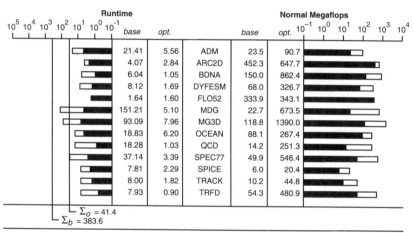

	Runtime				Normal Megaflops	
	base	opt.		base	opt.	
	21.41	5.56	ADM	23.5	90.7	
	4.07	2.84	ARC2D	452.3	647.7	
	6.04	1.05	BDNA	150.0	862.4	
	8.12	1.69	DYFESM	68.0	326.7	
	1.64	1.60	FLO52	333.9	343.1	
	151.21	5.10	MDG	22.7	673.5	
	93.09	7.96	MG3D	118.8	1390.0	
	18.83	6.20	OCEAN	88.1	267.4	
	18.28	1.03	QCD	14.2	251.3	
	37.14	3.39	SPEC77	49.9	546.4	
	7.81	2.29	SPICE	6.0	20.4	
	8.00	1.82	TRACK	10.2	44.8	
	7.93	0.90	TRFD	54.3	480.9	

$\Sigma_o = 41.4$
$\Sigma_b = 383.6$

Key:

Runtimes: Times are in seconds. Hollow bar denotes baseline time. Solid bar denotes optimized time. Σ_b = total baseline runtime. Σ_o = total optimized runtime.

Megaflops: Solid bar denotes baseline performance. Hollow bar denotes optimized performance.

Statistics   Let t_i, m_i, and f_i, denote the runtimes, megaflops rates, and flop counts for n codes. Then instability = $\max\{m_i\}/\min\{m_i\}$, harmonic mean = $n/\Sigma\ 1/m_i$, geometric mean = $(\prod m_i)^{1/n}$, arithmetic mean = $\frac{1}{n}\Sigma m_i$, and benchmark megaflops = $\Sigma f_i /\Sigma t_i$.

Center for Supercomputing Research and Development   *November 20, 1991*

Figure 8.3.   Perfect 1 Cray YMP-8 Data

were used to evaluate sequential workstations, but the SPEC 92 reports now show multiprocessor workstations and servers as well as sequential machines. SPEC is beginning to measure the parallel performance of one code run on more than one processor, and many manufacturers present "homogeneous capacity" numbers resulting from multiple SPEC codes run independently to indicate multiprocessing job-throughput rates.

The Perfect 1 suite [BCKK89] has been used to evaluate some 40 or 50 high performance systems. Fig. 8.3 shows results for the eight processor Cray YMP-8, obtained in 1991 [Poin90]. Runtime and megaflops (rate) are shown in the bar charts for the baseline and optimized codes. A summary at the top of the figure shows system characteristics and performance results. By comparing this to a one-CPU chart, speedup can be observed. Peak system speed allows the reader to estimate the efficiency of each code. The harmonic mean of the 13 numbers gives an estimate of overall performance, and the instability metric shows the ratio of the best to the worst performance of the 13 codes on a given system (cf. Table 8.3).

Comparing baseline and manual (optimized) results gives an idea about how well the compiler performs, relative to what is achieved through a moderate amount of hand tuning by others than the original authors of the codes. The performance of the optimized codes gives an indication of how well a system satisfies PPT1 for the Perfect codes. The stability index gives an indication of how well the system does relative to PPT2. The baseline codes give an indication of PPT3 satisfaction. The Perfect 2 suite, begun in 1993 and now being carried ahead by SPEC-OSSC, contains several data sizes, and thus will give some results concerning data-size scalability as discussed in PPT 4.

Regardless of their utility to date, it is easy to see that the SPEC and Perfect benchmark suites can be improved to allow the community better insight into the PPT's and beyond.

8.2.3 Practical Parallelism Test 3

Practical Parallelism Test 3: Portability and Programmability
The computer system is easy to program and to port codes to, for a general class of applications.

PPT3 adds another serious difficulty to the demonstration of practical parallelism, namely that parallel systems must be easy to use. While the above argues that PPT1 has been met long ago and that PPT2 is being met at this time, PPT3 is still causing much confusion.

Portability and programmability are indeed subjective terms, as they include interpretations by a broad user community of what is easy vs. hard to do. Because there are so many possible manual tuneup strategies (recall the PPT1 discussion), we can say that, unless tuneup can be regarded as easy work, one wants *speedup/tuneup* to be high for PPT3 to be passed. If tuneup *is* easy work, then we can regard it as normal computer use and be happy when most of the performance gains are due to a vanishing tuneup concept (recall Section 3.5). For present purposes, we will avoid discussing the merits of particular programming styles and languages, tuning strategies, or code development tools, and stay with evidence that is measurable. This discussion of PPT3 centers on the performance levels that can be obtained by using compilers for parallel systems, and compares these performance levels with those obtained in demonstrating PPT1. The tuneup factor can be removed from consideration by using a reasonable definition of compiler use, that excludes major human effort. This also supports the compiler goal of high delivered performance with low tuneup benefits, which must be a goal of practical parallel processing.

While the Perfect 1 rules required baseline results to be compiler obtained, we break those rules for Cedar here and in the PPT2 discussion. The Cedar Fortran compiler group has developed several compiler enhancements that were first applied manually to the Perfect codes in the design of a next-generation compiler [BEHP94]. These "automatable," but hand compiled results are reported here to indicate what may be regarded as state-of-the-art compiler-achievable results (see Sidebar 23).

Fig. 8.4 shows the speedup of Cedar and the Cray YMP-8 running the compiled Perfect codes; Cedar using the automatable codes and Cray using a production compiler. As expected, in contrast to Fig. 8.1 these results show that a number of codes have lower performance on both machines than for the manually tuned codes. Fig. 8.5 shows a scatter plot of Cray YMP-8 vs. Cedar efficiency for the baseline-automatable Perfect codes, and should be compared to Fig. 8.2. The automatable Cedar codes reflect our view of the state of the art of the best compiler technology today.

Using the performance categories defined earlier, Table 8.4 summarizes the data just as Table 8.2 did. Note that the 8-processor YMP has no high performance codes, while about one-half have intermediate performance and one-half have unacceptable performance. Cedar has one code with high performance, ten with intermediate performance, and two with unacceptable performance.

This data is also reflected in the harmonic mean rate efficiency (using megaflops) and arithmetic mean time efficiency shown (recall Eqs. 8.3 and 8.7). Cedar gives acceptable performance with both measures, just meeting the threshold for the harmonic mean rate efficiency. The Cray performance is unacceptable for the harmonic mean rate efficiency but is acceptable for the (generally more optimistic) arithmetic mean time efficiency.

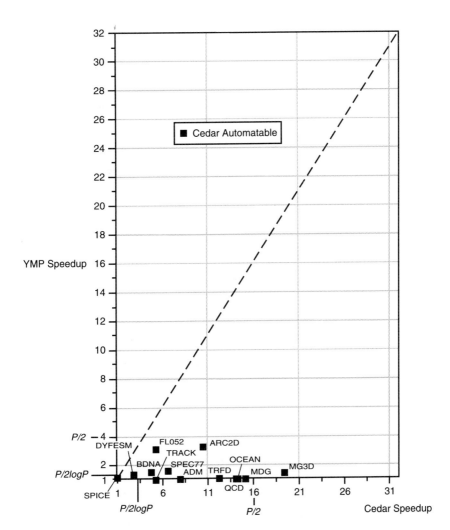

Figure 8.4. Perfect Baseline (Automatable) Speedup — Cray vs. Cedar

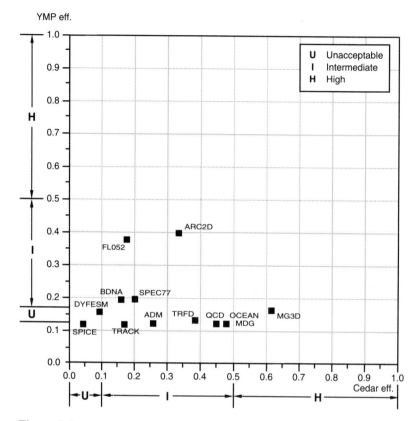

Figure 8.5.   Perfect Baseline (Automatable) Efficiency — Cray vs. Cedar

We conclude from this that the state of today's compiler art is just reaching acceptable levels for the Perfect codes.   In the next few years we can expect PPT3 to be passed by more and more parallel systems for wider ranges of applications codes.

Sidebar 23: Practical Parallelism Test 3

The previous sidebar gave an overview of how the Perfect and SPEC benchmarks can be used in evaluating the PPT's.   But, of course, many measurements beyond those taken in SPEC and Perfect will be necessary in future open-performance efforts (recall Section 3.7). Furthermore, the PPT's will have to be refined and enriched as time passes.   We have started by modifying some of the existing measurement rules, in order to make predictions about future system

Performance Level	Cedar	Cray YMP - 8
High	1 code	0
Intermediate	10 codes	6 codes
Unacceptable	2 codes	7 codes
$E^{Hm}(P, M_f)$	$.5 \geq .10 \geq .1$ Intermediate	$.17 > .13$ Unacceptable
$E^{Am}(P, T_K)$	$.5 \geq .28 \geq .1$ Intermediate	$.5 \geq .18 \geq .17$ Intermediate

Table 8.4.   Perfect PPT3 Summary

performance.

CSRD researchers have developed a number of systems including the Parafrase I, Parafrase II, and Cedar restructuring compilers, aided by measurements of the weaknesses of existing compilers, and hand-compiling benchmarks to study two subjects:

- Possible new compiler transformations.

- The performance effects of such new transformations.

This has been a fruitful approach over many years, and the Perfect 1 codes have been particularly helpful in developing future Cedar compiler ideas. Some would complain that such an effort is merely "tuning the compiler to the Perfect 1 codes," but as benchmark suites become more and more comprehensive and broadly representative, such "tuning" can capture almost all real-world code constructs. It is possible to write horribly performing codes ad infinitum, for which compilers will never offer performance improvement. The problem is to tune compilers and to tune parallel programming style, so that good performance is eventually achieved by ordinary users with little effort most of the time. Recall the discussion of Section 3.5.

We call compiler transformations **automatable** if they appear to yield good performance boosts, as well as being reasonable to implement in the context of a given compiler. In Section 8.2.3, automatable transformations are invoked in discussing potential compiler performance. While this procedure yields state-of-the-art performance expectations, it also leads to apples vs. oranges comparisons if done, say, relative to machine selection. However, the point here is to compare the Cray compiler used, with what may be available in the near future. Other modifications to Perfect and SPEC measurements, and rules to aid in performance improvement, will be suggested elsewhere in the book.

8.3   Glossary of Notation

In this chapter the notion of statistically summarizing *perf* function values was introduced using two approaches: *perf* of statistical data, and a statistical combination of *perf* values, as shown in Table 8.5. The former led us to use other representations than data size for *code* in the *rel perf* function. These included computational rate (ρ in Eq. 8.1), running time (T in Eq. 8.6), and a code's state of tuning (hand-tuned or untuned in Eq. 8.8); recall that we have also used the number of codes in a suite (N_K, in Chapter 6 with stability). Table 8.5 is a continuation of the glossary series begun in Chapters 6 and 7, that will be concluded in Chapter 9.

8.4   Conclusion

Throughout the book it is assumed that people want higher system performance; this chapter centers on how to measure current performance, with the goal of future system performance improvement. However, there are many difficult issues concerning what to measure and how to measure it. In the past, users of all types knew that if a particular problem was just beyond current performance capabilities, it would be handled with next-generation performance increases, because raw hardware performance increases were continuous. But a few expert users were always able to exploit the performance potential of a given system far better than ordinary users by properly structuring their codes.

Performance Observed			
Type	Symbol	Name	Definition
Statistical Combination	$Hm(\rho_K)$	Hm of Computational Rates	Eq. 8.1
of *perf* for a Suite	$Am(Sp_K)$	Am of Speedups	Eq. 8.5
Rel perf of Statistical Combinations for a Suite	$Sp^{Hm}(P, \rho_K)$	Hm Rate Speedup	Eq. 8.2
	$Sp^{Am}(P, T_K)$	Am Time Speedup	Eq. 8.6
	$E^{Hm}(P, \rho_K)$	Hm Rate Efficiency	Eq. 8.3
	$E^{Am}(P, T_K)$	Am Time Efficiency	Eq. 8.7
Relative Perf	$Tu(syst,$ $code\ tuned,$ $code\ untuned)$	Tuneup Gain	Eq. 8.8
Perf	ρ	Computational Rate	Section 8.1

Table 8.5.   Performance Functions Glossary

Now, because future hardware clock speed increases are debatable, system architecture has arisen as a necessary hardware alternative for system performance enhancement. However, if everyone must exploit architectural features to obtain performance gains in the future, it must become possible for ordinary users to exploit systems to the same degree that was possible only for a few experts in the past. If single source programs are to be usable across architectures, powerful compilers and libraries are required, and these are still being developed. Until now, this situation has led to a diversity of programs, each written for a specific architecture. These programs initially are a burden on users to write, and later confound the performance analyzers because there are multiple, diverse versions of programs that do the same work in different ways on different systems. The natural selection process of evolution is clearly at work in this man-made, high-tech setting, but it seems obvious that the diversity of evolved results is too broad.

From the ordinary users' perspective, obtaining performance has been a burden borne in many forms. In the context of vector/pipelined system performance, this issue arose in the mid-1960s on the CDC STAR. Ken Iverson had developed the APL language, which showed the power of vectors and other data structures, functional programming, and more. With the STAR and Cyber 205 systems, CDC developed hardware that supported a powerful memory-to-memory vector instruction set that mimicked parts of APL, allowing arbitrarily long (dense or sparse) vector operations (via Q8 CALLs). In contrast, the Cray 1 offered hardware vectors that were only dense and of length 64, provided a weak vectorizing Fortran compiler, and placed much programming burden on the user.

During the same 1970s time frame, users were awakening to structured programming and software engineering notions that the way programs were written affected their cost of development and maintenance, as well as their performance and lifetime. Thus, writing sequential programs in a vector style did not seem to be so difficult, and certain notions about good programming style caught on in subtle ways. The net effect in supercomputing was that the Cray hardware prevailed – mainly because of its fast scalar speed – and despite the inferiority of richness in its vector architecture, and its weak compiler, even non-experts learned to write effective vector programs manually. For ordinary users, it may have been easier to program CDC systems, but scalar performance dominated most codes and the Cray was a clear winner on that front. As time passed, vectorizing compilers improved as Cray flourished, vectors found their way into Fortran 90, and pipelined architectures have trickled down to RISC microprocessors.

A great diversity of Fortran programs are now presented to RISC systems, some are written mainly in a pre-1970s style, others use an inherent vector programming style, and some are now being written with Fortran 90 arrays. Some people now argue that Fortran 90 is too little, too late, because writing vectorizable scalar programs for today's vectorizers is sufficient, others say that parallelism extensions are needed, and still others say that Fortran 90 provides too little support for object oriented programming (which in turn may weaken its ultimate use in parallel programming) – users who care about the debate only need to wait for Fortran 95 or Fortran 2000 to appear, to get an answer. Meanwhile, Unix carried the C programming language to most platforms and promises of the powers of abstraction, object orientation, and reusability led C programmers to C++. All of this evolution has been governed by some natural selection rule resembling the Principle of Immediately Usable Change (Section 3.5), with different user communities evolving in different ways.

Parallel language extensions have been widely discussed and developed in the past decade. The Parallel Computing Forum (PCF), an industrial consortium formed in the late 1980s, designed the PCF shared-memory Fortran parallelism extensions [LRKI92]. These ideas have been assimilated into many vendor parallel-Fortran dialects and led to forming the ANSI X3H5 standards committee. In the 1990s, similar efforts arose for distributed memory systems (first, via message-passing libraries) and have led to the High Performance Fortran (HPF) effort [KLSS94], which has had wide participation by academia and industry.

A major difficulty with HPC systems has arisen as architectures have diverged (especially in parallel systems), in that a code that has been optimized for one HPC system may perform poorly on another (recall the discussion of Section 3.6 for now-outdated, relatively simple vector systems). This makes the programming task increasingly difficult because distinct tuning is required for each architecture.

More insidious is the fact that some of these codes are becoming relatively easily portable, but their structure usually offers substantial performance advantages to one class of architectures over the rest. Obviously, program designers have in mind design constraints that may sharply favor a given architecture, and even a genius software designer who might design something that performs well on *all* existing systems, cannot anticipate tomorrow's new architectural designs.

It is clear from this that anyone measuring performance is confronted with a diverse universe of source programs and a wide range of systems to study. As users' reliance on compiler capabilities has risen, compilers have come to play a central role in performance studies. But the complexity of modern architectures and compilers, together with the diversity of evolved programming styles, has led to a wizardry factor in obtaining good performance, and even in *using* compilers. To eliminate the wizardry factor, the SPEC workstation rules have now added a baseline measurement, wherein basic compiler options must be unchanged across the benchmark suite. Previously this restriction was only necessary in supercomputing (as in the Perfect 1 rules), but as technology trickles down and extracting performance becomes more difficult, such issues are arising among personal computers.

There are vexing issues here, made more difficult by the evolution of programming styles, the shift of hardware speed improvement from the clock to the architecture, and compiler performance features that are not as effectively controllable as they must become. Performance measurement and analysis is a crucial necessity for the process of architecture and compiler performance enhancement, so these difficult issues must be faced.

It is obvious from history that what seems logically correct and forward looking (CDC vectors) sometimes loses out to simple practicality (Cray 1 scalar speed), and that pioneering technology difficulties can sometimes trickle down to become widely assimilated (pipelines from supercomputers to RISC processors) or in other cases shift sideways (from hardware clock speed to architectural complexity). The time frames for these changes can vary widely and make market timing all important. Sometimes changes are rather slow in coming, as when user programming style leaves dusty decks and legacy codes that endure for decades, but other changes can be too rapid for some designers as when RISC processors eventually succeeded in the marketplace in the 1980s, causing a CMOS microprocessor revolution that propelled new companies to leadership positions in the marketplace. Currently we are in the midst of a parallelism revolution that has been slow in forming, but which now apparently will only require a few years to change the architecture of all high-performance desk-top systems, whether RISC, CISC, or hybrid.

Instead of getting easier, the problem of performance understanding will continue to grow in complexity, especially if it is not decomposed into manageable pieces. Manufacturers are now faced with architecture and compiler challenges that they have not seen before, and these serious challenges are in fact becoming their great hopes for the future. Fearless reliance on highly promising but poorly understood technology is not a sure-fire recipe for success, but very often for failure. The PPT's are an attempt to sort out some of the issues and guide measurements that will help to simplify and analyze various pieces of the overall problem. Chapter 8 has dealt with issues that are becoming important on all high performance computer systems, from desktop to large parallel systems. Chapter 9 deals with issues that are most relevant in the near future for large parallel systems.

CHAPTER 9

DEMONSTRATING PPT'S 4 AND 5

9.1 Practical Parallelism Test 4

Parallel system performance can vary widely as a function of both the number of processors used and the size of the problems being solved. For a fixed, medium data size, too few processors will saturate immediately and too many processors will incur intolerable overheads; the right number is between these and yields good performance. Similarly, for a fixed processor count, too small a data size will not be able to exploit the machine's capabilities, and too large a data size will overload the system so that performance falls off. Intuitively, the system scalability metric must capture the notion that there is a region of good performance as the number of processors grows for a fixed data size, and it must also capture the notion that good performance reaches and later falls below an acceptable threshold as the data size is increased for a particular processor count.

More difficult to quantify, but more challenging to designers than data-size and processor-count performance variation is the system performance response to varying program structures and data structures (recall Section 5.1). With present understanding, we can hope to capture these variables only by selecting a range of applications areas and specific codes for analysis. As defined in Chapter 7, system scalability requires the scalability of a range of programs, where each program's scalability requires a sufficiently broad range of scalable computation points, that is, data-size and processor-count scalability. This leads to:

Practical Parallelism Test 4: System Scalability
For computations ranging widely over useful applications and codes, a
P-processor system is scalable if it is both
a) Data-size scalable:
a sufficient range of data sizes can be effectively run on each chosen $p \leq P$, *and*
b) Processor-count scalable:
a sufficient range of processor-counts, $p \leq P$, *can effectively run each code.*

Differing expectations among various users and system purchasers make it impossible to specify fixed processor-count or data-size ranges and performance

223

levels for PPT4. Instead, we will discuss measured performance levels and ranges (in Chapter 7 terms) for several example programs, and leave value judgements about sufficiency and effectiveness to the reader. In the end, satisfying PPT4 means demonstrating system scalability over a sufficient range of programs, processor counts and data sizes at performance levels regarded as effective by the community.

PPT4 can be discussed in terms of hand optimized codes or of automatically compiled ones, i.e. either PPT1 or PPT3 can be assumed to have been passed. In this chapter, some data of each kind will be presented, however, we reserve the "practical parallel system" label for those cases where PPT3 has been passed.

It is important to underscore the fact that the results in this chapter are out of date in that they were obtained in the 1992-1993 time frame, and represent only a tiny fraction of the experimental data necessary for analysis in applying the practical parallel system label to any real machine. This discussion is presented not so much for what it *is* as for what it *represents*; it is a small example of what future performance analysis might be.

9.1.1   Chapter Overview

To preview the data that one can expect, Fig. 9.1 shows performance contours in $(perf, p, n)$ space, and generalizes the efficiency contours of Fig. 7.9. Those contours with negative slopes represent speedup, megaflops, etc., and we refer to them as **performance contours**. Those with positive slopes (as in Fig. 7.9) represent efficiency, megaflops per processor, etc., and we refer to them as **processor-normalized performance contours**; they occur in pairs as in Fig. 7.9. Note that the performance contours can be either absolute or relative, whereas the processor-normalized performance contours are normalized by processor count.

The most desirable performance contours would represent the highest levels of performance or cost/performance and lie closest to the axes in Fig. 9.1, i.e., have the least area under them. The most desirable processor-normalized performance contours would represent the highest levels of performance and contain the maximum overall area, as in Fig. 7.9. In Fig. 9.1 we show fragments of the left sides of contours, which would most desirably lie closest to the p axis, and would have the greatest slope. The unshown right side would correspond to very large n values, where performance is dropping.

In Sections 7.1 and 7.2 we presented detailed definitions of computation scalability CSc in terms of data-size scalability DSc and processor-count scalability PSc. Now we will use those definitions to present and analyze experimental data for real computations on several systems: first, PSc in Section 9.2, then DSc in Sections 9.3 and 9.4, and then CSc in Section 9.5. In contrast with the PPT's discussed in Chapter 8, there is not much historical or sequential system data upon which to base this discussion, so we can only discuss a combination of desired

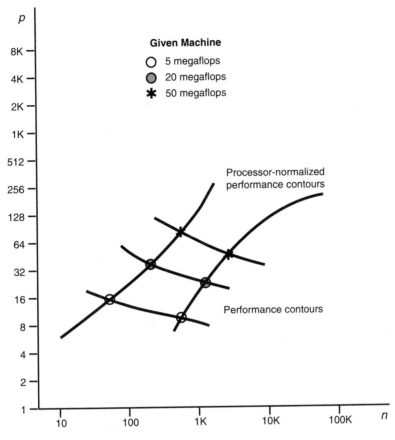

Figure 9.1. Performance Contours

goals for performance scalability and measured current parallel system behavior. We show experimental data for various comparable computations on Cedar, the Cray YMP, the CM-5 and the nCUBE/10. This will serve to begin the process of evolving useful practical metrics for parallel computation and system scalability.

9.2 Processor-Count Scalability $PSc(p,N)$

For any reasonable fixed data size, a small parallel system should operate in a system-saturated mode, but as p increases it will reach a point of diminishing performance returns. Intuitively, one wonders how well performance increases as p increases. An obvious and natural metric for expressing this relationship is efficiency, $E(p, N) = \frac{Sp(p,N)}{p}$, which often approximates the slope of the (Sp vs. p) curve in its initial, linear rise. Since our range of interest is the processor-count scalable region, (recall Section 7.1) we define **processor-count-scalable efficiency** (using Eq. 7.4) as

$$E^{PSc}(p, N) = \frac{Sp(PSc^{max}, N)}{PSc^{max}}. \tag{9.1}$$

Thus if $p^{dr} \leq P$, $E^{PSc}(p, N) = E(p^{dr}, N)$, and if $p^{dr} > P$, $E^{PSc}(p, N) = E(P, N)$. In either case, we are also interested in the maximum processor counts at which threshold and high efficiency are achieved, namely $p^{max}(E^H)$ and $p^{max}(E^{Th})$, respectively (see Eq. 7.6). At this point, we must also define a numerical value for π^{dr}, to apply the definitions of p^{dr} and E^{PSc}. One possibility is to choose p^{dr} so that $E^{PSc}(p^{dr}, N) \geq E^{Th}(p, N) = \frac{1}{2 \log P}$. Another possibility is to require $Sp(p, N) - Sp(p/2, N) \geq 1$. The following examples work for either of these choices.

We now present some example data from four codes for the Cedar system, which has $P = 32$. Table 9.1 summarizes the processor-count scalability information of this section. For each code, the data size of each computation is shown, followed by maximum scalable processor count, the corresponding efficiency and maximum high-efficiency scalable processor count. First, two examples of algorithms are given: a conjugate gradient code [MeSa88] for solving symmetric linear systems and a row projection code [BrSa92] for solving nonsymmetric linear systems. A survey of Cedar algorithms appears in [GaGS94].

9.2.1   Conjugate Gradient

For the conjugate gradient (CG) algorithm, we first consider a matrix derived from a 2D physical problem of size $N = 191^2 (= 36K)$. This turns out to be a data-size scalable problem size, where $p^{dr} > P$, so $PSc^{max} = 32$ and as shown in Fig. 9.2,

$$E^{PSc}(p, N) = E^{PSc}(32, 191^2) = \frac{Sp(32, 191^2)}{32} = \frac{21.56}{32} = .67. \tag{9.2}$$

Furthermore, in this case $p^{max}(E^H) = 32$.

Next we discuss $N = 31^2 (= 1K)$, which results in a data starved computation, as shown in Fig. 9.3. In this case, $p^{dr} = 8 < 32$ so $PSc^{max} = 8$ and

$$E^{PSc}(p, N) = E^{PSc}(8, 31^2) = \frac{Sp(8, 31^2)}{8} = \frac{3.48}{8} = .44. \tag{9.3}$$

Furthermore, in this case $p^{max}(E^H) = 6$.

Note that the smaller data size leads to a computation that is processor-count scalable on fewer processors and at lower efficiency, than the larger data size

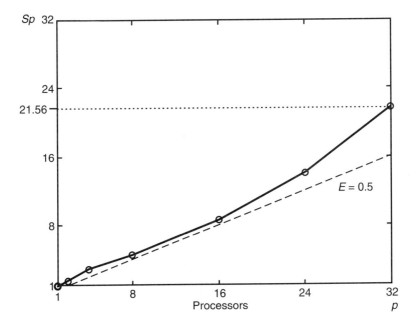

Figure 9.2. Conjugate Gradient Sp vs. p $(n=191)$

computation. The smaller data size saturates the system at high performance over only about $\frac{1}{5}$ of the processor range, whereas the larger data size yields high-performance saturation through all of Cedar's 32 processors.

9.2.2 Row Projection

The row-projection algorithm is applied to matrices derived from 3D physical problems, and results are presented in Fig. 9.4 for two data sizes: $N = n^3 = 12^3 (= 1.7K)$, and $N = n^3 = 36^3 (= 47K)$. Key results computed as for the conjugate gradient algorithm are presented in Table 9.1. Note the general similarity between the larger data sizes for the two algorithms, and between the smaller data sizes.

9.2.3 FLO52

Now we consider a Perfect code, FLO52 [Jame83], which solves 2D transonic fluid flow problems using a multigrid algorithm. Cedar performance results are shown in Fig. 9.5. The manually tuned version, using the Perfect data size $N = 33 \times 161 (= 5K)$, performs in the data starved region for $p > 16$ on Cedar. Nevertheless, we have $p^{dr} > P$, so

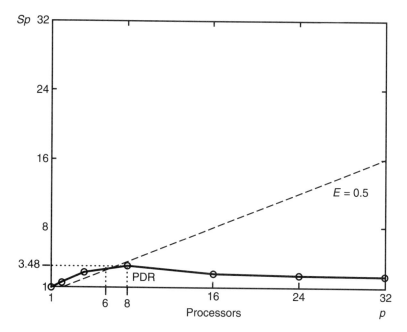

Figure 9.3.   Conjugate Gradient Sp vs. p $(n{=}31)$

$$E^{PSc}(p,N) = E(P,N) = E(32,5K) = \frac{Sp(32,5K)}{32} = \frac{10.5}{32} = .33. \qquad (9.4)$$

Furthermore, $p^{max}(E^H) = 16$.

Fig. 9.5 also shows the automatable version of FLO52 using the Perfect data size, $N = 5K$. Again $p^{dr} > P$, so

$$E^{PSc} = E(P,N) = E(32,5K) = \frac{Sp(32,5K)}{32} = \frac{5.3}{32} = .17. \qquad (9.5)$$

Furthermore, we have $p^{max}(E^H) = 6$, in this case. These results are summarized in Table 9.1.

Note that the manual version of FLO52 has about twice the processor-count-scalable efficiency of the automatable version, and $p^{max}(E^H)$ is nearly three times as high for the manual as the automatable version. This can be regarded as an example of the expected benefits of manual algorithm changes over compilers, or as a challenge to compiler writers to obtain some of this performance. In fact, it should be regarded as the goal of parallel software engineering to provide maximum performance with as little user effort as possible.

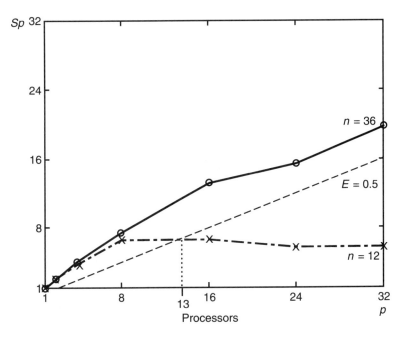

Figure 9.4. Row Projection Sp vs. p

9.2.4 GFDL-OCEAN

The final example is an ocean circulation modelling code from the U.S. Government's Geophysical Fluid Dynamics Laboratory, in Princeton, N.J. We refer to a version manually optimized for Cedar [DeGG93] as the GFDL-OCEAN code. Two data sizes representing the total number of mesh points in the 3D grid are shown in Fig. 9.6; $2K$ represents a tiny debugging sized run, and $71K$ represents a small production run. For $N = 71K$, $p^{dr} > 32$, whereas for $N = 2K$, $p^{dr} = 16$, and the results are shown in Table 9.1.

9.2.5 Summary PSc(p,N)

Table 9.1 summarizes the $PSc(p, N)$ results discussed in this section and indicates that relatively modest data sizes are scalable to the full 32 processors of Cedar. Note that a data size of only about $1K$ or $2K$ per processor is required. However, debugging sized runs are only scalable on a portion of the processors.

There are also some differences between the four examples. In the smaller data size case, the row projection algorithm has $PSc^{max} < p^{max}(E^H)$, while the other examples all had the inequality reversed, so scalability and high efficiency have

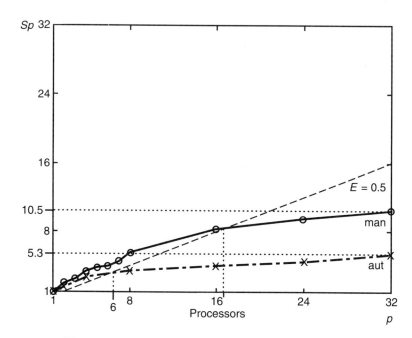

Figure 9.5.   FLO52 Manual and Automatable Sp vs. p

Code	Data Size N	Maximum Scalable Processor Count PSc^{max} (Eq. 7.4)	Processor-Count-Scalable Efficiency E^{PSc} (Eq. 9.1)	Maximum High-Efficiency Processor Count $p^{max}(E^H)$ (Eq. 7.6)
Conjugate	36K	32	.67	32
Gradient	1K	8	.44	6
Row	47K	32	.61	32
Projection	1.7K	8	.84	13
FLO 52				
manual	5K	32	.33	16
automatable	5K	32	.17	6
GFDL-	71K	32	.57	32
OCEAN	2K	16	.44	12

Table 9.1.   Cedar Processor-Count Scalability Summary

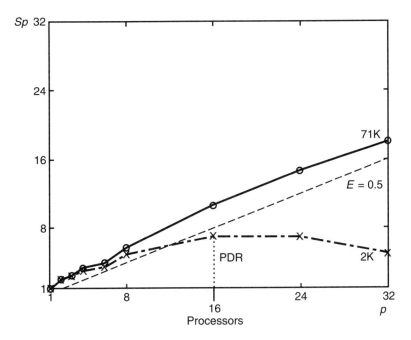

Figure 9.6. GFDL-OCEAN Sp vs. p

qualitatively different implications. Real computations can be data-size scalable without delivering high efficiency, or deliver high efficiency without being data-size scalable. Processor-count-scalable efficiency (Eq. 9.1) can have a wide range of experimental values, varying by a factor of 5 in Table 9.1 across the codes.

Of course, there is far too little data here to draw any general conclusions. To move the field ahead, comprehensive data of this nature must be compared across many systems. This will allow designers to draw their own conclusions about architectures and system software, and how they work together, based upon their own design constraints.

9.3 Data-Size Gradient and Scalabilty

The total data size required to reach threshold and higher saturated performance levels is an indicator to applications people of the types of computations for which a system may be useful. The saturated data size also specifies for system designers how large a memory is needed. Another important indicator is the amount of data used per processor when a parallel machine reaches its threshold. The smaller this number, the more impressive is the fact that threshold performance has been achieved.

This leads us to consider the scalable data-size range $DSc^X(P, n)$, and associated saturated speedup level $Sp^{Xsat}(P, n)$, as discussed for various performance levels X, in Sections 7.2.1, 7.2.2, etc. This defines the $MADS$ and $LADS$ data sizes, and in addition, we want to know the $SADS$ value and have some notion of the gradient of the speedup curve between $SADS$ and $MADS$. This tells us the data-size at which threshold performance begins $(SADS)$, and by how much we must increase the data-size to reach saturated performance $(MADS)$.

The above discussion has a natural correspondence with the $PSc(p, N)$ discussion of the previous section except for the "gradient" of the curve between $SADS$ and $MADS$. In the $PSc(p, N)$ discussion, efficiency has a slope-like nature, and while it was natural to begin that discussion at $Sp = 1$ and $p = 1$, there is no natural starting point for n, since $n = 1$ is meaningless. The most obvious choices are $n = SUDS$ or $n = SADS$, and because $SADS$ is the only objectively determinable value, we shall use it here. While a slope is normally the ratio of two differences, because of the wide range of practical data sizes across applications, it would be difficult to compare differences of normal slopes among applications, and the ratio of data sizes seems more useful for comparisons. The ratio of two ratios will therefore be used to define the data-size performance gradient of a given program for a set of computations on some system using various data sizes.

Just as $E(p, N)$ represents the efficiency of processor-count performance, we will represent the **data-size performance gradient** between data sizes n^- and n^+ by $G(P, n^-, n^+)$ and define it formally as

$$G(P, n^-, n^+) = \frac{Sp(P, n^+)/Sp(P, n^-)}{n^+/n^-}. \tag{9.6}$$

As with the performance definitions of Chapter 7, we may define the performance gradient at various levels, and we denote the gradient for speedup level X at data size n^+ as $G^X(P, n^-, n^+)$. Of particular interest here are the points $n^- = SADS$ and $n^+ = MADS$, so in the high performance case, the **high performance data-size gradient** is

$$G^{Hsat}(P, SADS, MADS) = \frac{Sp^{Hsat}(P, MADS) / Sp^{Th}(P, SADS)}{MADS/SADS}$$
$$= \frac{log P}{MADS/SADS}. \tag{9.7}$$

Thus

$$G^{Hsat}(P, SADS, MADS) \geq 1, \quad if \ MADS/SADS \leq logP; \tag{9.8}$$

otherwise,

$$G^{Hsat}(P, SADS, MADS) < 1. \tag{9.9}$$

Another interesting issue is how $SADS$ is related to the user defined small data size $SUDS$; if $SADS/SUDS \leq 1$, users will obtain acceptable performance for their smallest debugging runs. In summary, for indicators of the data starved but acceptable performance range, three useful numbers are: $SADS$, $SADS/SUDS$, and $G^{Hsat}(P, SADS, MADS)$. Furthermore, for the data-scalable range, $MADS$, $LADS$, $DSc^X(P, n)$ and $Sp^{Xsat}(P, n)$, are useful characterizations.

9.3.1 Data-size Gradient and Efficiency

For certain computational time-complexity classes (recall Section 6.4), we can bound the data-size performance gradient $G(P, n^-, n^+)$ with a **theoretical data-size performance gradient**

$$G^{atc}(P, n^-, n^+) = \frac{Sp^{atc}(P, n^+)/Sp^{atc}(P, n^-)}{n^+/n^-}. \tag{9.10}$$

We define the **level-X data-size efficiency**

$$DE^X(P, n^-, n^+) = \frac{G^X(P, n^-, n^+)}{G^{atc}(P, n^-, n^+)} \leq 1, \tag{9.11}$$

which measures how well a parallel system performs with respect to data size, relative to the best possible performance. Recall that the traditional processor-count efficiency definition of Chapter 7 and Section 9.2 is denoted as $E(p, N)$.

To establish a theoretical performance limit for codes with linear time-complexity $T^{atc}(1, N) = O(N)$, where N is the data size, consider a large problem of size n^+ and a small problem of size n^-. Then

$$Sp^{atc}(P, n^-) = \frac{T^{atc}(1, n^-)}{T^{atc}(P, n^-)} \tag{9.12}$$

and

$$Sp^{atc}(P, n^+) = \frac{T^{atc}(1, n^+)}{T^{atc}(P, n^+)} = \frac{\alpha T^{atc}(1, n^-)}{T^{atc}(P, n^+)}, \tag{9.13}$$

where $n^+ = \alpha n^-$, and where

$$T^{atc}(P, n^-) < T^{atc}(P, n^+). \tag{9.14}$$

These equations yield

$$\frac{Sp^{atc}(P, n^+)}{Sp^{atc}(P, n^-)} = \frac{\alpha T^{atc}(P, n^-)}{T^{atc}(P, n^+)} < \alpha, \tag{9.15}$$

so

$$G^{atc}(P, n^-, n^+) = \frac{\alpha T^{atc}(P, n^-)/T^{atc}(P, n^+)}{\alpha} < 1. \tag{9.16}$$

Therefore, for codes with $T^{atc}(1, N) = O(N)$ time-complexity, data-size efficiency is

$$1 \geq DE(P, n^-, n^+) = \frac{G(P, n^-, n^+)}{G^{atc}(P, n^-, n^+)} > G(P, n^-, n^+). \tag{9.17}$$

Using Eqs. 9.7 and 9.17 we can write

$$\frac{log\ P}{MADS/SADS} = G^{Hsat}(P, SADS, MADS) < 1, \tag{9.18}$$

so for the linear time complexity case,

$$MADS/SADS > log\ P. \tag{9.19}$$

By similar analyses one can compute $G^{atc}(P, n^-, n^+)$ bounds for other time-complexities. To discuss and compare total data-size growth we shall state each problem "size" N in such a way that a multiplier α can be used as a characteristic data-size growth factor. For example, a vector of size N, or banded matrix of size $N \times N$, will be called a problem of size N since each contains $O(N)$ nonzero elements. A dense matrix of n^2 elements will be called a problem of size $N = n^2$. For codes whose problem size can be characterized as growing linearly with parameter N, we have:

Data-Size Gradient Rule

If

$$Small\ Data\ Size = N, \quad Large\ Data\ Size = \alpha N \tag{9.20}$$

and

$$Abstract\ Time\ Complexity = T^{atc}(1, N) = O(N^\beta), \tag{9.21}$$

then, assuming that $T^{atc}(P, n^-) < T^{atc}(P, n^+)$

$$G^{atc}(P, n^-, n^+) < \alpha^{\beta-1}. \quad \square \qquad (9.22)$$

As in Eq. 9.17, for this case,

$$1 \geq DE(P, n^-, n^+) = \frac{G(P, n^-, n^+)}{G^{atc}(P, n^-, n^+)} > \frac{G(P, n^-, n^+)}{\alpha^{\beta-1}}, \qquad (9.23)$$

and letting $\alpha = MADS/SADS$, by Eqs. 9.7 and 9.11,

$$\frac{\log P}{\alpha} = G^{Hsat}(P, SADS, MADS) < \alpha^{\beta-1}. \qquad (9.24)$$

It follows that

$$\sqrt[\beta]{\log P} < \alpha, \qquad (9.25)$$

which provides a lower bound to estimate the minimum data-size increase required to drive performance from the threshold to the high level. For example, for an $O(N^2)$ computation, with $P = 1024$, the computation cannot rise from threshold to high performance without a data-size increase of at least a factor of $\sqrt{10}$, whereas a linear algorithm would require a data-size increase of at least a factor of 10.

It is also useful to observe that following Eqs. 9.11, 9.24 and 9.22,

$$DE^{Hsat}(P, SADS, MADS) = \frac{\log P}{(MADS/SADS)G^{atc}(P, SADS, MADS)}$$
$$> \frac{\log P}{(MADS/SADS)^{\beta}}. \qquad (9.26)$$

In the next section we turn our attention to experimental problem-size performance sensitivities for various real programs on Cedar.

9.3.2 Problem Sizes and Practical Complexity

It is extremely important to know that a system can deliver good performance over a range of problem sizes that can be regarded as reasonably complete by the applications people who will use the system. There are various ways of viewing problem size and the total data size upon which one computes; it depends on the original physical problem, as well as how one carries out the process of transforming the physical problem into a computational problem. The following is a list of various aspects of the size of a computational problem, which lead to the data-size definition used for estimating practical and theoretical time complexity.

Problem Size Definitions

- Physical Problem Size: This refers to the physical world, e.g., in terms of the number of points at which data is measured in a global weather model of the earth, or the number of transistors in a circuit being simulated.

- Mathematical Problem Size: This refers to mathematical objects derived from the physical world. For example, a $P \times Q$ mesh discretization of a physical object, a dense $N \times N$ matrix, or a tridiagonal $M \times M$ matrix.

- Computational Problem or Data Size Approximation: This refers to the time-dominant data structure size in a computational process. In rough estimations (as we are doing in this book) it may suffice to use this as an estimate of computational data size, so we refer to it as either a problem size or data size. (For more accuracy, see below.) Examples are: an explicit computation on a 100×100 physical mesh, a dense 100×100 matrix, and a tridiagonal $10^4 \times 10^4$ matrix, which would all have a computational problem or data size approximation of 10^4.

- Computational Coefficient: This is a coefficient of computational problem size that is derived from the physical and mathematical formulations of the problem. For example, an explicit 2D mesh computation with three physical variables (temperature, pressure, and two velocity components) and one temporary array would have a computational coefficient of $4 + 1 = 5$. A symmetrical tridiagonal matrix would have a coefficient of 2, whereas a nonsymmetrical tridiagonal matrix would have a coefficient of 3.

- Total Computational Data Size: This is the product of the computational problem size and the computational coefficient. It is the complete estimate of what should be used as a data size term. If a mesh size is $N \times N$ and the coefficient is as above, the total computational data would be $5N^2$. An $N \times N$ symmetrical tridiagonal matrix would have total computational data of $2N$.

9.3.3   Summary

This section has presented definitions that extend Chapter 7 into the data starved but acceptable performance region between $SADS$ and $MADS$. While the discussion of data-size gradient does not strictly cover the range of data-size scalability, data-size gradient does provide the doorway to scalability, and therefore is quite relevant to PPT4. Data-size efficiency provides a measure analogous to traditional processor-count efficiency, but it can only be applied when Sp^{atc} is known, i.e., for well understood algorithms. As more data becomes available, intuition about absolute data-size gradients should develop, and if more codes were subjected to careful algorithm decomposition, their time complexity and hence, data-size efficiency, would be known. The next section presents a few examples indicative of the results of such analysis.

9.4 Examples of Data-Size Gradient and Scalability

This section summarizes results for Cedar performance as a function of data size, using a given number of processors. Note that the performance stated for P processors does not refer to the best performance measured for $p \leq P$, but rather to whatever performance is measured on exactly P processors. The codes range from algorithms to a whole application. The data sizes range from small ($SUDS$ debugging runs) to medium and large ($MUDS-LUDS$ production runs), although these interpretations vary from one user to another. As in Section 9.2, we begin with algorithms: a conjugate gradient code (for solving symmetric linear systems) and a row projection code (for solving nonsymmetric linear systems) and evaluate the high performance data-size gradient for these codes.

9.4.1 Conjugate Gradient

First, consider the conjugate gradient (CG) algorithm. Note that for Cedar from Eq. 9.7,

$$G^{Hsat}(32, SADS, MADS) = \frac{log\ P}{MADS/SADS} = \frac{5}{MADS/SADS}. \quad (9.27)$$

Fig. 9.7 shows the $Sp(32, n)$ and $Sp(16, n)$ performance curves for the conjugate gradient algorithm. For $Sp(32, n)$, using linear interpolation between measurements, $SADS = 1.15K$ and $MADS = 12.6K$, so $MADS/SADS \approx 11$. It follows that for Cedar,

$$G^{Hsat}(32, SADS, MADS) = \frac{5}{11} = .45 . \quad (9.28)$$

The basic step of the CG algorithm consists of 2 inner products, 3 saxpys, and a matrix • vector product for a narrow band matrix, which leads to time-complexity that is linear in matrix size N. The algorithm is iterative and may require N iterations, but typically requires only $log\ N$ or $N^{\frac{1}{2}}$ iterations. So a practical upper bound on the time-complexity would be $O(N^{\frac{3}{2}})$ and from Eq. 9.21, $\beta = \frac{3}{2}$.

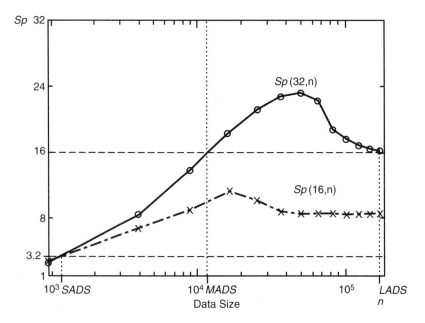

Figure 9.7.   Conjugate Gradient Sp vs. n

From the above, using Eq. 9.26, we have for the conjugate gradient algorithm on Cedar:

$$DE^{Hsat}(32, SADS, MADS) > \frac{log\,P}{(MADS/SADS)^{\beta}} = \frac{5}{(11)^{3/2}} = .14. \quad (9.29)$$

With these approximations, for Cedar we are within a factor of seven of the best possible performance growth that could be expected for an idealized parallel system in the unsaturated data-size range.

From Fig. 9.7 it may be seen that $DSc^{Hsat}(32, n)$ covers the range from about $12.6K$ to $172K$, so matrices ranging from about rank 115 to 415 define the data-size scalable high performance range on Cedar.

9.4.2   Row Projection

Fig. 9.8 shows the $Sp(32, n)$ and $Sp(16, n)$ performance curves for the row projection (RP) algorithm. For the $Sp(32, n)$ case, using a linear extrapolation below the smallest measured value, $\frac{MADS}{SADS} = \alpha \approx 10$. Following Eq. 9.27 for Cedar:

$$G^{Hsat}(32, SADS, MADS) \approx 5/10. \quad (9.30)$$

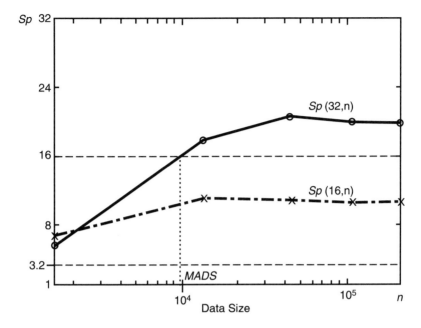

Figure 9.8. Row Projection Sp vs. n

The row projection scheme is iterative, where each iteration requires the solution of $O(N)$ least squares problems of size $N^{\frac{1}{3}}$, so the time-complexity per iteration is $O(N^{\frac{4}{3}})$. As with the CG algorithm, in the worst case N iterations are required, but in practice $O(log\ N)$ or $O(N^{\frac{1}{2}})$ iterations suffice. Thus we can assume that $O(N^{\frac{1}{2}})$ is a practical upper bound on the number of iterations, so the practical complexity is:

$$O(N^{\frac{4}{3}}) \bullet O(N^{\frac{1}{2}}) = O(N^{\frac{11}{6}}) \ < \ O(N^2). \tag{9.31}$$

From this and Eq. 9.26, we have for the row projection algorithm on Cedar

$$DE^{Hsat}(32, SADS, MADS) > \frac{log\ P}{(MADS/SADS)^{\beta}} \ \approx \ \frac{5}{100}. \tag{9.32}$$

Table 9.2 shows the comparative performance of the CG and RP algorithms on Cedar.

Since $DSc^{Hsat}(32, n)$ begins at $MADS$ (see Fig. 9.8) and continues off the figure, it ranges from less than 10^4 to much greater than 10^5. Thus, the data-size scalability of row projection exceeds that of the conjugate gradient on Cedar, while the data-size efficiency of RP is worse than the CG.

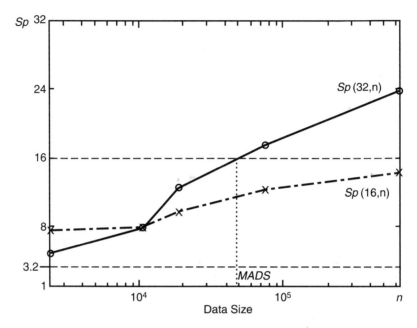

Figure 9.9. GFDL-OCEAN Sp vs. n (p=16,32)

9.4.3   GFDL-OCEAN

Fig. 9.9 presents $Sp(32, n)$ and $Sp(16, n)$ data for the GFDL-OCEAN code. The general shape of these curves is similar to those of the two algorithms above. The width of the high-performance saturated region appears much broader here than for CG and RP, perhaps due to the greater amount of work per data point. For 16 processors, this program and RP deliver better performance than CG, for data sizes well below 10^4. The effect of insufficient data per processor to overcome overheads is shown by the crossover of the $P = 16$ and $P = 32$ curves at $n = 10^4$. It is beyond the scope of this discussion to analyze GFDL-OCEAN further and there is insufficient data to estimate the gradient and data-size efficiency here.

9.4.4   Data-Size Summary

Table 9.2 displays salient points for the $Sp(32, n)$ results for the conjugate gradient and row projection algorithms; note that these are estimated and extrapolated values. Relatively little data is required per processor to reach threshold and saturated performance levels for each algorithm. This is an important aspect of system scalability that should be studied for all computations over a range of processor counts.

Performance Characteristic	Algorithm	
	Conjugate Gradient	Row Projection
Threshold		
Mathematical Problem Size	$(34)^2$	$\sim(10)^3$
Computational Data Size (*SADS*)	1150	~1000
Computational Data Size per Processor	36	~31
High		
Mathematical Problem Size	$(112)^2$	$(22)^3$
Computational Data Size (*MADS*)	12.6K	9.69K
Computational Data Size per Processor	393	303
Summary		
MADS/SADS	11	10
$G^{Hsat}(32, SADS, MADS)$	.45	.5
$DE^{Hsat}(32, SADS, MADS)$	.14	.05
$DSc^{Hsat}(32, n)$	12.6K to 172K	10K to >300K

Table 9.2. Cedar Data-Size Scalability Summary

The general shapes of the CG and RP $Sp(P, n)$ curves are similar. The $Sp^{max}(16, n)$ values are a fraction of the $Sp^{max}(32, n)$ values, in both cases. One would expect a factor of two shift from considering n/p as the axis instead of n, and the additional overhead of twice as many processors can account for a further shift. In both cases there is insufficient data to compute the gradient for $P = 16$.

The crossover of the curves for $P = 16$ and $P = 32$ exhibits the use of too many processors for small data sizes in the case of $Sp(32, n)$. All three figures reach high $(P/2)$ performance at lower values of n for $P = 16$ than for $P = 32$, which can be explained as in the above paragraph. Both algorithms appear to have wider saturated high-performance ranges for 16 processors. There is insufficient data to compare gradients between processor counts.

While there is insufficient data to observe as much of the GFDL-OCEAN curves' shapes as we can see for the algorithms, the parts of the curves shown match the general nature of the curves for the above algorithms. Data-size scalability for $P = 32$ ($MADS$ to $LADS$) begins at about $10K$ for the algorithms, and below $50K$ for GFDL-OCEAN. In the case of the algorithms, it continues to well beyond $100K$, while for GFDL-OCEAN, the range appears to go well beyond 10^6.

9.5   Computation Scalability *(CSc)*

We now vary both p and n as was done in Fig. 9.1, for several codes and systems. This presents the basics of computation scalability for a meager collection of data. As discussed in the introduction to Chapter 7, system scalability depends on program scalability, which in turn depends on individual computation scalability.

9.5.1   FLO52

Fig. 9.10 shows $E^H(p, n)$ results for FLO52 on two different parallel systems: Cedar and the nCUBE/10. The two systems have 32 and 512 processors, respectively, and peak speeds of over .35 Gf and .2 Gf, respectively, so the peak speeds per processor are widely separated at about 11 Mf and .4 Mf, respectively. The codes run are also different in that the Cedar effort involved hand tuning the original Fortran code, while the nCUBE effort involved a complete rewrite [BCJT89] including the use of new algorithms. Thus the nCUBE results can be regarded as an estimate of the achievable upper bound on performance for that system, while the Cedar results are representative of hand tuning existing codes.

It should also be observed that relative to PPT1 and PPT3, FLO52 represents a code with intermediate Cedar and Cray performance for the Perfect data size ($5K$) performance, as shown in Figs. 8.1 and 8.5.

9.5.2   Relative Performance: CM-5 and Cedar

Now we turn to a comparison of the Thinking Machines CM-5 with Cedar, and because there is little comparable data available, we drop to the level of algorithm studies again.

Table 9.3 shows measured Cedar results for a conjugate gradient solver, which involves a 5-diagonal matrix-vector product as well as vector and reduction operations for arrays of dimension N. Cedar exhibits high performance data-size scalablity for the range shown in Table 9.2, and scalable intermediate performance for smaller data sizes ranging down to about $N = 1K$.

In [FWPS92], a number of linear algebra experiments are reported on the CM-5. For comparison, we quote data for matrix-vector products with bandwidths (BW in the table) 3 and 11. The CM-5 used did not have floating-point accelerators. For the range of data sizes run, between $16K$ and $256K$, high performance was

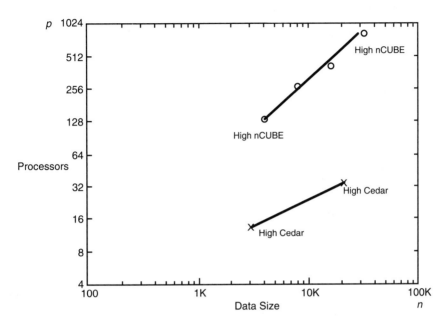

Figure 9.10. FLO52 (p, n) Contours

	Cedar $(2 \leq P \leq 32)$	Connection Machine 5 $(32 \leq P \leq 512)$	
	Conjugate Gradient $(1K \leq N \leq 172K)$	Sparse Matrix x Vector $(16K \leq N \leq 256K)$	
Performance Level	BW = 5	BW = 3	BW = 11
High	$(N < 15K \text{ to } 172K < N)$	?	?
Intermediate	$(N = 1.1K \text{ to } N < 15K)$	$(N \ll 16K \text{ to } 256K < N)$	$(N < 16K \text{ to } 256K < N)$
Unacceptable	?	?	?

Table 9.3. Banded Matrix PPT4 Summary

not achieved relative to 32, 256, or 512 processors. The communication structure of the CM-5 evidently caused these performance difficulties [FWPS92]. The CM-5 exhibited scalable intermediate performance with these three processor counts for problems evidently smaller than $16K$ for bandwidth 11, and evidently much smaller problems for bandwidth 3. No unacceptable performance was observed in the ranges reported.

The conjugate gradient algorithm is important in many large applications, and the matrix-vector product is an important part of CG. Thus, we conclude that for these components of realistic applications codes, Cedar achieves scalable high performance over problems ranging from modest data sizes up to large data sizes, and intermediate performance down to tiny data sizes. The CM-5 did not deliver high performance but appears to have achieved intermediate performance on modest-to-large data sizes, although no problem below $N = 16K$ was run. No unacceptable performance was observed on either machine. Thus we conclude that, for the number of processors studied, the CM-5 is scalable with intermediate performance, while for up to 32 processors, Cedar is scalable with high performance for many problems and with intermediate performance for debugging sized runs. Before any system can claim to have passed PPT4, data of the kind discussed here must be presented for many whole applications, and PPT3 will have to be considered as will performance levels (high vs. intermediate).

9.5.3 Absolute Performance: CM-5 and Cedar

The 32-processor Cedar delivers between 34 and 48 megaflops as the CG problem sizes range from $10K$ to $172K$. On the banded matrix-vector product, the 32-processor CM-5 delivers between 28 and 35 megaflops for BW=3 and between 58 and 67 megaflops for BW=11, as the problem sizes range from $16K$ to $256K$. Thus, the per-processor megaflops of the two systems on these problems are roughly equivalent.

9.5.4 Summary

In this section we have presented merely the beginnings of several ways to compare system scalability for multiple codes and diverse systems. Deciding whether or not a given machine passes PPT4 is a subjective matter involving a number of parameters and the functions discussed in this chapter. As we have stressed throughout the book, the suite of codes that one tests is very important. We have presented scalability ranges for single programs, but in practice it is necessary to test a suite of programs. Finally, the relative scalability of all the leading current systems is germane. Given that no one knows how well it is possible to scale various applications on real systems, definitions of acceptable standard levels of scalability await future comparative scalability studies. Section 9.7 summarizes the PPT's and the discussion of Fig. 9.11 provides more context for the fragmentary data of this section.

9.6   Practical Parallelism Test 5

As stated in Section 5.6, it is necessary that any practical parallel system should pass reimplementability tests. **System reimplementability** can be accomplished in two distinct ways. **Architectural scalability (or reimplementability)** requires that systems with a sufficiently broad range of processor counts must be implementable using the same basic hardware and software system architecture, without varying the underlying hardware technology. This allows a range of system performance levels to be implementable with a given technology. Note the distinction between this and PSc of PPT4: PPT4 deals with varying the processor count (p) use in an existing P-processor system, while PPT5 deals with enlarging the size of P in building a new system.

The final test that practical parallel systems face, is **reimplementability via technology**, because a successful system architecture should not depend uniquely upon any given technology for its implementation. When a new technology mix becomes cost-effective, a successful system must be reimplementable using much larger processor counts, and as low processor count, low cost systems, as well. One way of failing this test is by using very fast, unusual hardware in one part of the system, relative to the remainder of the system, so that if the remainder of the system is reimplemented in a faster, new low-cost technology, the one part, having no new faster technology base, becomes a bottleneck. The two ideas of this paragraph form the basis of PPT5.

Practical Parallelism Test 5: System Reimplementability
A system architecture must be capable of being reimplemented with:
a) a sufficiently broad range of processor counts, using current technology, and
b) new, faster or less expensive technologies as they emerge, using much larger processor counts than current technology allows.

To illustrate PPT5, consider three similar but distinct computer design studies that use the existing Cedar system design as a basis example, plus a fourth, related question:

1. Cedar has 32 processors in 4 clusters. How effective would it be to build a 1024 processor Cedar-like system using 32 clusters of 32 processors each?

2. Cedar contains 4 Alliant FX/8's as clusters and an ECL gate array global shuffle-exchange interconnection network. How effective would it be to reimplement Cedar using 16 current SGI systems as clusters interconnected with a custom-CMOS global shuffle-exchange interconnection network?

3. Intel licensed Alliant shared-memory parallel system technology and is now moving in the direction of more parallelism into its products. As Intel builds parallel system boards or chips, whole clusters may become commodity parts. Could these parts become the dominant PC's or workstations of the future?

4. Both Alliant and SGI explored clustered Cedar-like systems based on their, respective, existing parallel systems, by using commercially available high-speed networks, e.g. HIPPI networks, for global interconnection. Are such systems cost-effective?

In terms of the notation of this book, study 1 concerns a processor-count increase issue, in which the number and size of clusters is varied to study PSc. Thus, it is a PPT5a study (although the Alliant and Cedar technologies are now out of date). Study 2 includes examples of both aspects of PPT5. SGI builds systems that are similar to the original Alliant systems used in Cedar, so using larger SGI clusters would be an architecture reimplementation study (PPT5a). Redoing the network using custom CMOS instead of ECL gate arrays would be a technology reimplementation study (PPT5b). Study 3 is a PPT5b example, wherein a dozen 20 inch boards from the 1980s would be reduced to a few chips or small boards in the 1990s (in reality some architectural changes would be inevitable, of course, bringing in PPT5a). Study 4 concerns new architectures and goes beyond PPT5. Here, companies have one architecture (Alliant, SGI), observe another architecture (Cedar), and try to improve upon both by using their existing systems plus new, off-the-shelf hardware components (e.g. a crossbar switch replaces a shuffle-exchange network for global interconnection).

All four studies concern new system designs that go beyond existing systems. None should be undertaken without a comprehensive understanding of the systems upon which hoped-for improvements are based. Study 1 is a sensitivity study of the Cedar architecture, and is assumed not to involve new hardware, but would likely require new compiler and algorithm technology. Study 2 involves the relation of SGI to Alliant system performance, as well as how the global network architecture and speed affect system performance. Study 3 is a pure hardware technology-spin, and in principle may not need much new software. Study 4 is a system-wide architecture change, which potentially involves all aspects of the system. As stated, studies 1, 2 and 3 are covered by PPT5, and study 4, by moving sufficiently far from existing systems goes beyond specific PPT's for existing systems.

When a company is starting to build a new system there is a thin line between PPT's 4 and 5. Initially, all performance demonstrations are by simulation and thus can be regarded as PPT5 issues. Once a system is in production, practical, cost-effective values of P are determined, and demonstrations of PPT4 are made on real machines using the largest values of P possible. Then, building a larger system using the same architecture may be possible with approximately the same technology, but mainly a physical redesign (PPT5a), or by introducing major technology changes (PPT5b).

This book will not deal with PPT5 in any detail. As has been stated repeatedly, PPT's 1-4 still need substantial effort before they are well understood for most systems. If they were well understood, then solving design problems centered on PPT5 would become easier. Furthermore, designing completely new systems, as with study 4, requires having as much data as possible about the PPT's, plus the full range of HPC design intuition and opinion that is available.

Sidebar 24: Future Applied Practical Parallelism

The cost-effectiveness of any proposed R & D project can be debated in terms of many criteria (including those of Section 8.1 for computers). The cost-effectiveness of any developed product can be evaluated by a potential customer in many of these same terms, with uncertainty about the future centering on what new products might appear. Both are difficult subjects that involve technology and money. One aspect of both cost-effectiveness discussions is the set of tradeoffs between general purpose and special purpose systems.

It has been known for decades that special purpose parallel systems could be much faster, at the same cost, than a general purpose system. People have made paper designs of systems ranging from partial differential equation solvers to checkers playing machines. But there were almost never development budgets for special purpose systems, because the development and production costs would have been too high to support sales volumes.

This has all changed in the 1990s. People can now build special purpose consumer products that perform many specialized operations simultaneously, and there are mass markets for such products. The confluence of PC's, multimedia technology, global computer networks via the "information superhighway," and satellite megachannel TV broadcasts, have created new market turmoil. Should TV manufacturers push a new kind of TV set with built-in computing, or should computer and game technology try to swallow the TV set business? How do the mass-market manufacturers and suppliers deal with the diversity and overlap of mass entertainment (e.g., yesterday's TV and computer games), large group communication (e.g., yesterday's educational TV and home shopping networks), small group communication (e.g., yesterday's telephone and e-mail), and computer problem solving (e.g., yesterday's word processing, databases, spread sheets, and engineering design)?

No one knows how technology, government regulation, and consumer preferences will ebb and flow in the evolution of new products and services in these areas. High sales volumes will drive parallel computer architectures into many areas that were not even considered in the past. Special purpose parallel architectures will become commonplace commodities.

This implies many new R & D projects that will require huge investments of money and high-powered talent. And while these special purpose projects will be economic golden eggs, they have their roots in general purpose parallel computing R & D. Although they will generate new ideas that feed back and enrich general purpose parallelism, they will remain corollaries of the overall field.

Until general purpose parallel computing is very well understood, it must continue to be regarded as the goose that lays the golden eggs. Academia, industry, and government must not lose sight of its central importance, and none of the three should waver in supporting it.

9.7   Practical Parallelism Test Summary

Table 9.4 summarizes the above comparative system discussion of PPT's 1-4. The first three tests were discussed for the Perfect codes and compare Cedar to the Cray YMP-8. Both machines pass PPT1 at the intermediate performance level and Cedar passes PPT2 with 2 exceptions, whereas the YMP-8 fails. Thus it may be argued that Cedar demonstrates the Fundamental Principle of Parallel Processing using almost all of the Perfect codes. With as yet unimplemented compiler transformations, Cedar just achieves intermediate performance for PPT3 while the YMP-8 with a production compiler fails. In terms of scalable performance, we considered banded matrix operations on Cedar and the CM-5. Cedar achieves scalable high performance for a wide range of data sizes, whereas the CM-5 achieves scalable intermediate performance for approximately the same data-size range.

The PPT's address a number of aspects of system performance. Fig. 6.7 showed a performance sweet spot which intuitively combines speedup, efficiency and stability from the perspective that might be found in manufacturers' advertising; it represents the range of p and n that provide speedup and efficiency above some desired level. Fig. 7.9 refined the idea by representing system scalability in terms of efficiency contours on a (p, n) plot. Fig. 9.1 shows performance contours (e.g., speedup) and processor-normalized performance contours (e.g., efficiency), and Fig. 9.10 presents efficiency threshold data for real systems. Now we combine these ideas in Fig. 9.11, which formalizes the sweet spot concept.

Test	Cedar	Cray YMP-8
PPT 1	**Intermediate** for Perfect	**Intermediate** for Perfect
PPT 2	**Stable** for Perfect with 2 exceptions	**Unstable** for Perfect (Cray 1 Stable with 2 exceptions)
PPT 3	**Intermediate** for Perfect (Automatable compilation)	**Unacceptable** for Perfect (Production Compiler)
PPT 4	**Scalable High/Intermediate** Performance for Conjugate Gradient (most data sizes) $(P \leq 32)$	**Connection Machine 5** **Scalable Intermediate** Performance for Banded Matrix x Vector $(P = 32, 256, 512)$

Table 9.4. Comparative System PPT Summary

Adding a constant speedup threshold constraint, i.e., a speedup contour, to Fig. 7.9 yields Fig. 9.11. Points within the shaded sweet spot should appeal to everyone. Individual users want high performance (guaranteed by a speedup threshold), system managers and groups of users want good system throughput (guaranteed by the efficiency and memory hierarchy thresholds), and manufacturers want happy customers (so they promise to raise the reimplementability threshold).

Two basic types of questions can be raised about such plots. The first types of questions concern the relative merits of systems being compared for particular workloads. The eventual benefits of the macroperformance analysis discussed in this book depend on the availability of extensive data. A fragment of such data is shown in Fig. 9.10. Extensive amounts of this data would allow us to develop comparative system intuition about the shape and size of these curves for system selection and design purposes.

The second types of questions concern how this region can be given a particular shape or be made as large as possible. Section 7.5 outlined some relations of Fig. 7.9 to system design, and that discussion will be continued here. The parallel scalability threshold has been modified, showing the constraint of Fig. 7.9 as an efficiency constraint, and adding the speedup constraint. For certain data sizes, parallel performance can be improved upward or downward, which corresponds to finding a better system match for a given code.

At the architectural level, in the upward direction a system might be given better global communication, for example, by introducing a faster global network, while in the downward direction better local communication might be supplied by introducing clusters or enhanced cluster communication. Better algorithms, or compilers that restructure the programs for given algorithms, can help as follows. Upward expansion on a given architecture could be achieved by modifying a program's global communication pattern; downward expansion could be achieved by modifying local communication patterns.

Some changes help in both directions, for example, finding more parallelism will decrease parallel time and allow the same speedup with fewer processors (dropping the lower curve) as well as allowing the same efficiency with more processors (raising the upper curve). Increasing processor cache size will allow the parallel time to drop relative to sequential time (because more cache space is available, overall) and provide the same effects.

Expansion to the left means better small-data performance; larger cache size and better cluster-level performance will help this. In general, reducing critical time latencies can help in fine tuning performance. Expansion to the right can be achieved through hardware by reducing I/O latency or increasing bandwidth, or by adding main memory to reduce I/O requirements. It can also be achieved through software, by reducing I/O requirements through restructuring a program to block its loops for better addressing locality, or by using a different algorithm. Upward expansion can also be provided by reimplementing the system using more processors, when that constraint is hit.

These changes have interactions and the constraints slope, so up-down and right-left are interrelated concepts. Satisfying the PPT's means defining and then expanding the sweet spot area as much as possible, and to do this we must first measure its size on existing systems. The fragmentary discussion and plot of Section 9.5 is what we are capable of today. To pass the PPT's it will be necessary to have much better data upon which to base future system designs.

9.8   Glossary of Notation

Concluding the glossaries of Chapters 6, 7, and 8, Table 9.5 presents a final list of *perf* functions. The types of functions match those of earlier chapters, with the exception of $DE(P, n^-, n^+)$ which combines theoretical and observed values.

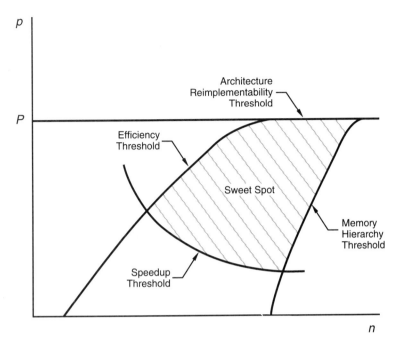

Figure 9.11.   Scalability Thresholds

9.9   Conclusions

The material presented in Chapter 9 merely scratches the surface of what is necessary to assess the status of PPT4. We discussed too few programs, with too small a dynamic range of data sizes, on too few systems. While we were able to evaluate a number of the metrics discussed in Chapter 7 for real examples, the discussion was system-centered rather than user-centered. Architecture-defined data sizes, $SADS$ and $MADS$, were discussed, but only a few intuitive statements were made about user-defined data sizes $SUDS$ or $MUDS$; in reality, these are subjective to particular users. Little was said about $LADS$ because of the unavailability of experimental results for a large dynamic data-size range.

The depth of measurements presented may be adequate for system selection, but, of course, is far short of the level of detail required in system design. Architects and compiler writers need details about the frequencies and latencies of many time-consuming aspects of computations. These range from cache misses, to interprocessor communication, to I/O; they were summarized abstractly in Section 4.4.

Performance Functions			
Type	Symbol	Name	Definition
Observed	$E^{PSc}(p,N)$	Processor-Count-Scalable Efficiency	Eq. 9.1
	$G(P,n^-,n^+)$	Data-Size Performance Gradient	Eq. 9.6
Observation Depends on Parameter	$G^{Hsat}(P,SADS,MADS)$	High performance Data-Size Gradient	Eqs. 9.7, 9.18, 9.24
Theoretical	$G^{atc}(P,n^-,n^+)$	Theoretical Data-Size Performance Gradient	Eqs. 9.10, 9.16, 9.22
Combined Observed and Theoretical	$DE(P,n^-,n^+)$	Data-Size Efficiency	Eqs. 9.12, 9.17, 9.26

Table 9.5. Performance Functions Glossary

One should remember that the definitions upon which these chapters are based have an abstract nature that is sometimes difficult to relate to real systems; Section 5.2 outlined some of the issues. Nevertheless, real data, as presented in this chapter, takes on the general shape of the abstract plots of Chapter 5. Stairstep performance has been measured on several cluster-based systems, including Cedar and Dash, for example.

The performance graphs of Chapters 8 and 9 capture certain characteristics of parallel performance. While these are revealing, especially when comparing several codes and several systems in a performance analysis, they present static summaries. Imagine all of the data presented here to be snapshots from a comprehensive performance database. If this data arose as the result of dynamic queries, the user would be able to explore the range from gross to subtle performance questions, following intuitive leads. Each program could be studied for one or many data sizes on a given machine, or various competing programs could be compared on a given system. Alternatively, a given code could be compared across a range of competing systems. Such studies could be conducted by end users or system designers whose interests range from architecture to software, and whose purchasing and design constraints vary widely.

As mentioned earlier, this chapter is a summary and empirical demonstration of some of the abstractions presented earlier in the book. It is also an appeal to the reader to accept the challenge of developing and using tools and databases that further the cause presented here. Sections 3.7 and 10.4 outline more details of a database and performance understanding system that would enable and accelerate various aspects of progress toward practical parallel systems.

This concludes the main technical presentation of the book. The definitions of Chapters 6 and 7, and the experimental results of Chapters 8 and 9, are an answer to the question "How, best, can practical parallel processing be advanced?" It is hoped that the reader can appreciate the merits of the case presented, despite any conceptual weaknesses and the obvious incompleteness of the experiments discussed. Further developing these notions, and building large publicly available databases, would put parallel system design on a quantitative, open-performance basis. It seems obvious that this would improve the field, relative to its current intuitive and qualitative state. In particular, it would move designers' intuition from low-level localized performance issues to macroperformance issues, eventually allowing passage of the PPT's and a solution of the GGC.

CHAPTER 10

THE FUTURE OF HIGH PERFORMANCE COMPUTING

10.1 Scenario 2000

It is possible to construct a number of different scenarios for the future development of high performance computing based on the ideas presented in this book. We will present one here which is intended to be both appealing and alarming, but which seems quite plausible and most likely. Regardless of the precision of its details, the general accuracy of what follows seems hard to refute, given early-1990s facts about the future.

By the early 2000s the clock speeds of uniprocessors and parallel computer systems will have flattened off in the neighborhood of 1 ns (Chapter 4 discussed a range). Without good prospects for future clock speed increases, system speed increases will have come to depend on parallelism within processors and across processors. In deciding what to put on a chip and how to package multiprocessor chips into boards and whole systems, engineers will have made the necessary trade-offs among issues ranging from packaging to compiling technology.

Achieving more speed by using more parallelism will require increases in problem size and hence in physical memory size. Thus, as the feature sizes of circuit microlithography reach saturation, component and board packaging reach heat density limits, and clock speeds stop increasing, computer sizes will increase in proportion to their processor count and memory size, which will increase in proportion to their speed requirements. It is not a new observation that faster machines are larger than slower ones, but this simple dependence of speed on processor count and memory size will be a novelty.

It need not be inferred from this that every high speed computation will require a room full of hardware, even if packaging densities stop growing. An alternative is to rely on a building full of distributed equipment. As more people rely on more computation to do their work, it seems plausible that there will be more excess computing capacity at any given moment. Just as most 20th-century American households have adopted the two-car, three-telephone, four-radio, mentality over

255

time as prices have dropped and reliance on technology has increased, we can assume that each office building of the 21st century will be very well equipped with computing cycles in some highly connected, distributed form. Fiber optic bandwidths can be made sufficiently high to allow us to dismiss transmission rates as a problem, but transmission delays (latencies) imposed by unchangeable laws of physics are a problem at the microlevels of a computation. Nevertheless, for nanosecond-clock-speed computations that run for minutes, latencies of several hundred nanoseconds to transmit data between floors of a building are acceptable, if they are properly located in a large computation. Even when focused on interactive computing, with clock speeds frozen at 1 ns and signals travelling less than a foot in 1 ns, we can still take advantage of the fact that human reaction time does not change and is measured in seconds, not nanoseconds. Thus, if properly exploited, the unused cycles in a building full of high performance workstations could be used for a single, large, time-sensitive computation. People and organizations do not, currently, worry much about possessing large amounts of unused capacity—in vehicles, telephones, or even office space —if there is purpose to their use only at peak-load times. However, large computations may be able to consume cycles remotely and at almost no incremental cost, either during peak hours or in off hours, and in this sense, computing resources are similar to electric power.

The ideas above combine in complementary ways. For those people who need ever faster computers, physically larger machines will become a necessity. On the other hand, assuming that office sizes will remain fixed, as will individual offices' cooling capacity and their occupants' tolerance for fan noise, the desktop, desk-side, . . . office-full systems of the past will reach a speed limit. Nevertheless, any individual employed by a large organization with a tightly interconnected computing capacity will have periodic access to a major fraction of the total available on-site computing power. This will include office-based as well as departmental and building-wide computing facilities. From the individual computer user's perspective, this scenario is not much different from what the short-term perspective has been at any time in the past. The major difference, and one that will affect every HPC user, is that new hardware speed increases within single systems will not appear like clockwork, as in the past; in fact, they will not appear at all. Furthermore, the plausibility of an individual computation gaining performance by using a building full of equipment does not demonstrate its feasibility; many difficult problems remain to be solved.

Sidebar 25: Global/Local Machines

In the beginning, there were huge, expensive, difficult-to-use Electronic Automatic Computers that replaced the 1930s computers — humans with electromechanical calculating machines. These machines were rare and programmed in machine language. By the 1960s, programming languages and operating systems development allowed wide access to time-shared central computers, and hardware development led to the availability of minicomputers that could be used in dedicated roles; Digital Equipment was founded and flourished in this marketplace. Thus after the first 15 years of development, computers were available for use in a wide variety of ways, and debates began about which mode of use would dominate in the future. In reality, all sides in these debates were right because all viable approaches continued to develop; but all sides were wrong in that a myriad of new use styles and forms of computing developed by the 1980s.

The wonder of the early computer marketplace was that every useful new approach to computer use created a new market without destroying previous markets. Over the years there has been a tremendous technology trickle down; all of the useful historical supercomputer and large time-shared system ideas now appear in desktop systems. This, together with open systems ideas, made it difficult to maintain or expand certain earlier markets as had been done previously. By the 1980s the ubiquity of computers had saturated most markets, and in the 1990s the computer business is being dealt several serious shocks.

Large central time-shared systems are unnecessary now except in very special situations, for example, airline reservations, and even these are moving toward distributed processing. Large mainframes are under severe price attack, except when age-old software makes them the least unpleasant alternative. Large supercomputers have hit a flat-market wall, but being *the fastest* are still crucial for some users.

Efficiency and economy of use have forced computer system companies to reexamine all of their basic assumptions. Food and commodity marketing executives are now chosen to run major computer companies (Gerstner at IBM, Sculley for 10 years at Apple), whereas insiders-only was the rule in the 1960s and 1970s. Commodity marketing will become more widespread in computing, so these are good, short-term choices. Today, however, more complex technical decisions are being made than in the past, knowingly or by default, at the highest management levels of computer companies. In the past, such decisions determined the general health and well-being of the company; today's decisions will most likely decide the *survival* of the companies in the next decade.

As high-performance single-user computing approaches its technical asymptote (from minicomputers to PCs), and single-user performance requirements force engineers to build these systems from the same technology used in supercomputers, a common hardware base is being forced onto the industry. Software alone will determine whether a user accesses a limited amount of the common hardware base for small computations or a maximum amount of it for supercomputer speeds. This will again shift the services and technology provided by computer companies in new directions and eventually end the debates about whether to buy a large or small system. A large, fast system will simply *be* a collection of smaller systems, plus commodity interconnection hardware and software. Whether these individual systems are in separate offices or in a collection of special rooms will be irrelevant.

10.1.1 Software Dependence

All of the above leads to an absolute dependence on software that goes well beyond what is currently available. Software to manage memory allocation is rooted historically in memory hierarchy management, cache management, and register allocation. Software to manage parallelism is rooted in the vectorizing and parallelizing compilers of the 1970s and 1980s. And the software to manage hybrid fast-memory/slow-memory distributed processing must be invented, based on the above as well as the slow-memory distributed processing of today. Compilers and libraries will play central roles in ensuring that required data advances to the right processors and retreats to the right memories at appropriate times, and that there is sufficient parallelism in the computation to exploit the parallelism in the system. Problem-solving environments (PSEs) can be expected to shield most users from thinking about these issues. By specifying their problems and using PSE systems that are specialized to their application areas, users will be able to think in terms of their own disciplines rather than in terms of the computer's structure. Technology now in place is sufficient as a basis for making these predictions. However, developing it to meet the needs of the above scenario will necessitate major efforts and changes of focus in the computing R & D community over the next few years.

As time passes the percentage of programmed computers is dropping considerably. This follows from two lines of reasoning: first, the computer (PC) explosion of the 1980s was fueled by simple PSE systems, such as for word processing, spreadsheets and CAD. As PSEs become more widely developed for all fields, even Computer-Aided Research (CAR) environments will appear [Kuck92]. Thus a smaller percentage of users will need to be programmers. Second is the point made throughout this book that modern high-performance computer systems have become more complex and difficult to program. As parallel systems become universal, users will naturally become less able to exploit them without using advanced system software, and as such system software becomes well developed, advanced PSEs will rely on it more heavily. The overall argument, then, is that as time passes, users expect better software in the form of PSEs, and simultaneously as advanced computer performance becomes difficult to understand, the number of users who are skilled programmers flattens or drops off. Because the number of users is growing rapidly, the percentage of programmers using machines drops sharply. Thus the future dependence of the community on advanced software is inevitably growing.

10.1.2 Scenario Summary

This scenario offers great promise to computer users: computer system speed increases with unlimited potential for growth independent of clock speed growth; PSEs that largely free users from programming chores available in each field; and high utilization of installed equipment through locally distributed computing. On the one hand, it seems reasonable that after 50 years of development, computers should mature to the point where they offer very powerful, easy-to-use, and low-cost service to all types of users. On the other hand, we must carefully examine the likelihood of reaching this scenario by 2000.

As a nation we are well on our way toward these goals, but the scenario raises several important questions.

- Do we have a plan to reach these goals?

- If not, how can we establish paths with high probabilities of success?

- As we proceed, how do we know if we are on course toward reaching the goals?

- At any time along the way, what are the serious open issues that may prevent us from reaching the goals?

As innovators in a synthetic field, computer scientists and engineers have a great storehouse of ideas and techniques that can be used to produce a wide variety of possible systems with many possible user features. The market is efficient in distinguishing the useful systems among those that have been built, but it does little to plan or prescribe what is needed for the future. Nor can these matters be left in the hands of government employees, panels, and book writers. There must be strong cooperation between the producers and consumers of the equipment to focus on these issues, and the process can benefit from the ideas and assistance of the R & D community in industry and academia, with some government financial support.

Sidebar 26: Future Costs of Speed via Parallelism
    Predicting future product costs and prices is difficult to do in any high technology field because of the large number of independent variables, ranging from the cost of the technologies used to the demand for the products. Moreover, there are differences between the past,

which was driven by technology speed increases, and a future that will be driven by speed increases via parallelism.

To produce circuits with a faster clock often required enormous financial investments in research that included physics, chemistry, electrical engineering, and materials science. To package these circuits with 100 or 200 leads emerging from a square inch, and mount a hundred or more packages on a board required the above plus such technologies as microlithography, micromachining, and robotics. Hundreds of millions of dollars could easily be invested in developing the process and manufacturing facilities. The market for the resulting faster products has been so huge that such large investments could be amortized over several years, reducing the cost of new circuits and boards to those of the previous generation. Thus the mips and megaflops per dollar exponentiated over time. However, as these numbers approach an investment of one billion dollars per plant, they become another market force that opposes the development of ever faster circuits.

Instead, consider a hypothetical future that is free of circuit speed growth and in which the basic problems of parallelism have been solved. Hardware manufacturers would concentrate entirely on miniaturization and cost reduction — a subject filled with tradeoffs — but the dollars per mips or megaflops of delivered products could be imagined to flatten off, eventually. The enormous costs of solving the parallelism problems will also require amortization, but let us assume that has also happened at some future time.

Future speed increases would then come at the cost of using additional hardware resources. So, even though the system hardware and software had reached rock-bottom prices, faster computation would require more resources, and thus be incrementally more expensive. There is one last redeeming feature of parallel computation in a world of ubiquitous computers: idle facilities are free to use, except for power and communications costs. If there were productive uses for all of the idle telephones, radios, or automobiles in a firm or household today, productivity would rise for very little incremental cost. This is exactly what power systems do by keeping production rates high at off-peak times, and selling the excess power in other time zones or by causing shifted work-schedules in heavy-use industries. It is similar to keeping an automated factory operating around the clock instead of building additional manufacturing facilities. Thus, the inevitablity of using idle computer cycles via high bandwidth networks seems certain.

Skyrocketing performance/cost increases have driven the computer revolution of the past half century. As the fundamental forces that drove those increases disappear, we will have to depend on hardware parallelism. If the required architecture and software are developed, we can ride a second stage performance/cost rocket into the indefinite future. The importance of this goal requires the ultimate in planning and execution.

10.2   Software Prospects

There is absolutely no disagreement with the conclusion that software is today a key missing ingredient of practical parallel systems. Because software plays so many roles in computing and takes so many forms, definitions of the exact nature of this missing ingredient can be very controversial.

Two distinct scenarios to achieve practical parallelism are the bottom-up and top-down approaches to software change. Both approaches would follow the Principle of Immediately Usable Change (cf. Chapter 3). A bottom-up approach would follow the path of selecting good parallel programming languages, designing powerful restructuring compilers and a parallel operating system, and developing sound parallel software engineering principles; practical parallel software would evolve over time from today's sequential software.

In contrast, the top-down approach would burst onto the scene Lotus 1-2-3-like (or Visicalc-like). It would break all the rules that were made for sequential computing, but that constrain practical parallelism, and leverage all of the sequential ideas that work. Problem-solving environments would be developed for the applications requiring parallelism, allowing parallel systems to compete with today's sequential PSEs in ease of use. Thus the need for every user to learn parallel programming would be skipped over in favor of the "direct" implementation of parallelism through libraries and data structures that support PSEs for whole codes across a range of parallel systems. These technologies would be developed by a few experts, thus eliminating the need to invent widely acceptable parallel programming languages, powerful restructuring compilers, or parallel software engineering principles, as required with the bottom-up approach.

This latter approach seems wildly optimistic, but some experimental engineering and scientific computing systems today are pointing in that direction [HoPR90]. On the other hand, while the traditional bottom-up approach seems slow and pessimistic, it is the way most progress has been made in the past (cf. Chapter 1). Although it is not clear that we have learned enough in the past 40 years to break this mold, it does seem quite possible that for certain applications, the top-down PSE approach may be successful in the 1990s. In the area of databases and transaction processing, easy-to-use commercially successful systems have been in use for many years; for example, recall the earlier Teradata discussions. More top-down successes in limited contexts together with solid progress on bottom-up tools could accelerate the whole process to a top-down scenario by 2000.

10.2.1   Problem-Solving Environments (PSEs)

This section outlines some top-down PSE approaches to practical parallelism and follows the outline of [Kuck92]; for related ideas see [HoRV92] and [GaHR94].

Adaptation

Adaptation is an important aspect of large software systems, and the idea has been in use for some time. Historically, people have attempted to write software systems that were flexible enough to allow easy human modification, e.g., using top-down, structured, object-oriented programming ideas. Reusable software is a current buzzword that describes such systems. For high-performance machines people have attempted to write programs that were easily adaptable to various architectures by automatic program restructurers (e.g., by writing vector-style code). Collectively, these are examples of what we shall refer to as:

Type 1 Adaptation, a new *use* or *performance level* for an old software system.

Of course, defining a "new use" is difficult, and over time people come to expect more and more impressive behavior from software systems.

Sidebar 27: Square Root Finding

   A simple example of Type 1 adaptation is a root-finding routine. In the 1950s a SQRT routine might have accepted two arguments, the number whose square root one wanted to find and an initial guess of its square root, and it returned a more precise square root. By the late 1970s much more flexible, portable, and general-purpose libraries had evolved — indeed they were adaptive libraries. As shown in Fig. 10.1, the arguments now may include the machine word length w, a function f and its derivative, the dimensionality of the array (or scalar) to which f is to be applied, and the type of arithmetic to be used (e.g., single precision, complex), and the result is just what the user wants on whatever machine is being used.

Type 1 Adaptive Systems are written for engineering and scientific applications, using the best ideas of software engineering and incorporating the best numerical methods (e.g., numerically stable, vectorizable, parallelizable). Examples include: computational fluid dynamics codes that operate on a wide range of geometries,

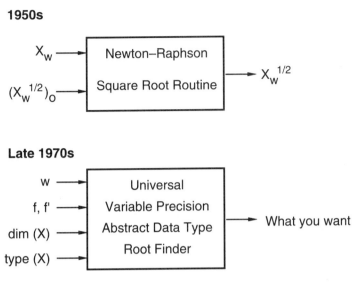

Figure 10.1. SQRT Routines

Reynolds numbers, etc., as in the cases of N3S from Electricité de France and FIDAP; a circuit simulation code that is later modified for radiation-hardened settings; or a structural dynamics code that is modified to handle the analysis of earthquake response. The systems must be written with flexible use in mind, but then some work may be involved in actually adapting the code in the future. One software system is more adaptive than the other if less work is required to make these adaptations with one than another.

More difficult to implement, but more useful future systems would exhibit:

Type 2 Adaptation, a new system use derived from the *merger* of two old systems.

As with Type 1 adaptation, a "new use" is also difficult to define here. Possibilities are easy to list, however. Suppose we had a molecular dynamics code and structural dynamics code. Using Type 2 adaptation we could merge these to study the crashworthiness of vehicles, taking into account the molecular structure of materials used in key components of the vehicle. Other examples include combining the simulation of VLSI circuits and printed-circuit board electromagnetics to simulate board-level packaging, or space station dynamic control plus meteorite probabilities and dynamics to simulate space station lifetimes.

The overall model of PSE that we use is shown in Fig. 10.2. As input we can expect either a program or a specification (e.g., equations, a domain). The

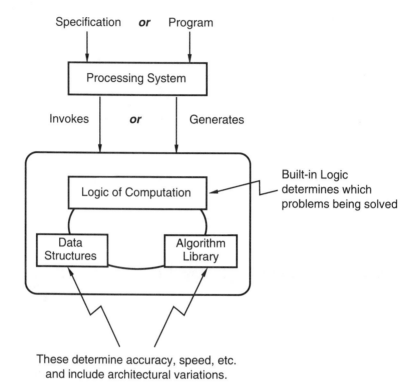

Specification   *or*   Program

Processing System

Invokes   *or*   Generates

Logic of Computation

Built-in Logic
determines which
problems being solved

Data
Structures

Algorithm
Library

These determine accuracy, speed, etc.
and include architectural variations.

Figure 10.2.   PSE Model

processing system generates or invokes (depending on the input) a three-part software system.

The topmost box is the Logic of the Computation, and this determines which problems are being solved. For adaptation, we must incorporate the logic of all methods of solution for a class of problems, e.g., linear algebra or Monte Carlo, for all of the architectures on which we plan to run the system.

The Data Structures and Algorithm Library boxes are the key elements in determining the speed and accuracy of a calculation and are generally very machine-dependent. Thus, for adaptation, the data structures must support all algorithms on all machines, and the algorithm library must support all methods of solution on all machines. Both the data structures and algorithms would be fine-tuned to particular parallel systems to exploit various processor counts and data sizes. Of course, we can write the system to allow modifications over time, but at any moment the scope of the data structures and algorithm library define the performance limitations of the system.

Data Structures

The Data Structures part of a PSE can be broken into a number of levels for understanding and implementation. Consider the four-level data structure repesentation of Fig. 10.3: the problem, algorithmic, program, and computation levels. The problem level is the level of the physical world, and here we define data by giving specific geometries with the number of space dimensions, time, etc. The algorithmic level defines data in terms that algorithms can use, e.g., vectors and matrices for linear algebra, finite element or finite difference meshes for partial differential equation solutions. At the program level we have integers and reals, arrays with given dimensions and pointers. Finally, at the computation level, data is allocated to memory, for example, in dense, structured sparse, or random sparse arrays and with certain dynamic properties (e.g., fill-ins). There are well-known transformations, which can be used to transform one data structure to another at each level and between levels. Software that implements each of these transformations is widely used, although it is not integrated in any way today. The feasibility of various basics necessary to support the principle of adaptation has been demonstrated, but much research remains to develop practical systems.

Algorithm Library

Currently, libraries are popular with some users, but are generally underutilized for several reasons:

1. Most libraries are not functionally complete. For example, Linpack, Eispack, and LAPACK, contain nothing that is effective for solving sparse problems, which are in fact the main workload in most scientific and engineering computations.

2. Most libraries do not give high performance on advanced architectures. Most commercial libraries contain only generic routines that are not aimed at high performance on vector or parallel machines, for example. Machine-specific algorithms and proper data structures are generally crucial to providing high performance.

3. Interfacing with libraries is often a problem. For example, most commercial packages use unique calling sequences, and special effort may be required to substitute a routine from one library for one from another library.

4. Scientists and engineers often write their own numerical algorithm libraries. Partly for the above reasons and partly because of human nature, people who understand an area often prefer to "do it themselves." Notice that this is seldom done in other areas — for example, graphics and windowing libraries and standards are widely accepted by ordinary scientists and engineers.

FOUR DATA STRUCTURE LEVELS

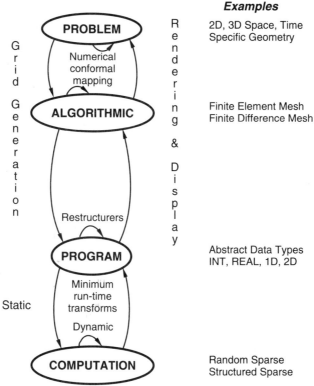

Figure 10.3. PSE Data Structures

From the above, it can be concluded that some work is needed at the library level to provide performance portability across a wide range of applications and HPC machines. However, it is promising to observe that libraries are used without question under the right circumstances, e.g., in graphics.

10.2.2 Software Review

The topic that presents the most difficult technical challenges for practical parallelism is also difficult to summarize. Top-down and bottom-up approaches to the software challenges were sketched at the beginning of this section. Section 10.2.1 gave some details of the top-down approach; bottom-up approaches have been discussed throughout the book. The following is a list of basic topics and recommendations with references to some of the other discussions in the book.

Languages create strong user followings for various reasons. The psychological aspects of what a user already knows and is comfortable with, or of a language's expressive powers and elegance of expression, will develop for practical parallel systems as they have for sequential systems. Similarly, the economic aspects that relate to the costs of using one language or another for individual or group programming efforts must be considered.

The performance aspects of practical parallel languages are difficult to deal with. On the one hand, the above paragraph must not be ignored, but on the other hand, if higher performance is possible there is a great temptation to implement language features that put this performance within the users' reach. The problem here is that for practical parallelism to emerge and prevail, user burdens must be relieved (e.g., by means of compilers or PSEs), not increased. Furthermore, the limited national talent pool available to work on software problems should not focus on regressive issues, for example, attempting to mask the difficulties of poor architectures by inventing language "features." Section 3.5 dealt with this (Principle of Immediately Usable Change), as did Sections 2.7 and 4.5.

Restructuring Compilers have been held out as a promise and dream for two decades. They exist today in a practical sense, but they are still far too weak. Their importance is growing as they have become necessary for single microprocessors, all of which have pipelined and multi-instruction issue capabilities, features once found only in supercomputers.

The performance strengths of compilers rest on the cumulative effect of their power as more transformations are added over time, and in the potential performance growth indicated by Amdahl's law as discussed in Section 5.3. The current performance state of parallel compiler development is expressed via PPT3, and examples were given in Section 8.2. The overall importance of compilers, including their role in performance portability, was summarized in Section 5.5.

Libraries have been discussed throughout the book as a labor saver for users, as a method of enhancing performance portability, and as a building block for PSEs; these are characteristics they share with compilers. Numerical libraries have been available for decades, and many other types of libraries have come into wide use more recently, but as with restructuring compilers, most libraries are too weak to support practical parallelism's needs. New algorithms have had major performance impact from time to time, but the systematic development of portable parallel libraries is needed. Library functionality must be enhanced to include algorithms which cover most cases that users need (e.g., sparse linear algebra) and open performance standards across the full library must follow. Libraries and parallel algorithms were discussed in several sidebars of Chapter 2 and Section 4.5, their crucial role in PSE development was presented in Section 10.2, and the potential for academics is further discussed in Section 10.3.2.

Data Structures, Scheduling, Operating Systems, and Parallel Software Engineering have been mentioned throughout the book. The first two are technical subjects and the last two involve technical issues as well as programmer preferences, psychology, and conventions. These topics were introduced in Section 4.5.

Inventing and using the right data structures to match algorithms to architectures needs careful attention, as does their integration with programs to produce portable codes. Object-oriented programming is under wide development now and fits in nicely here. Some ideas about data structures were discussed in Section 10.2.1, and the subject was introduced in Sections 2.3 and 3.4.

Scheduling was traditionally an operating system issue, but for parallel systems the OS can introduce fatal overhead. Scheduling loop iterations can be done by hardware and compilers, while the higher level scheduling of tasks and jobs can be shared between the OS and compiler. This topic was discussed in Section 4.3.

Operating systems are important to parallel computing in two ways: as they affect performance (e.g., in scheduling) and as they affect the human interface. The former was discussed briefly in Section 4.5.6. The latter has become their major importance in sequential computing, such as on PCs and workstations, where "openness" has led to major lawsuits. This has implications for practical parallel computing as a follow-on technology.

Software engineering is a very broad topic, and we have added "parallel" to evoke images of programming style and standards that help to produce practical parallel programs. Although the topic of parallel software engineering has received little attention, if users were cautioned against or prevented from using certain data structures (e.g., unstructured dynamic pointers), program structures (e.g., unstructured ifs and gotos), and algorithms (e.g. those with nonlinear recurrences), compilers would be able to do a much better job of restructuring for parallelism than if such constructs were used. Other constraints can be useful in the performance portability of resulting codes. This point returns us to notions similar to those discussed under languages: programmers' personal choice, psychological issues, and employers' policies all come together in software engineering. These are slowly changing matters, often steeped in tradition and personal prejudice, but they can have major performance influences and must be addressed (see Section 10.3.2 for an academic role).

Sidebar 28: CSE-PSE

Anyone can use smart computers, but too many smart people use dumb computers.

Consider the computational insights available to students of science and engineering since World War II and the invention of computers. From the 1940s into the 1960s, students used hand computation aided by slide rules. They looked at plots in textbooks and made their own graphs to develop insights about the relationships between variables. Next came a series of increasingly powerful hand-held calculators that made the process quicker and reduced drudgery. By the 1980s, students could afford personal computers that provided two-dimensional monochrome graphics plotting packages, which allowed the exploration of much broader design spaces. In the 1990s, symbolic manipulation of input formulas, CAD systems, and 3D color graphics allow much easier use and greater insight.

In the same time frame, the leading computational scientists and engineers have had available increasingly powerful supercomputers, with increasingly easier to use input languages and 3D color graphics for output visualization as well as input modification. However, clerical workers have had the greatest benefits, moving from typewriters and electromechanical calculators to computers with multimedia I/O devices and do-what-I-mean problem-solving environments for word processing, spreadsheet analysis, desktop publishing, and presentation production. The size of the clerical markets and the relative simplicity of these systems explains why such systems have advanced most quickly.

It seems likely that there will be a confluence of these three lines of development in the 1990s. With the acknowledgment that the most advanced research users will always be pushing the system technology envelope and therefore will demand more than is provided by the most advanced commercially available systems, students will be the major beneficiaries of the technology trickle-down from both supercomputer and clerical users. The notion of employing CAD/CAR technology to automate textbook examples and homework problems opens potentially amazing new vistas for future students. For one's favorite field, imagine that major subsystems of an engineering design can be modified, the complete system reconfigured and driven with new inputs, and that the results can be visualized via 3D color graphics. This would enable students in the future to do experiments that in the past advanced researchers were able only to imagine. Subject to their pushing the commercial state of the art, advanced researchers will benefit similarly.

10.3   The Future Role of Academic CSE in Advancing the GGC

10.3.1   Computer Science and Computer Engineering

The future roles of academic computer science and computer engineering are currently under increasing debate [Bore92], [HaLi92], [Parn90]. Simply put, the field arose a few decades ago because computers were being built and used to solve a growing range of real-world problems. Initially, these problems and the computer systems themselves provided a tremendous stimulus for the field. Subsequently, computer science (CS) has slowly turned its back on its roots, and to a lesser extent computer engineering (CE) has done the same. There were probably several reasons for this, including:

- The desire of computer scientists and engineers to free themselves from the subservient role of machine builders and programmers for other well-established academic fields that used computers and wanted help.

- The fact that new, interesting and indeed useful problems were discovered which could occupy the attention of many CS/CE reasearchers; these included the theory and practice of algorithms, artificial intelligence, databases, and language and operating system theory.

- The crush of new students in the 1980s whose curiosity was probably stimulated by the novelty of home PCs and was fueled by the excitement of these new fields of CS/CE research.

- The growing importance of computers in the world, adding to the budgets, publicity, and importance of the field; this led computer scientists and engineers to feel confident that they could chart their own courses.

The growth of the computing field in size and importance has surely been aided by CS and CE research. In turn, the growth of the field has justified the need for these disciplines. But rapid growth and change in industry as well as academia, can lead to divergences that are damaging to both sides. As education fails to match real-world demands, and research fails to relate to real world problems, academia tends to become irrelevant to the real world. The roots of CS and CE are well-grounded in real-world problems, as the sidebar points out, but over time there has been too much divergence from these realities and problems.

In the early 19th century, Michael Faraday could state that while he did not know specifically where his electromagnetic research would lead, he was confident that government support for it would lead to new government tax revenues a few years hence, and Carl Friedrich Gauss was equally at home doing mathematical research (which is still useful today) or applying it to, and deriving it from, the real world. In some branches of mathematics, and arguably in parts of physics as well, the research topics of the present leaders are so far removed from reality that there is little hope of ever applying the ideas in the real world. Whereas in mathematics and physics this has taken 150 years, some computer scientists have made the same transition to irrelevance in a mere 25 years.

Sidebar 29: University-Industry Cooperation

Universities have repeatedly pioneered in HPC developments. Beginning in 1937, Harvard University built a series of computers under the leadership of Howard Aiken, which involved the cooperation of IBM after 1939. This got IBM interested in computers, in addition to punched card machines. The University of Pennsylvania built ENIAC, the first successful electronic computer, which was completed in 1946. The project was led by John Mauchly and J. Presper Eckert. Eniac spawned EDSAC, which was built in a project led by Maurice Wilkes at Cambridge University, England. EDSAC, completed in 1949, was the first operational stored-program computer. ENIAC also led to the Institute for Advanced Study machine (in Princeton, N.J.), a very influential system, that was begun by John von Neumann and was completed in 1952. Over the following decades, many university projects and ideas have had major influences on computer systems. We shall focus on parallel computing efforts in universities that directly affected industry in systems design.

Beginning in 1965 with ARPA support, a University of Illinois team designed the architecture and wrote initial software for the Illiac IV parallel computer. Burroughs designed and built the system, and Texas Instruments did the memory subsystem, which was one of the first semiconductor computer memories. This evolved into a major collaboration between the Illinois group and a Burroughs group, in the design of the Burroughs Scientific Processor (BSP), and later also led to collaboration with Alliant Computer Systems, which produced the FX/8 series and others. Much effort at Illinois went into the Parafrase software system for analyzing Fortran programs; many of the architectural and compiler insights of the group came from or were verified by Parafrase. In the 1980s, the Illinois group designed and built the parallel Cedar system [GKLS83, KDLS86]. Faculty members who had long-term involvement with these activities include Ed Davidson (Cedar), Dan Gajski (BSP and Cedar), David Padua (Cedar), Duncan Lawrie (all), Ahmed Sameh (all), Dan Slotnick (Illiac IV), and the author (all). These projects have many alumni who have subsequently made significant contributions to the field; for example,

Steve Chen spent nearly ten years in the Illinois group and on the BSP before joining Cray Research to design the X-MP and Y-MP.

The Parafrase system was originally intended (in 1970) to analyze programs to help infer good parallel architectures, but became an excellent compiler model as well. In the late 1970s, a copy of Parafrase was given to IBM, Yorktown Heights, where it helped launch Fran Allen's group as a major research leader in parallel system compilation. After spending a sabbatical year in this group, Ken Kennedy returned to Rice University and began what has become a leading parallel software research group. The Rice group was influential in the design of the Convex Computer Corp. compilers which have shown vectorizing and parallelizing strength over the years. In the 1990s, Kennedy became a leader of the High-Performance Fortran (HPF) effort for MPP's, that spanned industry and academia.

Hypercube interconnection networks were discussed in an early University of Michigan paper [SqPa63]. The hypercube implementations at Cal Tech and in several West Coast companies arose from the initial ideas of Carver Mead and the long-term efforts of Geoffrey Fox and Chuck Seitz. This group also benefitted from a strong collection of computationally oriented faculty and graduate students in various departments. The Cal Tech team initially built the Cosmic Cube systems [Seit85, FJLO88] and became involved in system design efforts at nCUBE, Ametek, Intel, and elsewhere. The Intel supercomputer line today is in its fourth generation of direct descendents of the original Cal Tech efforts.

New York University has had a long-term leadership role in HPC through its Courant Institute of Mathematical Sciences. Beginning with Richard Courant himself, this group has pioneered in developing algorithms for the numerical and computational solution of partial differential equations, which model many of the laws of nature. The NYU parallel computing efforts have been led and inspired by Jack Schwartz since the 1960s. In the 1980s, this group built the MIMD Ultracomputer system [Schw80, GGKM83] and played a major role in the IBM RP3 project at Yorktown Heights (the IBM group had extensive interactions with both the NYU and Illinois groups before launching RP3). Mal Kalos and Allan Gottlieb have played major, long-term roles in the NYU projects. IBM has built several parallel research machines over the years, and the MPP distributed-memory SP-1 and SP-2 systems of IBM have arisen from these roots.

The groups at CalTech, Illinois, and NYU were all able to build their 1980s prototypes because of major funding commitments by the Department of Energy, as well as other agencies and companies. These projects each consumed on the order of $5 million per year and in addition to prototype systems, supplied important ideas to companies and produced several hundred graduate students.

MIT has been involved throughout the history of HPC. In the 1980s, the Ph.D. thesis of Danny Hillis, written in the AI group there, led directly to the formation of Thinking Machines Corp. and long-term consulting relationships for some MIT faculty members. MIT has also pioneered in dataflow parallel computers, in projects led by Jack Dennis and Arvind, which, while not producing commercial successes, have influenced a number of industrial groups to study the issues and in some cases build prototypes.

Thus university research has had direct, short-term payoffs for industrial projects many times in the history of parallel computing. As the field matures and system building (especially the software) becomes increasingly expensive and demanding, universities can play major roles in performance measurement and analysis, as well as in traditional system design and prototyping. It is frequently suggested that if university researchers are given free access to HPC systems (e.g., via the NSF supercomputing centers), the HPC field will reap great benefits. In fact, various scientific and engineering disciplines have benefitted from widely available, low-cost HPC access, and some insight may have been gained by the HPC community. The key missing point is that HPC researchers in universities must be funded to carry out major projects concerning system design and analysis, not the mere use of existing machines. It must be realized that *design* and *analysis* are equally important in our drive toward practical parallelism.

As things have developed in the 1990s, we face a crisis in computer science and computer engineering education on three fronts:

A. Enrollments are down, probably partly because of demographics and partly because of a cooling of student interest in the field.

B. Funding is in question as the economy, peace, and the interplay among academic disciplines ebb and flow.

C. Future research directions are debated as on one hand the field matures and on the other, new technical problems arise.

Our purpose here is not to deal broadly with these issues, but rather to focus on one important piece of the whole puzzle.

10.3.2   Computational Science and Engineering

Computational science and engineering (CSE) is now being called the third branch of science and engineering, along with theory and experimentation [Pool92]. We view CSE as the direct extension of those subjects that led to the academic computing field in the 1940s and 1950s, and, beginning in the 1960s, led to the formation of academic computer science departments and caused many electrical engineering departments to change their names, becoming electrical and computer engineering departments.

We define **computational science and engineering** as the study of the *whole* computational process of solving problems in science and engineering. On one hand the name is a generalization of "computational chemistry," "computational electronics," "computational physics," "computer-aided design," etc. On the other hand, it is a variation on "computer science" and "computer engineering" that refers to the application of scientific and engineering principles (rather than the current, generally used intuitive approach) in designing systems for the whole computational process of solving problems. It does not include the theoretical and experimental aspects of the discipline to which computing is being applied. Nor does it include those parts of modern theoretical or experimental computer science that are completely divorced from the principles of designing computer systems to solve general problems, (e.g., artificial intelligence as a theory of human thought processes, or abstract complexity theory). A variety of interpretations of CSE has led to the establishment of a number of diverse university programs [Rice94].

There are several subjects that have not been of the greatest interest in computer science and computer engineering in the recent past, but that are now essential to the future of high-performance computing. The advent of commercially available parallel computer systems in the 1980s must be regarded as a major milestone in the history of computing. Parallel systems are being built, of necessity, to achieve high-performance; the fastest clock speeds have improved relatively little recently, so parallelism is the architect's only hope. Thus for the first time in history, computer architecture is not simply another interesting academic subject; instead, the future of high-speed computing depends on it. Computer architecture of the future must become a discipline that is deeply rooted in the performance analysis of earlier systems; architectures with flaws as deep as those found in most MPP systems cannot be patched up via software. Furthermore, compiling for well-balanced parallel machines is a major challenge. Whereas compiler research for sequential machines was pretty much a closed subject by the early 1980s, parallel compilation has blossomed in the past decade and is currently a very important and popular subject.

Finally, parallel algorithms need substantial development and implementation in useful libraries. As architectures become more complex, algorithms to exploit them become more difficult to understand. Unfortunately, numerical library research and development have not kept pace. Much attention has been placed on reimplementing and repackaging algorithms for traditional problems (e.g., LA-PACK from Eispack and Linpack), but little effort has gone into such difficult topics as sparse algorithm libraries, or any libraries for parallel machines.

These basic subjects together with material that integrates the various aspects of large parallel codes should form the core of CSE course offerings. Integrating material might include:

1. Large-Scale Computations and Their Performance Implications: program structures, data structures, data generation and analysis, visualization [SaRi93],[CACM94].

2. Great Equations and Their Parallel Solution Techniques: Maxwell's, Navier-Stokes, Boltzmann's, and others; Monte Carlo, Linear Algebra, Numerical Integration, Table-Lookup.

3. Parallel Software Engineering: the structure of codes for high-performance parallel computation, data structures for parallel memory, good parallel programming style.

4. Performance Evaluation and Improvement: performance measurement and analysis tools, comparative system performance analysis, system component performance improvement techniques.

5. Problem Solving Environments: problem oriented libraries, data structure transformations, adaptation principles, application visualization [GaHR94],[Comp94].

10.3.3 PSEs in CSE

An excellent starting point for cooperative research and development between CS, CE, and other engineering and science departments would center on existing computer-aided design (CAD) systems. Consider the benefits and problems of adapting existing CAD systems to automate the figures and expand the homework in an engineering textbook. There would be manifold benefits in enabling students to see dynamic, 3D color graphics rather than static, 2D black and white textbook illustrations. Futhermore, the students could manipulate the figures by changing the load on a beam or the input voltage to a circuit. Similarly, all homework could consist of machine problems that were based on the figures and text as built into a CAD system.

The first challenging problem here would be to use the CAD systems to build up simple designs (discipline-oriented work) and then to develop new user interfaces for interacting with the figures and for solving the homework exercises (computer science-oriented work). This use of CAD systems makes them effectively Computer-Aided Simulation (CAS) systems. The potential payoff of the above should be enough to encourage the CAD system companies to cooperate by releasing (parts of) their source code for academic enhancement, which in turn would allow academics to build software on top of the existing CAD systems for user interfaces, to interface two CAD sytems, and to study their structures for adaptive use. The real goal of computer science research would be in developing tools, software engineering methods and frameworks, to allow this kind of activity to proceed easily. It could also open the CAD companies to academic cooperation in developing parallel versions of their systems for higher performance.

This scenario could also open the door to building Computer-Aided Research (CAR) systems which differ from CAD systems as follows. Given an input specification, a CAR system produces answers for which, if they appear plausible, the user seeks to study their derivation. In other words, a CAD system is treated like a black box — problems go in and solutions come out — whereas a CAR system is a transparent box full of smaller transparent boxes, each of which bears examination and enhancement in building better models and thus better understanding the real world. Examples of CAR system use include modeling a weather system, the folding of a protein, or the heart pumping blood. Notice that a CAR system will spin off CAS systems to be used in accurate simulators of engineering designs or of the physical world.

10.3.4   CSE Summary

Much work is needed in curriculum development for CSE, and it is necessary that computer engineers, computer scientists, and a wide range of applications people be involved in the effort. The subject is controversial today because it seems to attack and compete with current academic computer science and computer engineering activities in terms of A, B, and C in Section 10.3.1 [HaLi92]. It must be realized by people within CS and CE that their academic disciplines will be revitalized by cooperation with CSE. Developing CSE will have immediate payoffs in helping to solve a number of the problems discussed above. It will also have long-term benefits in educating a new generation of people to think in new ways that will, in the end, solve the greatest grand challenge.

**Sidebar 30: How to Break the Computational
Science and Engineering Gridlock**

The statement that computational science and engineering (CSE) is central to all future technological R&D, and that new educational programs are crucial to the development of CSE, today raises very little objection in forward-looking academic settings. However, more is necessary than plausibility, consensus, and central importance to bestir most academic institutions.

New money, new people, new attitudes, and new leadership are necessary to implement new ideas. Especially in times of tight budgets, academic departmental wagons circle about their traditions while merely offering verbal support for great new ideas like CSE. University administrators, being broadly ignorant of the detailed facts about CSE, fall back on their long-standing traditions of avoiding risks. Academic institutions support mostly bottom-up decision making, whereby an idea with wide intellectual support or merely local financial support can easily gain widespread institutional agreement. In contrast, industrial organizations support mostly top-down decision making, whereby the management develops ideas that are passed down the organization for implementation. In any case, for a new and far-reaching idea like CSE, deans and department heads favor verbal support while maintaining the status quo with their actions.

Joint projects between academic units can break this gridlock by taking actions that cost little, but make practically irreversible changes at low levels. Three examples of projects that follow this strategy are:

- Development of CSE courses (cf. Section 10.3.2) across two existing departments, so that both departments want the course and want to teach it. Established courses are difficult to erase from the books, and joint teaching maintains interdepartmental dialog. Ideally both will agree that a professor with new CSE skills will be hired to teach the course, but this does cost money.

- Development of PSEs (cf. Section 10.3.3) within or between departments, to be used in conjunction with regular course materials. If done well, this approach will irreversibly change teaching methods, because students will demand more of it and professors will find it a great teaching aid. This costs money but will promote solicitation of industrial funds and perhaps joint activities with industry. In the past, academic application software systems like SPICE (circuit simulation) and Gaussian (computational chemistry) have arisen in universities and enjoyed wide acceptance in academia and industry.

- Development of joint research projects within or between academic departments to further the cause of CAD and CAR. This technique has benefits similar to those above and certainly advances CSE, but it is transitory as people and ideas come and go. Its best effects are in attracting Ph.D. students in new CSE areas and creating CSE proposal pressure on various agencies. Good new cooperative R & D work is much easier to continue when it has broad discussion and support, and when each participant stands to gain something substantial in his own field from the cooperation.

Finally, some warnings and cautions must be observed; if certain problems are not solved or avoided, CSE programs will not succeed.

1. Section 10.3.1 mentioned a wariness of computer scientists even to the appearance of subordinating themselves to others, professionally. Cross-disciplinary teams must have explicitly stated, win-win goals. For example, a senior biologist or physicist must not look at a junior CSE person as an employee, but as a peer. There are a number of success stories, historically, to rely on here, but there have also been many failures. Explicit agreements and candid reviews by the participants and administration are important to keep such academic teams together.

2. All scientists and engineers work — in a day-to-day way — on idealized problems that are abstracted from other sources. Most physical scientists have problems that are abstracted from nature; most computer scientists and computer engineers have problems that are abstracted from computing. If these problems from various fields are sufficiently formal and mathematical, there is a tendency to think that the difficulty, rigor, and quality of the work is equivalent, and is therefore justified as a proper academic activity. Merely producing new software is, on the other hand, thought to be inferior academic work because "everyone can program." Ultimately, this comes down to the same distinctions made between theoreticians and experimentalists in all fields. It is just as easy and useless to do bad theory as it is to do bad experiments (although bad theory may take longer to dismiss). Furthermore, Nobel prizes to experimentalists count just as much as they do to theoreticians.

3. People in CSE deal with computational problems that are derived from other scientists and engineers. The nature of the real world for CSE *is* other peoples' programs, computers, and computations. The complexity of these human-synthesized problems is enormous, as is the value to the world of solutions to these CSE problems. We must avoid thinking that "Mathematicians and physicists work on problems posed by God, but computer people only work on problems posed by Charlie in the physics department."

4. CSE students must eventually be regarded as being in a new field, not as being in one or another traditional field, with an outreach in some direction, just as electrical engineers are neither overeducated

electricians nor failed physicists. Some unifying themes of CSE have been sketched in the text, and must evolve over time. Ph.D. students in CSE should eventually have programs and exams that diverge from traditional areas, even though this causes great suspicion and threatens many established academics.

5. The relationship between CSE and computer science (CS) or electrical and computer engineering (ECE) presents serious practical difficulties. CSE bears a relationship to established academic departments, that is very similar to the relationship that CS had with other departments in the mid-1960s. As the text elaborates, CS has charted its own course, and most CS departments now have a culture in which it is impossible for CSE to prosper. Similar statements can be made about most ECE departments. CSE deserves and will eventually command a major role in academia. It may be argued that CS, ECE, and CSE eventually will become three branches of one large engineering department, although based on size alone this would seem wrong, because more than half of the enrollment in an engineering college might be in one department. The details about how to initiate CSE programs depend on the organization and politics of various academic institutions (some have merged CS and ECE, others are separating them, while in still others, both survive — either at arms length or in cooperation with one another). Administrations with foresight will chart a course that fits their own institutional constraints, but establishes a vigorous, well-funded CSE program.

There is little reason to expect dramatic changes based on present conditions. However, as the urgency of the problems of developing practical parallelism become more obvious to all, and as the academic role in the process evolves, the pressures to change should become irresistible.

10.4 National Performance System

Comprehensive and comparable data are necessary to improve performance in parallel computer systems. For maximum benefits, the data should also be widely and easily accessible. These needs were referred to and discussed in Section 3.7, where open performance progress was discussed and in Section 5.4, where some performance and benchmarking issues were discussed.

In the history of science and technology, it is clear that progress has been strongly correlated with the availability of quantitative data. Section 1.2 outlined this traditional process of progress, and contrasted it with the typical process used in high performance computing. The substitution of arm waving and hype for quantitative data and analysis has been a major contributor to the tragedies in the field, including the long list of failed companies and wasted resources of Section 4.1.

Historically, empiricism in science and technology has often led to theory and abstraction. In successful fields this process has flourished along the lines of the cycle in Section 1.2. This book has outlined some empirical approaches that must be taken in HPC and has proposed some simple abstractions — the practical parallelism tests — that can be used as guidelines and milestones towards future progress.

Performance data have long been available in HPC design, but data are usually only collected about one part of a system, and therefore are not comprehensive. Such data are often proprietary or only partially presented, and then they are presented in whatever form the people involved choose. It is remarkably frustrating when trying to compare several systems, that papers about the various machines use plots and units that require substantial effort to compare; furthermore, this is the rule rather than the exception in HPC today. Comparable data are essential. We must be able to understand easily the details of what it is about computation X that makes it better than computation Y.

Availability of data to a wide audience is obviously necessary. With the growth of science and technology has come a wide proliferation of technical journals that makes it difficult for people in any field to keep abreast of progress. But in HPC, the results come in dozens of computer journals and conferences, plus uncounted numbers of applications-oriented journals and conferences. No individual can keep track of these sources of information, much less which performance data actually appear in them.

It does not take deep insight to realize that comprehensive performance databases available on national networks would be an excellent step in the required direction. Ideally, the data would be freely available to all, but in practice, qualified users would easily be able to pay access fees to help provide support.

This data would have to meet the requirements presented in Section 3.6 or explicitly state any shortcomings; otherwise the data could be misleading and have negative effects. Various performance reports have been made available in the past, some via network, but the content and organization of the data do not come close to meeting the requirements. Proper steps have not been taken for several reasons:

- The work is difficult at the intellectual level; exactly what should be stored and in what relationships?

- The work is difficult at the implementation level; how should the data be measured, validated, and updated?

- The data itself is controversial and can be damaging to particular systems and their proponents.

- The database must be broad-based to be useful, so the project is large in scope and requires a major commitment of high-quality effort and funding, and the cooperation of many people.

Nevertheless, such a project is of central importance to the field. Consider the design of a **National Performance System** (NPS) that would provide performance information to the entire community. The contents of this database and the groups that it is designed to serve, will be presented in the next two sections.

10.4.1   National Performance System Contents

A wide range of NPS users should be able to find detailed answers to their queries, which means that the database must contain a large amount of timely, as well as historical, information. Eight categories of NPS contents follow; the details of how this should be organized remain to be developed.

1. Source Programs

   Original source programs must be available with a level of documentation that enables casual NPS users to understand the problems each program solves, the methods used, and the general organization of the program. Also necessary are the names of the programs' authors, where the program has been used, and the name of a person to be contacted concerning its operation.

2. Algorithm Decomposition

   Each program should be represented in terms of its most time-consuming algorithms. Information presented about each algorithm should be similar to 1. More details might be expected here concerning published papers about the algorithms, and analyses of their merits. It is expected that algorithm replacement should be possible within these programs, so necessary details should be provided for this process.

3. Data Sets

   The actual data used must be available for rerunning the codes. Furthermore, the data sizes should be discussed in the sense of LADS, MUDS, and other characteristics discussed in Section 6.6. Some discussion of the origins of the data and its meaning and significance should be provided.

4. Architectural Details

Architectural details must be provided for each system on which there are performance runs. The hardware and software must be documented in sufficient detail so that the performance experiments can be reproduced. The complete state of the system, including compiler options and any performance instrumentation used, as well as any other load on the system during the runs, must be explained.

5. Performance Summary

Canonical measurements must be included for each run, in a simple summary, as Perfect and SPEC have done. This should be as comprehensive as possible, including speedup, stability, and scalability information. This basic summary should also include information about 1. through 4. above.

6. Performance Analysis

Performance analysis must include some form of macroperformance matrix (MM of Section 4.6) that divides performance into analyzable pieces. Recall that the MM contains profile-type information, as well as attribution of time to system hardware and software components. This data opens the door to system performance improvement by means of further analysis. Analysis tools may be thought of as outside the database, but basic ones should be available within the NPS.

7. Performance Details

In the long run, performance details that enable performance improvement efforts should be linked into the NPS. For example, in key performance bottlenecks, engineers want address traces, and high resolution cache miss and memory delay information. It may not be necessary to store all of this, but it should be easy to rerun the code and generate such information on demand. This capability requires an instrumented, executable code and access to the original system upon which the runs were made. If long runs under special circumstances (e.g., single-user system access and hardware instumentation) are required, it may be desirable to collect and store this information initially, and periodically increment it using batched analysis requests. As systems change over time (e.g., via new software releases), it becomes increasingly difficult to reproduce old system states, which of course increases the importance of this topic.

8. Archival History

The NPS must be regarded as an archival database. As systems go out of production, their performance information may become more rather than less valuable. This is especially true of systems with unusual features and high performance in particular areas. Thus NPS will become the only source of information that is needed for comparative performance studies of out-of-production systems.

Database access methods must provide flexible retrieval of information for the range of users discussed next. Analysis software must also be part of NPS, but we will not discuss it further here.

10.4.2 NPS Audiences

Consider the following examples of how a National Performance System would be used and what its benefits would be to the whole community.

A. System Purchasers An obvious use of an NPS would be for rational computer system selection. Today one can listen to sales pitches, talk to other users, study standard benchmark results (too limited), or run one's own benchmarks (too difficult and time consuming). If the results of 50 or 100 real codes, each with various data sizes, were available in an NPS together with well-designed methods of accessing the data, one should be able to get a reasonable approximation of one's own workload. This would allow decision making to move from today's nearly random selection process to a fairly accurate, rational process.

B. Algorithm Developers A key to exploiting parallel systems is matching the computational algorithms to the systems. Among a class of good parallel algorithms, the proper choice may depend strongly on the system architectual details. Even for a very high quality architecture, the number of processors in the system may dictate the choice between two good algorithms.

Suppose that you are an algorithm researcher, say a developer of new fast Fourier transforms (FFT's). These algorithms are useful in signal processing, image processing, and partial differential equation solution, so it is unlikely that you would be able to know more than a fraction of the real codes in that FFT's are "enabling" algorithms. The algorithms can be arranged to deal with local data for part of their running time, but ultimately they must move data across the entire system. Thus, FFT's are very performance-dependent on system architecture.

If you had invented a new FFT algorithm and wanted to find a class of real application codes that depended upon FFT's and which were yielding poor performance on a class of parallel systems, the NPS could serve as a perfect matchmaker. If the codes were arranged properly, you would be able to insert your algorithm into several codes, run them on several systems, and observe performance changes. For those cases that were most improved, if performance measurements could be taken easily, you would also be able to understand the details of how your technique better exploited the system than previous FFT's did, which might allow you to make further progress.

C. Compiler and Language Developers Compilers are universally fundamental to the good performance of parallel systems. They are more broadly important than any particular application algorithm because they are used for *every* computation; however, particular algorithms can provide bigger performance gains for particular computations. Compiler developers look for program and data structures that cause performance blockages across all codes on a given system. Language designers should have the same motives (cf. Section 3.5: Principle of Immediately Usable Change) to help parallel processing.

If the NPS contained performance information in the form of the Performance Matrix (PM) of Section 4.6, a compiler or language designer could zero in on specific code segments or the particular language syntax that caused wide-ranging performance bugs. Progress in the field would then be dictated by addressing the most important of these performance bugs. Parallel software engineering ideas could evolve from analysis of the syntax and style of poorly performing programs.

D. System Architects Suppose that designers could probe more deeply into the NPS (recall the ideas of Sections 4.4 and 4.5) to understand much more about the Cedar and Cray computations than was discussed in Chapters 8 and 9. Assume that the interplay among algorithms, data structures, compiler, and architecture could be characterized for a number of performance outliers. Assume further that this could be done for a number of systems. In this manner one could start to understand what improvements should be made to a given system to make its performance more like superior systems. In particular, if several systems were improved in this way, the process would tend to converge toward better performance than any of the original systems. The complexity of the process and the difficulty of global convergence on high performance are serious considerations in designing the NPS.

Today, each manufacturer pursues ad hoc strategies based on often superficial and spotty performance information, as they independently inch toward better systems. Comparative design (cf. Section 4.6) based on comprehensive data can help eliminate local optimizations in favor of global ones. One analogy might be shopping for a TV set in a small store vs. a large dealer with a wall full of sets tuned to the same program: we can easily compare picture quality, then pick the easiest controls among the best pictures, and finally buy the lowest priced set among the survivors. The attackers' advantage (Section 1.5) is clear in this design scenario.

E. System Funders Suppose you have the critical job of funding the development of the HPC systems; venture capitalists, computer company executives, and Washington bureaucrats all share this important responsibility. In the past none of these groups has demonstrated remarkable insight or strength of purpose in moving the field ahead through difficult times, which is the basic reason for the enormous number of failures listed in Section 4.1. If, as such a decision maker, you had the ability to know exactly how your systems were performing and to compare this performance to your competitors', several aspects of the present process could be vastly improved.

- You would know performance facts and not need to rely on mere opinions.

- The basis for these facts would be knowable, either directly from the database or more likely through further experimental and analytical work by system engineers.

- Decisions to drop projects, modify designs, or start new projects could be based on the verifiable results of performance analysis, rather than on tradition, opinion, and chutzpah.

These scenarios are typical of how an NPS could benefit the community. It would at once serve as a *Consumers' Report*, National Bureau of Standards, and *Racing Form* to the many constituencies that depend upon HPC. Using a collection of supercomputers across the country together with the NPS would form a National Performance Metacenter, allowing many uses for all existing HPC systems. A worldwide version of the NPS is needed, ultimately. The book describes a U.S. NPS, which eventually could be integrated with a **Multinational Performance System.**

Sidebar 31: Pruning and Testing

In high-performance computing, analogies with everyday situations and historical technologies are easy to develop and perhaps to learn from.

Novice gardeners often find it difficult to distinguish young weeds from young flowers, but as time passes, the distinction becomes more obvious and it becomes necessary to pull the weeds. As they develop a green thumb gardeners also learn how to select and nurture new flowers. In the 1980s, when every HPC system design of the 1970s was germinating as a new company, the nation could afford to let 100 flowers bloom. But now we must selectively and intensively cultivate only the most promising new developments. Just as we have field guides to edible wild plants, we must develop a field guide to HPC performance, upon which to base future system decisions.

In the early decades of the automotive industry, there were hundreds of automobile manufacturers, a few of whom innovated, survived, and grew. Parallel computer systems are much more complex than automobiles in the number of parts they contain and in their operation. They require more subtlety in their design and performance analysis. Furthermore, even in the automobile industry no one considered putting experimental cars on the street in the hands of any driver who came along. Instead, proving grounds and race tracks were built, professional drivers were hired, and engineers attempted better designs based on the results of these stress tests. Again, detailed peformance data must be gathered and disseminated for HPC as it has been for automobiles.

10.5   Budgeting and Rebudgeting for Parallelism

The science and technology community has become conditioned to look to Washington for help in paying its R&D bills. Federal funds have supported a number of major advances in the history of computing. The enormity and importance of parallel computing are such that the whole community — industry, academia, and government — must participate in solving the problems of practical parallel computing. The National Performance System of the previous section is an example of the first step that the community should take toward solving these problems. How the work would be organized and managed, and how it would be paid for are major questions. In this section we outline some ideas about the flow of R&D cash and past records in the management of industry-wide R&D efforts.

10.5.1   R&D Costs

The importance of performance data in parallel system design and the difficulty of obtaining these data are recurring arguments throughout this book. An item of good news that has not been emphasized is that the dollar cost of this work is relatively minor. A basic performance database with network access could be established and maintained for $1 million - $2 million per year. As the contents of the database grow, the software necessary to generate and analyze it becomes more complex, and the types of use increase, the total cost could grow to $10 million-$20 million per year. But as the key driving force and monitoring point for the $1 billion per year Federal government HPCCI, as well as a much larger private sector annual investment in HPC, this is a minor cost. And it becomes vanishingly small when contrasted with a multi-hundred billion dollar worldwide computer business. In summary, the performance database is like the proverbial horseshoe nail, for want of which the entire computing kingdom is at risk.

Sidebar 32: Performance Data and the GAO Report

The U.S. General Accounting Office (GAO) conducted a study of HPC in 1993 and issued a report [GeAO93] to the House Committee on Armed Services concerning the role of the Advanced Research Projects Agency in HPC. The Executive Summary states that: "The lack of widely available performance data on new designs slows technological progress because the research community remains uncertain about the merits of the new designs." Chapter 3 is entitled "ARPA's HPC Program Would Benefit from Greater Collaboration with the HPCC Research Community." It ends with three sections from which we quote here.

"Conclusions:... Unaccustomed to dealing with such a broad constituency, ARPA has focussed on interacting chiefly with its own principal investigators. ... Establishing a database of performance and program data would go far to resolve the agency's information dissemination shortcomings."

"Recommendations: ... We recommend that the Secretary of Defense direct the director, ARPA to

1. Establish and maintain a public database of information about the status and results of the agency's ongoing HPC projects as well as performance data for different MPP systems, and

2. Sponsor annual or semi-annual conferences ..."

"*Agency Comments*: ... ARPA officials said they are considering alternatives for improving information dissemination ... . However, they stated that they do not consider their current information dissemination activity to be lacking. ..."

At this point the GAO authors reiterate their concerns about ARPA's inadequacies. While this document is specifically about ARPA, other agencies are equally vulnerable.

For example, in a survey conducted by a National Research Council group chaired by the author in the late 1980s, it was observed that university users of supercomputers had relatively little understanding of performance. Indeed, it took U of I researchers at CSRD several *years* to convince the NSF-sponsored NCSA management that a Cray hardware performance monitor was a worthwhile purchase; in fact, little can be known about performance without one.

There are two basic aspects of human nature that cause and per-
petuate these problems. The first is ignorance and naiveté, which
cannot be faulted in the short run, but which should only be a short
run issue. The second is fear of the unknown, and more specifically,
fear of exposure in view of massive budgets. The fact that HPC systems do not perform well in spite of much effort, should motivate
only non-believers to obscure performance results. Those who believe that parallel processing is necessary and that it will eventually
perform well, must make every effort to share detailed performance
information as widely as possible, to aid the development of practical
parallelism.

10.5.2   Federal Funds

It is easy and popular to criticize research-oriented agencies and organizations for
misspent money and technical misjudgments. Because hindsight can be perfect,
outsiders may easily misinterpret a subject, and most taxpayers love a whistle-
blower, the cast of characters playing this role continues to grow: from Representative John Dingell, to Pentagon ex-employees, to a Stanford University auditor.
Symmetrically, it is easy to administer Federal funds in an R&D agency whose
decisions are largely based upon peer-reviewed proposals or in mission-oriented
agencies where insiders review proposals. Each technical community *knows* what
it needs to do next, who the good people are, and how to judge well-written
proposals.

It is hard for Congress or Federal research administrators to look at a variety
of broad technical subjects that have wide popularity and decide which should be
funded and which should be dropped. It is also hard for the research community
itself to change directions, when the present direction has many important, unan-
swered questions. Human nature keeps us all moving in familiar (if difficult) and
popular (if not unanimous) directions. Nevertheless there are times when major
changes are necessary.

To collect, analyze, disseminate, and act upon parallel computer macroperformance data is a key recommendation of this book. This is an unpopular idea for
several reasons which we list in Section 10.4, but it must be done. If money were
made available for this work, it would attract major academic and industrial attention and would proceed. There are several possible sources for such money. As the
scientific community itself is now recommending, hard decisions must be made in
the zero-sum government game of science and technology funding. For example,
a joint study by the National Academy of Sciences, Institute of Medicine, and
National Academy of Engineering chaired by Phillip A. Griffiths [Hilt93] recommended that we remain "at the forefront of science in all major fields, and clearly

ahead in at least a few." High-performance computing is an area whose importance has been discussed throughout this book and which almost always appears on lists of top priority, traditional leadership topics in American science and technology.

When looking for reassignable Federal funds, two agencies are easy to single out, but others could be discussed as well. In recent years the U.S. Department of Defense's Darpa (ARPA: Advanced Research Projects Agency) has received much criticism, especially for sponsoring the purchase of HPC systems whose research and development phases it has also supported. This is an easy criticism, and it is also an easy place to find $5 or $10 million per year to reassign. Unfortunately ARPA has accepted the criticism and responded by buying other machines as well as ARPA-supported ones. This costs more money, not less, and does not address the facts of the issue. The point is that we need both widespread experimentation with existing machines *and* the analysis of this experimentation to build better future systems. No one knows which MPP performs best for which class of computations or, based upon global experimental analysis, how to build improved systems. New machines are launched based upon detailed analyses of small, idealized parts of an existing system, plus a lot of intuition.

The other agency that we shall discuss is the National Science Foundation (NSF). Over the past decade the NSF, through its Advanced Scientific Computing program, has spent about one-third of its $100-200 million annual computing budget to support four or five supercomputing service centers. These centers have provided important network access to critical computing resources that would not have been available or affordable otherwise. There are two issues here; first is the obvious question of how much of this we need. The program is popular because users in universities across the United States have benefitted, so endorsements for the centers can easily be garnered in Congressional districts in every state.

Second, how should this money be labelled? To a first approximation, in computational science and engineering, a (super)computer plays the same role that instruments play for experimental researchers, or that pencils and paper play for theoreticians. As infrastructure, it should be supported from the budgets of each NSF Directorate whose researchers benefit from it. In fact, the NSF originally allocated "new" money for this program and simply placed it in the Computer and Information Science and Engineering (CISE) Directorate for management. This might have been the right approach if it had been separated physically and in everyone's mind from supercomputing research per se. But it was not; in fact the Advanced Scientific Computing program of CISE has repeatedly attempted to use some of this money for "research" within the supercomputing service centers. Although work has progressed on networking and computer graphics, two facilitating technologies that needed development for the users but are not supercomputing per se, very little worthwhile supercomputing research has arisen within the centers.

Thus, in two important cases, major amounts of supercomputing money have been spent on crowd-pleasing activities that have advanced neither research nor development in HPC system performance improvement. Under the aegis of high-performance computing budgets, both ARPA and NSF have simply provided computing facilities with few strings attached — certainly none concerning system-level performance analysis and improvement. As a result, we have lost a decade of experimental data that could have been crucial toward the making of better HPC systems. Furthermore, many people have come to believe just the opposite about this funding. Besides government sponsors who feel that they are advancing supercomputing by these programs, it is most unfortunate that many of the participants in these programs seem to feel the same way. The hacker mentality leads some people to believe that merely by using these systems they are advancing the supercomputing field. In fact, they may be advancing their own disciplines by their results, but by absorbing computer system research money and in many cases cheerfully using poorly designed systems, they send a message of hope, where loud complaining is in order.

10.5.3   Industrial Funds

It is not obvious that the Federal government should be the agency of change in developing practical parallelism. In matters of advanced development, the private sector has more motivation, and much better insight and mechanisms for proceeding. In Chapter 3, we have already referred to SPEC and Perfect — low-budget, direct-action performance consortia. To date they have not gotten beyond the benchmarking and data dissemination phase of open performance, but future joint efforts could have a major role in moving practical parallelism forward. The Microelectronics and Computing Consortium (MCC) is a high-budget activity that was initiated by William Norris of CDC to encourage a number of U.S. companies to pull together and become more internationally competetive by cooperating. Several parallel processing efforts have failed at MCC, but it could yet recover a leadership role in parallel computing. The Semiconductor Research Corp. (SRC) is a lower-budget activity that attempts to bring industrial problems and academic researchers together. Companies supply problems and money, and academicians write proposals to obtain funds to work on the problems. This format could be an excellent one for expansion of the SPEC-Perfect type of effort to develop methodologies for performance analysis and improvement. Without strong participation by industry, some academic researchers have a tendency to get lost among challenging but irrelevant weeds.

Ideally, because there is a substantial Federal HPC budget, and the government owns a number of HPC systems and employs a large number of highly experienced supercomputer users, government participation in these programs would be welcomed. An agency with a tradition of neutrality in data gathering and dissemination is the National Institute of Standards and Technology (NIST) — formerly the National Bureau of Standards — which has been given substantial new funds under HPCCI, as well as the Advanced Technology Program (ATP). Furthermore, NIST has no HPC history and presumably no prejudices in the HPC field. This might make NIST an ideal lead agency for Federal government participation. However, the direction of the effort must come from the real-world users and system designers, so management of the activity would best reside outside the Federal government.

Companies tend to be profit-oriented and thus have short-range views. However, in this case they would be developing and evolving data and software that is basic to everyones' future work. The performance data would cut across all systems and thus would expose each company equally. Basic performance analysis software could benefit all companies in equal measure. In this sense it can be viewed as CAD software. CAD software is a major SRC effort and because of its potential universality has been a relatively successful aspect of MCC cooperation. Because no one knows how to proceed and the costs of obtaining practical parallelism may still be quite high, each company should be happy to participate and share the development risks as well as the results of an open National Performance System. The future winners, then, would be those companies who do the best job of exploiting the results of the basic open-performance development work, by building the first practical parallel systems.

10.6 Summary

Whether this book's assumptions are regarded as obviously true or merely plausible, the likely consequences of the assumptions can be summarized in a brief logical chain. The three basic assumptions are that:

1. The computer clock speed increases provided by known physics and technology will continue to flatten, leading to little further clock speed increase after the early 2000s.

2. People will seek system speed increases indefinitely, to provide more functionality and faster turnaround for future computations.

3. Faster parallel systems will always be physically larger than slower parallel systems (mitigated by Moore's Law), because they contain more processors and memories.

These assumptions lead to the following consequences:

A. Flat clock speeds (1. above) imply flat traditional sequential processor and system speeds.

B. Continued demand for additional system speed (2. above) and flat traditional system speeds (A. above) require the use of parallelism in each microprocessor and between processors in computer systems.

C. Flat clock speeds (1. above) imply that every type of computer system produced in volume will use the same basic type of hardware technology. In particular, traditional HPC dependence on ECL will not be cost-effective, and microprocessor CMOS/BiCMOS will become universal.

D. The combination of using one basic technology (C. above), requiring the use of parallelism in each system (B. above), and having faster systems be physically larger (3. above) erases the distinction among personal, departmental, and central machines, and attaches new importance to computing across physically distributed systems.

E. The demand for parallelism within each system (B. above) and among physically distributed systems (D. above) raises difficult and poorly understood questions that must be answered to develop practical parallel processing.

Sidebar 33: Surviving the 1990s

Computer manufacturers in the mid-1990s find themselves in extremely difficult positions. Many are losing money each quarter, and some are on the verge of bankruptcy. In addition, they must decide what to do as clock speeds are squeezed and the necessity of using parallelism threatens. Parallelism cannot be viewed by any surviving companies or CEOs as anything but a threat, because so many of their colleagues have failed in trying to make a business success of it.

Three markets now compete with one another: vector/parallel supercomputers, MPPs, and workstation clusters. The first of these has been declining, while the other two gain, but the total market size is variously estimated to be only in the range of $2-3 billion per year (see [BuWe93] for an estimate). Furthermore, some companies compete with themselves in several segments, and IBM competes in all three. Nevertheless, this market is rapidly expanding, especially when one anticipates adding PC clusters to the workstation clusters list. While these numbers are minor parts of the total computer market, they are probably comparable to the $1 billion per year Federal HPC budget, plus industrial HPC R & D funds. As this book has discussed extensively, the influence of these expenditures extends across the whole computing field.

One survival strategy in this marketplace is to apply parallelism in niche markets or at least in focussed markets. A very large market is provided by transaction and database processing, which has major parallelism; obviously employee X and employee Y want their checks processed independently, just as bank depositors want their statements processed separately. This market was developed by Teradata, which was bought by NCR, which in turn was bought by ATT in the early 1990s. Similarly, Oracle acquired a strong financial interest in nCUBE, Intel has a relationship with Unisys, and IBM is pushing its Power Parallel Systems, all in these areas. Markets can be found in digital signal processing, image processing, visualization, video image retrieval, and other applications with substantial inherent parallelism, and these have all attracted parallel system builders or special-purpose chip manufacturers.

Another survival strategy in exploiting parallelism is to go for the vector processing market that Cray Research and other supercomputers of the 1970s and 1980s developed. In the 1990s many users have well-tuned vector codes that they want to expand and speed up. Because SIMD systems may be regarded as scalable vector processors, successes in this area include early Thinking Machines systems, as well as follow-on vector customers who migrated to the MIMD CM-5, and more recently to MasPar and others. Cray Research itself has the T3D, an MPP MIMD system which, together with IBM's SP-2, Fujitsu offerings (mostly in Japan and Europe) and others, are being used as vector supercomputer add-on accelerators, and may capture a substantial part of this market.

But these are strategies for hanging on. The companies that prevail will be those whose strategy is to develop practical parallel systems for broad use. To do this they must first understand performance, develop high-quality architectures and compilers, and then demonstrate performance on a broad range of applications for their new systems.

10.6.1   Paradigm Shifts

It has become commonplace to underscore proposed changes by describing major redirections as paradigm shifts [Kuhn70], which sometimes are mainly name changes. Table 10.1 lists six technical areas that have been discussed throughout the book, together with their major focal points in the sequential and parallel eras. A brief recounting of previous discussions of each follows.

1. Hardware speed thinking will be inverted, from a major concentration on circuits, with architecture providing some boosts, to exactly the opposite as circuit speed increases become more difficult to obtain.

2. Compilers were originally a user convenience for getting programs written, and this convenience has been extended to debugging and development environments, together with program optimization. In the parallel era, compilers

Technical Area	Sequential Era	Parallel Era
1. Hardware Speed	Circuits (Architecture)	Architecture (Circuits)
2. Compilers	User Convenience	Performance Exploitation
3. Libraries	Breadth for User Convenience	Performance Portability (Specialized Functionality)
4. Software Engineering	Programmer Productivity, Software Reliability (Broad, General)	Library Use, Data Structures (Abstract), Program Structure (Focus on Performance, Portability)
5. Performance Evaluation	Benchmarks (fine-tuning), Queueing Models (Peripheral)	Eliminate Instability, Increase Delivered Performance (Central)
6. Performance/Cost, Technology Convergence	RISC (HW - Compiler), UNIX (open software), PSEs (specific areas)	Open Performance, System Scalability, Broad Usability via PSEs

Table 10.1. Sequential to Parallel Era Paradigm Shifts

will become the major providers of performance by conveniently exploiting the architecture for software developers.

3. Libraries originally provided users with the convenience of not having to think about implementing certain standard algorithms, and their breadth was of key importance. Breadth remains important, but their ability to permit porting codes while maintaining performance across architectures, is crucial for parallelism.

4. Software engineering has been a broad, general topic embracing a few (often loose) principles aimed at the productive programming of reliable software. In the parallel era, as with libraries, software engineering will focus more on performance portability between architectures, and programming principles that encourage high performance will evolve.

5. Performance evaluation has meant benchmarking various systems to fine tune performance or evaluate "horse races" between systems, and building abstract mathematical models of systems. In the parallel era, it is taking on a central role in eliminating instability and generally exploiting systems for high performance.

6. Technology convergence based upon usability and performance/cost has involved open systems, VLSI-based design, and the development of various

PSE systems. The performance aspects will become more important in parallel systems as open performance and system scalability, together with usability, take on central roles.

As we move from the sequential era to the parallel era, it appears that the overall areas of technical concentration will not change much, although performance per se will become more important because of its greater variability in parallel systems. The greatest changes will be in the subject matter dealt with in each area. As the contents of various topics change, thoughts and discussions among practitioners and policymakers must also change. Areas that may have been unworthy of much effort will take on important roles, and vice versa. Although it is not necessary to introduce new names for every topic, it is important to rethink the meaning and importance of each.

10.6.2 Recommendations

Thoughtful people in the computing world are generally aware of the separate pieces of this puzzle. But for a variety of reasons, far too little is being done to head off the resulting potential crisis. Wishful thinking and the knowledge that in the past we have always discovered new tricks to devise faster computers, are probably first on the list of reasons for inaction, with ignorance of the problem's breadth and the true difficulties of the individual technical problems a close second.

The top four recommendations of the book are to push ahead with:

1. **Open Performance** A comprehensive effort to collect and disseminate system performance information,

2. **Comparative System Development** A methodology for the use of this information in system performance improvement,

3. **Practical Parallel Processing** The resulting integrated practical parallel architectures and software, and

4. **Computational Science and Engineering** A revitalized university community of computational science and engineering people.

These may seem to be obvious and straightforward points. To computer insiders they may even seem hackneyed. The main point of this book is that the confusion in the community, demonstrated repeatedly by wasted time, money, and human resources, now demands cooperative action to solve the problems of practical parallel computing. Industry, government, and academia must carefully appraise the current situation based on facts, not opinions. Baseless competitiveness and self-interest, as well as self satisfaction and not-invented-here syndromes must be set aside. An open-performance plan must be broadly developed and used in future system designs. A newly educated crop of students must be trained and sought by industry to solve these problems. Solving the problem of practical parallelism depends on new depths of facts, new levels of effort, and new peoples' thoughts.

The parallel computing field today has the advantage of broad financial support, the involvement of the best technology companies, and many high quality people. However, there is a lack of good communication, or even of a language or method of communication within the field. There is no technical journal containing comprehensive computer system performance information, nor is there a comprehensive journal of computer system architecture. How long can these advantages hold together under such circumstances?

To put an even finer point on this, it appears that the complexity of the problems and the high technical quality of the people involved have led to large amounts of deception and self-deception within the field. Everyone in the field wants to solve the practical parallelism problem, and some have been trying for so long that they feel the next thing they try must be **it**. Unfortunately, some others are content merely to be trying one more thing. While competition is good, if every competitor can declare himself the winner, everyone loses. Without common metrics, benchmarks, and ground rules, that is exactly the self-destructive state of the parallel processing community today.

The good news here is that there is not a unique or perhaps, even, a narrow range of solutions to this problem. We are not looking for the Holy Grail (sought for 2000 years), a proof of Fermat's last theorem (which took 350 years), or even a particular subatomic particle (which typically takes a decade or two, as did new accelerators). We are looking for good engineering solutions to a set of very complex problems, in the tradition of putting a man on the moon, or tunnelling under the English Channel. The main difficulty is that these new problems are sufficiently different from traditional sequential computing problems that a seat-of-the-pants approach and a bit of good luck are not enough to make practical parallel systems happen. We have tried that for the past 15 or 20 years, but because of the sequential speed squeeze, time is now running out. It is now *necessary* to collect and compare facts publicly, develop new design methodologies, and act as a cooperative community.

The design of complex engineering systems is never a one-person activity, although personal inspirations and inspired leaders are necessary. As I began [Kuck78]:

> *Art is I*
> *Science is We*
> *Engineering is They,*

and it must be remembered that computer system design is all three. Scientific principles, engineering methods, and the experience of multiple designs are all crucial to success. Many well-designed, multicomponent subsystems are necessary for the synthesis of whole, practical parallel systems (recall Chapter 1). As the book has pointed out, many of these are missing in parallel computing today. Our recommendations are, in summary, to fill these gaps and solve the Greatest Grand Challenge as soon as possible.

References

[AbKL81] Walid Abu-Sufah, David J. Kuck, and Duncan H. Lawrie, "On the Performance Enhancement of Paging Systems Through Program Analysis and Transformations," *IEEE Trans. on Comp.*, 30(5), pp. 341-356, 1981.

[AgPa93] Dharma P. Agrawal and Lalit M. Patnaik, Guest Eds., *Journal of Parallel and Distributed Computing, Special Issue: Performance of Supercomputers*, 19(3), pp. 143-291, 1993.

[AlSm88] Robert C. Alexander and Douglas K. Smith, *Fumbling the Future: The Story of Xerox and Personal Computing*, William Morrow, New York, 1988.

[Amda67] G.M. Amdahl, *The Validity of the Single Processor Approach to Achieving Large Scale Computing Capabilities*, AFIPS Proc. SJCC, vol. 30, 1967.

[Bail92] J. Bailey, *First We Reshape Our Computers, Then Our Computers Reshape Us: The Broader Intellectual Impact Of Parallelism.* Proceedings of the American Academy of Arts and Sciences, vol. 121, no. 1, pp. 67-86, 1992.

[Bane79] Utpal Banerjee, "Speedup of Ordinary Programs," Ph.D. Thesis, Report DCS 79-989, Univ. of Illinois at Urbana-Champaign, Oct. 1979.

[Bane88] Utpal Banerjee, *Dependence Analysis for Supercomputing*, Kluwer Academic Publishers, Boston, 1988.

[BBFY92] Committee on Physical, Mathematical, and Engineering Sciences; Federal Coordinating Council for Science, Engineering, and Technology (FCCSET); White House Office of Science and Technology Policy, *Grand Challenges 1992: High Performance Computing and*

Communications. The FY 1992 U.S. Research and Development Program. Supplement to the President's Fiscal Year 1992 Budget, (Washington D.C.) 1992.

[BBFY93] Committee on Physical, Mathematical, and Engineering Sciences; Federal Coordinating Council for Science, Engineering, and Technology (FCCSET); White House Office of Science and Technology Policy, *Grand Challenges 1993: High Performance Computing and Communications. The FY 1993 U.S. Research and Development Program.* Supplement to the President's Fiscal Year 1993 Budget, (Washington D.C.) 1993.

[BBFY94] Committee on Physical, Mathematical, and Engineering Sciences; Federal Coordinating Council for Science, Engineering, and Technology (FCCSET); White House Office of Science and Technology Policy, *High Performance Computing and Communications: Towards a National Information Infrastructure* . Supplement to the President's Fiscal Year 1994 Budget, (Washington D.C.) 1994.

[BCJT89] E. Barszcz, Tony F. Chan, D. C. Jespersen, and R. S. Tuminaro, "FLO52 on Hypercubes," *Int'l. J. High Speed Computing*, 1(3), pp. 481-503, 1989.

[BCKK89] M. Berry, D. Chen, D. Kuck, L. Pointer, S. Lo, Y. Pang, R. Roloff, A. Sameh, E. Clementi, S. Chin, D. Schneider, G. Fox, P. Messina, D. Walker, C. Hsiung, J. Schwarzmeier, K. Lue, S. Orszag, and F. Seidl, "The Perfect Club Benchmarks: Effective Performance Evaluation of Supercomputers," *Int'l Jour. of Supercomputer Applications*, 3(3), pp. 5-40, Fall 1989.

[BDKK94] Gordon Bell, Jack Dennis, Ken Kennedy, and David Kuck, contributors, *International Journal of Parallel Programming: Special Issue*, 22(1), pp. 3-127, 1994.

[BEHP94] William Blume, Rudolf Eigenmann, Jay Hoeflinger, David Padua, Paul Petersen, Lawrence Rauchwerger, and Peng Tu, *IEEE Parallel and Distributed Technology*, Fall 1994, pp. 37-47, 1994.

[Bell92]   Gordon Bell, "Ultracomputers: A Teraflop Before Its Time," *Comm. ACM*, 35(8), pp. 27-47, 1992.

[Bore92]   Nathaniel S. Borenstein, "Colleges Need to Fix the Bugs in Computer Science Courses," *The Chronicle of Higher Education*, pp. B3-B4, July 15, 1992.

[BrSa92]   Randall Bramley and Ahmed Sameh, "Row Projection Methods for Large Nonsymmetric Linear Systems," *SIAM J. on Scientific and Statistical Computing*, 13(1), pp. 168-193, 1992.

[Broo75]   F. P. Brooks, *The Mythical Man-Month*, Addison-Wesley, Reading, MA, 1975.

[BuWe93]   "In Supercomputing, Superconfusion," *Business Week*, Nbr. 3311, pp. 89-90, Mar. 22, 1993.

[BuWe94]   "Wonder Chips," *Business Week*, Nbr. 3379, pp. 86-92, July 4, 1994.

[CACM94]   "High Performance Computing," *Communications of the ACM: Special Section*, 37(4), pp. 28-64, April 1994.

[ChVe90]   Hoichi Cheong and Alexander V. Veidenbaum, "Compiler-Assisted Cache Management in Multiprocessors," *IEEE Computer*, 23(6), pp. 39-47, June 1990.

[CoBO93]   Anon., Congressional Budget Office Report ISBN 0-16-041828-3, Washington, D.C., 1993.

[Comp94]   "Visualization," *IEEE Computer: Special Issue*, 27(7), pp. 18-88, July 1994.

[Corc91]   Elizabeth Corcoran, "Calculating Reality," *Scientific American*, vol. 264, no. 1, pp. 100-109, Jan. 1991.

[CyKu92]   George Cybenko and David J. Kuck, "Revolution or Evolution?," *IEEE Spectrum, Special Issue: Supercomputers*, 29(9), pp. 39-41, 1992.

[DeGG93]   Luis DeRose, Kyle Gallivan, and Efstratios Gallopoulos, "Status Report: Parallel Ocean Circulation on Cedar." In: *Parallel Supercomputing in Atmospheric Science*, Eds. Geerd-R. Hoffmann and Tuomo Kauranne, pp. 157-172, 1993.

[DeLS89]   Michael L. Dertouzos, Richard K. Lester, and Robert M. Solow, *Made in America: Regaining the Competitive Edge*, The MIT Press, Cambridge, 1989.

[FeMo93]   Charles H. Ferguson and Charles R. Morris, *Computer Wars: How the West Can Win in a Post-IBM World*, Times Books, New York, 1993.

[FJLO88]   G. Fox, M. Johnson, G. Lyzenga, S. Otto, J. Salmon, and D. Walker, *Solving Problems on Concurrent Processors, Vol. 1*, Prentice-Hall, Englewood Cliffs, NJ, 1988.

[Fost86]   Richard N. Foster, *Innovation: The Attacker's Advantage*, Summit Books, New York, 1986.

[FWPS92]   W. Ferng, K. Wu, S. Petiton, and Y. Saad, *Basic Sparse Matrix Computations on Massively Parallel Computers*. AHPCRC Preprint 92-084, University of Minnesota, July 1992.

[GaGS94]   Kyle Gallivan, Efstratios Gallopoulos, and Ahmed Sameh, "Cedar: An Experiment in Parallel Computing," *Proc. of HERMIS '94*, Athens, Greece, Sept. 1994.

[GaHR94]   Efstratios Gallopoulos, Elias Houstis, and John R. Rice, "Problem-Solving Environments for Computational Science," *IEEE Computational Science and Engineering*, pp. 11-23, Su. 1994.

[GeAO93]   Anon., High Performance Computing: Advanced Research Projects Agency Should Do More to Foster Program Goals, General Accounting Office Report GAO/IMTEC-93-24, Washington, D.C., 1993.

[GGKM83]   Allan Gottlieb, R. Grishman, C. P. Kruskal, K. P. McAuliffe, L. Rudolph, and M. Snir, "The NYU Ultracomputer – Designing an MIMD Shared Memory Parallel Computer," *IEEE Trans. on Computers*, C-32(2), pp. 175-189, Feb. 1983.

[GGPY89]   Patrick P. Gelsinger, Paolo A. Gargini, Gerhard H. Parker, and Albert Y.C. Yu, "Microprocessors circa 2000," *IEEE Spectrum*, pp. 43-47, Oct. 1989.

[GHNP90]   Kyle Gallivan, Michael Heath, E. Ng, B. Peyton, Robert Plemmons, James Ortega, C. Romine, Ahmed Sameh, and Robert Voight, *Parallel Algorithms for Matrix Computations*, SIAM Press, Philadelphia, 1990.

[GKLS83]   D. Gajski, D. Kuck, D. Lawrie, and A. Sameh, "CEDAR – A Large Scale Multiprocessor," *Proceedings of the 1983 International Conference on Parallel Processing*, pp. 524-529, August 1983.

[GlLi90]   Roland Glowinski and Alain Lichnewsky, eds., *Computing Methods in Applied Sciences and Engineering*, SIAM Press, Philadelphia, 1990.

[Gray93]   Jim Gray, ed., *The Benchmark Handbook*, Morgan Kaufmann Publishers, San Francisco, 1993.

[HaLi92]   Juris Hartmanis, and Herbert Lin, Editors. *Computing The Future: A Broader Agenda for Computer Science and Engineering.* Committee to Assess the Scope and Direction of Computer Science and Technology, Computer Science and Telecommunications Board, Commission on

Physical Sciences, Mathematics, and Applications, National Research Council, National Academy Press, Washington, DC, 272 pp., 1992.

[HePa90]   John L. Hennessy and David A. Patterson, *Computer Architecture: A Quantitative Approach*, Morgan Kaufmann, San Mateo, CA, 1990.

[Hill90]   Mark D. Hill, " What is Scalability?," *Computer Architecture News*, 18(4), pp. 18-21, 1990.

[Hilt93]   Philip J. Hilts, "For Some Scientists, Less Money is Just as Good," *New York Times*, p. A9, June 22, 1993.

[HoPR90]   Elias N. Houstis, T. S. Papatheodorou, and John R. Rice, "Parallel Ellpack: An Expert System for the Parallel Processing of Partial Differential Equations," pp. 63-73, in: *Intelligent Mathematical Software Systems*, E. N. Houstis and J. R. Rice, eds., North-Holland, Amsterdam, 1990.

[HoRV92]   Elias N. Houstis, John R. Rice, and Robert Vichnevetsky, eds., *Expert Systems for Scientific Computing*, North-Holland, Amsterdam, 1992.

[Hwan93]   Kai Hwang, *Advanced Computer Architecture: Parallelism, Scalability, Programmability*, McGraw-Hill, New York, 1993.

[Jame83]   A. Jameson, "Solution of Euler Equations for Two Dimensional Transonic Flow by a Multigrid Method," *Appl. Math. and Comp.*, 13, pp. 327-355, 1983.

[KDLP93]   David J. Kuck, Edward S. Davidson, Duncan H. Lawrie, David A. Padua, Robert Downing, Michael Haney, Pen-Chung Yew, Alexander Veidenbaum, Rudolf Eigenmann, Perry Emrath, Kyle Gallivan, Jeffery Konicek, and Thomas Murphy, "The Cedar System and an Initial Performance Study," *Proc. 20th Annual Int'l Symp. on Computer Architecture*, 1993.

[KDLS86]   David J. Kuck, Edward S. Davidson, Duncan H. Lawrie, and Ahmed H. Sameh, "Parallel Supercomputing Today – The Cedar Approach," *Science*, 231(2), Feb. 1986.

[KiKu93]   Lyle D. Kipp and David J. Kuck, "Newton: Performance Improvement through Comparative Analysis," *Proc. 1993 IEEE Intl. Conf. on Computer Design: VLSI in Computers and Processors*, IEEE Computer Soc. Press, Los Alamitos, CA, 1993.

[KLSS94] Charles H. Koelbel, David B. Loveman, Robert S. Schreiber, Guy L. Steele Jr., and Mary E. Zosel, *The High Performance Fortran Handbook*, The MIT Press, Cambridge, 1994.

[Kuck78] David J. Kuck, *The Structure of Computers and Computations*, John Wiley and Sons, New York, 1978.

[Kuck89] David J. Kuck, *Keynote Address 15th Annual Int'l. Symp. on Computer Architecture, May 30-June 3, 1988, Honolulu, HI*, Computer Architecture News, vol. 17, no. 1, pp. 5-26, March 1989.

[Kuck92] David J. Kuck, *A User's View of High-Performance Scientific and Engineering Software Systems in the Mid-21st Century*, pp. 69-87, in: *Expert Systems for Scientific Computing*, E. N. Houstis, J. R. Rice and R. Vichnevetsky, eds. North-Holland, Amsterdam, 1992.

[Kuhn70] Thomas S. Kuhn, *The Structure of Scientific Revolutions, Second Edition, Enlarged*, The University of Chicago Press, Chicago, 1970.

[KuMC72] David J. Kuck, Yoichi Muraoka, and Steve S.C. Chen, "On the Number of Operations Simultaneously Executable in FORTRAN-Like Programs and Their Resulting Speed-Up," *IEEE Trans. on Computers*, vol. C-21, no. 12, pp. 1293-1310, Dec. 1972.

[Lars85] John L. Larson, "CRAY X-MP Hardware Performance Monitor," *Cray Channnels*, pp. 18-19, Winter 1985.

[Lax82] Peter D. Lax, report of the panel on *Large Scale Computing in Science and Engineering*, Dec. 1982.

[LeeR80] Ruby B. Lee, "Empirical Results on the Speedup, Efficiency, Redundancy, and Quality of Parallel Computations," *Proc. Int'l Conf. on Parallel Processing*, pp. 91-96, 1980.

[LLGW92] D. Lenosky, J. Laudon, K.Gharachorloo, W. D. Weber, A. Gupta, J. L. Hennessy, M. Horowitz, and M. Lam, "The Stanford DASH Multiprocessor," *IEEE Computer*, pp. 63-79, Mar. 1992.

[Lohr93] Steve Lohr, "Present at the Transition of I.B.M.," *The New York Times*, pp. C1 and C18, Oct. 26, 1993.

[LRKI92] Bruce Leasure, Walt Rudd, Ross Knippel, Andrew Ingalls, and Cherri Pancake, *Parallel Processing Model for High Level Programming Languages*, Doc. No. X3H5/91-0023-G, X3H5 Technical Committee on Parallel Processing Constructs for High Level Programming Languages, American National Standards Committee on Computers and Information Processing (X3), Mar. 1992.

[McMa86] Frank H. McMahon, "The Livermore Fortran Kernels: A Computer Test of the Numerical Performance Range," Report UCRL-53745, Lawrence Livermore National Laboratory, Dec. 1986.

[MeSa88] Ulrike Meier and Ahmed Sameh, "The Behavior of the Conjugate Gradient Algorithm on a Multivector Processor with a Hierarchical Memory," *Jour. of Computational and Applied Math.*, vol. 24, pp. 13-22, 1988.

[MeSt93] Paul Messina and Thomas Sterling, eds. *System Software and Tools for High Performance Computing Environments*, SIAM Press, Philadelphia, 1993.

[Nowa94] Rachel Nowak, "Ignorance Is Not Bliss," *Science*, 264, p. 1538, 10 June, 1994.

[Noyc77] Robert N. Noyce, "Microelectronics," *Scientific American*, 237(3), pp. 63-69, Sept. 1977.

[NuAg91] D. Nussbaum and A. Agarwal, "Scalability of Parallel Machines," *Comm. of the ACM*, 34(3), pp. 57-61, 1991.

[NYT93] New York Times, p. 1, Oct. 14, 1993.

[Parn90] David L. Parnas, "Education for Computing Professionals," *IEEE Computer*, 23(1), pp. 17-22, 1990.

[PeZo89] Tekla S. Perry and Glenn Zorpette, "Supercomputer Experts Predict Expansive Growth," *IEEE Spectrum*, 26(2), pp. 26-33, 1989.

[Poin90] Lynn Pointer, ed., "Perfect Reports," CSRD Reports 964 and 1052, Center for Supercomputing R. and D., Univ. of Illinois at Urbana-Champaign, 1990, 1991.

[Poly88] Constantine D. Polychronopoulos, *Parallel Programming and Compilers*, Kluwer Academic Publishers, Boston, 1988.

[Pool92] Robert Pool, "The Third Branch of Science Debuts," *Science, Special Section:Computing in Science*, 256, pp. 44-62, 3 Apr., 1992.

[Reyn91] Terry S. Reynolds, ed., *The Engineer in America: A Historical Anthology from* Technology and Culture, The University of Chicago Press, Chicago, 1991.

[Rice94] John R. Rice, " Academic Programs in Computational Science and Engineering," *IEEE Computational Science and Engineering*, 1(1), pp. 13-21, Spring 1994.

[SaRi93]   Ahmed H. Sameh and John P. Riganati, Guest Eds., *IEEE Computer, Special Issue: Computational Science and Engineering* , 26(10), pp. 8-67, 1993.

[Saxe94]   Annalee Saxenian, *Regional Advantage: Culture and Competition in Silicon Valley and Route 128*, Harvard University Press, Cambridge, MA, 1994.

[Schw80]   J. T. Schwartz, "Ultra-Computers," *ACM Trans. on Prog. Lang. and Systems*, 2(4), pp. 484-521, 1980.

[Seit85]   C.L. Seitz, "The Cosmic Cube," *Communications of the ACM*, 28(1), 1985.

[Simo69]   Herbert A. Simon, *The Sciences of the Artificial*, MIT Press, Cambridge, MA, 1969.

[SPEC93]   *SPEC Newsletter*, Volume 5, Standard Performance Evaluation Corp., (c/o NCGA) Fairfax, VA, 1993.

[SqPa63]   J. S. Squire and S. M. Palais, "Programming and Design Considerations of a Highly Parallel Computer," *AFIPS Proc. SJCC*, vol. 23, pp. 395-400, 1963.

[WCHH93] Eugene Wong, George Cotter, Nico Habermann, Charles Holland, Gary Koob, David Nelson, Paul Smith, and Steve Squires, "Panel on the Federal High Performance Computing and Communications Initiative at ICS 92," *Newsletter of the IEEE Comp. Soc. Tech. Comm. on Supercomputer Applications*, 7(1), pp. 1-22, April 1993.

[Wolf89]   Michael J. Wolfe, *Optimizing Supercompilers for Supercomputers*, MIT Press, Cambridge, 1989.

[ZiCh91]   Hans Zima and Barbara Chapman, *Supercompilers for Parallel and Vector Computers*, ACM Press, New York, 1991.

Index